Spitfire Girl

JACKIE MOGGRIDGE served in the Air
Transport Auxiliary (ATA) during
World War Two, receiving a King's
Commendation for Services in the
Air. After the war she continued to fly
professionally whilst raising her two
daughters. She died in 2004; her ashes
were scattered from a Spitfire.

Spitfire Girl

My Life in the Sky

JACKIE MOGGRIDGE

HEAD
ZEUS

First published as *Woman Pilot* in the UK in 1957 by Michael Joseph Ltd

This revised edition first published in paperback and eBook in the UK in 2014 by Head of Zeus Ltd

9 7 5 3 1 2 4 6 8

A CIP catalogue record for this book is available from the British Library.

Paperback ISBN: 9781781859896
eBook ISBN: 9781781859889

Typeset by Ellipsis Digital, Glasgow
Printed and bound by CPI Group (UK) Ltd, Croydon, CR0 4YY

Head of Zeus Ltd
Clerkenwell House
45–47 Clerkenwell Green
London, EC1R 0HT

WWW.HEADOFZEUS.COM

To Reg,

You are my love, and my delight,
You are the thrill I find so sweet,
Wrapped in your arms I am complete.

1945

INTRODUCTION

> Earth, why should I return to you?
> The sky is such a lovely blue;
> Oh Earth, why should I return to you?

> 1940

MY MOTHER JACKIE WAS LIKE TWO WOMEN IN ONE: ARTISTIC, romantic, forgetful and disorganised, but when she climbed into an aeroplane she became focused, calm and very capable – not my mother at all! She loved many things: singing, dancing, sewing and painting, but her main passion in life was flying. Up in the sky is where she belonged.

On Saturday mornings, my little sister Candy and I would jump into our mother's bed and sit beneath the billowing duvet – the clouds – and play at being Spitfire pilots. As we held the pretend joystick she would say, 'just think right and it will go right, the Spitfire is so sensitive it should always be flown by a lady'. Candy remembered those duvet lessons fifty years later when she went up in Spitfire ML407, an aircraft Jackie had been the first to ferry, now owned by our great friend Carolyn Grace, who has kindly written the Afterword for this edition.

My mother's life of adventure began in South Africa, where she was brought up to be a good, prim Catholic girl by her grandmother, whom she adored. Although these codes stayed with her forever, she had a very open mind and a strong will. If she didn't agree with a teaching of the church she'd just say, 'well, a man made that rule up, not God, so you can ignore that one'.

From her first flight at fifteen, Jackie was hooked. When I was born, in 1946, she was determined to continue working – just as a man would have done. 'There's mummy dear,' our father would say as he pointed to an aircraft in the sky. For years after I was convinced all aeroplanes were called 'Mummy Dears'.

Even though Jackie flew aircraft for the ATA during World War Two, she still struggled to find work once peace was declared. Of course this got her down, but she refused to feel defeated, taking any and every opportunity to stay in the sky. So, from the age of about two, I would be strapped onto the back of her motorbike and sped off to various local airfields, singing all the way. When she was working for Channel Airways in the late 1950s, she would often sneak me onto the plane along with the other passengers. If there was no seat to spare, she'd just plonk me down in the doorway between cabin and cockpit – hang health and safety!

The summer I turned fourteen I joined her up in Perthshire where she was flying aircraft for Meridian Air Maps. Jackie was sick as a dog, but she wasn't ill, she was pregnant. Somehow she managed to hide it from everyone. She continued to work right up until Candy was born, two months early, never letting on she was expecting. Amazingly, she was back flying again six months later.

Growing up, Candy and I knew our mother was unusual, but we didn't realise how exceptional she was until much later. It's a credit to her that she always remained 'mummy' first and foremost, but like all children we sometimes found our mother excruciatingly embarrassing. I remember turning up terribly late for my first day at boarding school as Jackie had been flying all day. Into the school we burst, my mother in her Captain's uniform, closely followed by an airline hostess who was hitching a ride home with us. I was mortified, but everyone just assumed Jackie was a bus conductress. Candy didn't escape either, she had to suffer the pain of turning up at school every day in a horrid, bright blue helmet on the back of Jackie's Honda motorbike. Although she begged to be left at the end of the road, she was always dropped right in front of the school gates, for all to see.

My father, Reg, was the quiet strength behind Jackie. He fully supported her need to fly and was immensely proud of her achievements. They met at a dance in 1940 but the war kept them apart for most of their courtship and early married life. Like many lovebirds of their time they had to rely on letters. Jackie would often tell the story of how she attached a love letter for Reg to her 2oz bar of ration chocolate and dropped it from her aircraft as she flew over Aylesbury where he was posted at the time. Tied to her parcel was a note telling the finder to keep the chocolate, but please deliver the letter to Reg Moggridge! He always received his post.

Re-reading this book has made both of us appreciate, more than ever, the amazing things our mother achieved in what was, very much, a man's world. Jackie absolutely loathed housework and, at times, the dull routine of being a housewife would get her down. She just didn't think she was any good at it. She would rant and rave whilst wrestling with the washing-up saying, 'don't ever get married dear, you'll have to cook and clean for the rest of your life', but, as soon as it was done she'd become her cheerful self again.

It was in the sky that Jackie felt most capable. She was a loving and caring wife, mother and grandmother on the ground, and a vivacious, talented pilot in the air. She taught us to look at the clouds, the moon and the sunset: to take the time to rejoice in things and not just rush on by.

Not long before she died, Jackie was driving to visit me in central London when she was stopped by two young police officers for driving too slowly round Hyde Park Corner. If only they knew how brave and daring she really was, and what a hero she'd been during the war! We hope, by reading her book, you'll get an inkling of just how remarkable our mother, Captain Jackie Moggridge, really was.

Veronica Jill Robinson (née Moggridge)
with Candida Adkins (née Moggridge)

KEY EVENTS IN
JACKIE'S LIFE

1920   *1 March*: Dolores Theresa Sorour (Jackie) born in
        Pretoria, South Africa.

1935   *1 March*: Taken up for her first flight on her fifteenth
        birthday.

1938   *30 January*: Becomes the first woman to perform a
        solo parachute jump in South Africa, aged seventeen.

        24 June: Leaves South Africa for England in order to
        start training for her Pilot's Licence.

1939   *3 September:* Chamberlain announces Britain is at war
        with Germany.

        30 November: Joins the WAAFs and is stationed at
        Rye working as a Radar Operator.

1940   *26 June*: Meets Second Lieutenant Reginald
        Moggridge at a dance.

        29 July: Discharged from the WAAFs in order to
        take up duty with the ATA in Hatfield.

1941   *August*: First Spitfire flight from Crawley to
        Ternhill.

1944	Joins Number 15 Ferry Pool stationed at Hamble.
	29 April: Ferries Spitfire ML407 (the Grace Spitfire) to 485 Squadron at Selsey.
	24 November: Travels to South Africa to see her mother and family before marrying.
1945	*12 January*: Jackie and Reg are married at St George's Catholic church in Taunton.
	8 May: Peace is declared in Europe.
1946	*1 January*: Receives a King's Commendation for valuable service in the air for having ferried more aircraft during the war than any other man or woman.
	21 March: First daughter, Veronica Jill, born.
1949	*August*: One of the first women to become a commissioned pilot in the WRAF (VR).
1951	*26 May*: First recipient of the Jean Lennox Bird Trophy, awarded to the outstanding woman pilot of the year.
1953	*25 August*: Becomes one of only five woman to get full Wings from RAF.

2 June: Receives the Coronation Medal.

Campaigns to become first woman to break the sound barrier. The 'powers that be' would not lend her the Sabre Jet she needed in order for Britain to achieve this.

1954–56   Spitfire flights to Burma.

1957   Memoir first published by Michael Joseph.

1957–60   Becomes first female airline Captain to fly passengers on scheduled flights whilst working for Channel Airways.

1960   Summer: Works for Meridian Air Maps in Scotland.

1961   *3 January*: Second daughter, Candida, born.

1967   Pilots pleasure flights for tourists out of Weston-super-Mare.

1969   *22nd April*: Jackie's press plane is the first to spot Robin Knox-Johnston's boat arrive in Falmouth, making him the first man to successfully sail around the world solo.

1968–93   Continues to fly professionally for various organisations, maintaining her Instrument Rating yearly in order to pilot passengers.

1994	*29 April*: Last flight with Carolyn Grace in Spitfire ML407, re-enacting its inaugral flight 50 years earlier.
1997	Reg Moggridge dies.
2004	*7 January*: Dies at home in Taunton, surrounded by her family.
	1 August: Ashes scattered by Carolyn Grace from Spitfire ML407 over Dunkeswell Aerodrome.

PART ONE

PRE-WAR

When we are very young,
The grown-ups talk as though we cannot hear,
'Poor Jackie' mother says aloud,
With poor me standing near.

1938

1

SIX MONTHS BEFORE I WAS BORN MY WIDOWED MOTHER AND I moved to my grandmother's home. Six months after I was born my mother re-married. My grandmother, old-fashioned and strong-willed, was determined that I should not leave her orthodox Catholic home and influence. It is not difficult to imagine the arguments and promises that centred over my sublimely indifferent head like a tropical storm thundering high in the heavens over a placid lake, but when my mother moved to her new home in Durban I stayed at Pretoria with my grandmother.

The results were inevitable. I adapted myself, and was adapted, to an elderly woman. My behaviour, habits and interests were those calculated to make her happy. I was quiet, reserved and serious except when surrounded by octogenarians.

My grandmother's firm belief in the Roman Catholic version of faith was a deep-water harbour in which I moored without once slipping the anchor and venturing outside the harbour gates. To her it was a living philosophy to which she referred even on the most trivial matters. In her generation it was simpler to have only black and white. She, and I, were untrammelled by the greys of modern psychology, where, the point of sin and misdemeanour is counter-pointed by environment and hereditary influence. For

3

her, and me, this was right, that, unquestionably, was wrong. Admirable in a grandmother. Insufferable in a grand-daughter.

Thus when I was fourteen and my grandmother died I was a prig and a prude and ill-fitted to return to my mother's home and the extravagant high spirits of my two step-brothers.

Reviewing my life it seemed inevitable that I would fly, though, looking back, I cannot choose the precise moment and say *that* was when I was committed to the sky. Perhaps this was it:

'Sissy.'

'Baaaby.'

'Cry Baby.'

'You wait!' I cried, 'I'll show you.'

'Showing' my step-brothers was an empty gesture. I had been showing them for months but they refused to be impressed. Still fuming I left their calumny, jumped on my bike and rode out of Pretoria.

Calmer, I stopped on the dusty road that bordered Swartkop military aerodrome, leaned my bike against the fence and gazed pensively. Aircraft, the sun ricocheting sharply from their windscreens, rose gracefully and effortlessly into the sky. No longer pensive I cycled nearer to the hangars, parked my bike against a 'Trespassers will be Prosecuted' sign and looked closely at the pilots and pilots-to-be. I watched them until the last aircraft landed, the hangar doors closed and quiet returned to the aerodrome.

Riding home I wondered about the pilots. They seemed perfectly normal. Their hands into which they placed their lives were as mine. They had laughed and gestured ordinarily;

4

oblivious of the courage, nobility and many other virtues that my admiration lavished upon them.

After I had been told off for being late for tea I announced that I was going to be a pilot.

'Yah! You couldn't fly for toffee.'

It went on like this until, over my fifteenth birthday breakfast, my mother, entirely hoodwinked by my unwary and apocryphal affection for flying, announced that for my birthday present we were all to drive out to Rand airport for my first flight. She called it a joy-ride. The sudden departure of my appetite and an attack of biliousness were charitably attributed to excitement. I have never been so frightened in all my life.

The drive to the airport was purgatory. I prayed for an earth-quake, a flat tyre, anything to deter further progress as I wrestled with the problem of Scylla and Charybdis; the fear of flying or the humiliation of admitting the lies of the last few months. I chose, if such a word describes an almost involuntary action, the whirlpool of flying with its remote possibility of survival to the certainty of rock-like ignominy that would follow confession.

The wretched airport looked peaceful with an air of gentle laziness and shimmering quiet broken only by the departure or arrival of aircraft that, paradoxically, seemed to intrude. Irresistibly we drove through the gates to the excited and envious comments of my step-brothers. My mother had the smug expression of those who give. I tried very hard to wrench my ankle as I stepped out of the car but succeeded only in giving myself ineffectual pain.

I remember nothing of that first flight except the studied disgust of the pilot as he delicately avoided my breakfast and the feeling of unutterable relief when my feet touched soil again.

5

I contrived to avoid further combat but towards the latter part of the following year as I neared my sixteenth birthday, it was evident that my position as a 'pilot' needed strengthening. I requested a repeat performance. This time, on my birthday, we drove to Barragwanath airport, the headquarters of Johannesburg Flying Club, and I remember every minute of it.

The aircraft, de Havilland Moths, stood wing-tip to wing-tip in a neat line in front of the administration buildings. I was introduced to the veteran who was to transport me to another element. He was casually unconcerned as he showed me around the aircraft prior to our flight. Had he, I wondered, forgotten his first few flights. Rapidly he strapped me into the front cockpit immediately behind the engine and then climbed into the cockpit behind me. I sat, frightened, and gazed at the welter of instruments, wires and crash pad. Everything seemed oddly still. A mechanic appeared and, with the order 'Contact,' spun the propeller. The engine coughed into action and transformed the plane into vibrating animation. The tiny pointers on the instruments rose, registering goodness knows what. A laconic 'O.K.?' through the speaking tube attached to my helmet calmed my fear as we taxied out over the grass. The rattle of the tail skid on the uneven surface sent a series of judders through the frail structure; the wings curved and swayed with an action of their own. With a sharp turn we stopped at the far end of the field.

Another laconic grunt implied something, but before I could answer my back was pushed sharply against the back rest and we careered along the field. Fascinated, I saw the nose lower until I could see along the top of the engine. The wind thrust at my head and buffeted me like a punching bag. The airport buildings lurched and ran towards us. Closer they came until I could see our car parked nearby. They'll catch us, I thought childishly, thinking of a game of tag, when suddenly they gave up the chase and slid smoothly beneath us. Timidly I looked ahead and saw the horizon. The large horizon of pilots, with the earth sinking into insignificance beneath. We banked steeply and as I looked down the left wing and saw the ground I was conscious of the void beneath me. I wondered what I sat on, looked down between my feet and was horrified to see canvas and flimsy bits of wood. Panic-stricken I tried to hold on to the struts that supported the top wing; the wind tore my hands away and only another grunt from the rear prevented sheer hysteria.

Suddenly the unnerving roar of the engine subsided to the gentle caressing swish of wind against the wings. I relaxed and was sick. The saucer of the earth gradually flattened as we glided towards the field. Gently the plane transferred its weight from the air to the ground and the swish gave way to a rumble of wheels and tail skid as they creaked protestingly over the field. We stopped, and everything was still.

In the last few moments of that flight, after fear and panic departed, leaving a brilliance of perception that follows all malaise, I realized that now I *wanted* to fly. Wanted the exhilaration of fear and difference. A world beyond my step-brothers.

We had lunch at the airport and I spent the afternoon enquiring about the economics of learning to fly. To my dismay I learned that I could not qualify for a licence until I was seventeen. I could however commence flying lessons immediately. I was introduced to the Chief Flying Instructor who, as I watched in awe, spoke of pounds, shillings and pence. Fortunately my mother was with me and absorbed these essential matters.

That night and every night for weeks my mother and I

discussed and argued interminably. The entire family and all my relations were united in their opposition against my wish to fly. The four pounds a week, they suggested, could be more usefully spent on a finishing school, preparation for university or marriage, or scores of other estimable projects.

2

I HAD MY FIRST FLYING LESSON TWO MONTHS LATER. IT WAS A trial lesson with the Chief Flying Instructor prior to committing myself to the full course necessary for obtaining an 'A' licence. This first lesson was in a Hornet Moth, with side-by-side seating arrangements and an enclosed cockpit. Looking back I realize that most of my early difficulties were due to the lop-sided effect of sitting on one side. As the instructor levelled off high above Johannesburg he gestured to me to take over control. At that time I was about five feet tall and could barely reach the control column and rudder bars. I stretched, coupled my fingers around the joystick and clung on, hard. The following series of evolutions, a faithful exposition of all I had read in a book entitled 'Learn to Fly by Correspondence Course,' defy description.

'Try some straight and level flight,' said the instructor wearily.

'But I am,' I answered.

'Oh.'

We landed, I was sick again and we had a fatherly chat in his office.

Despite his advice I arranged to take the full course and had five rather unproductive lessons on the Hornet Moth before transferring to the illustrious Tiger Moth. This machine, vehicle of pioneering record-breaking flights, with its tandem seating and

9

open cockpit seemed more of a friend than an enemy to be conquered. Each Sunday, weather permitting, and in South Africa it usually did, I had one lesson lasting an hour and a lecture or two on ground subjects.

Getting to the airport, 45 miles from home, had become a problem so I bought a motor-bike or, rather, my mother bought one for me. This of course played havoc with her estimated budget of flying costs.

I failed to fulfil gloomy prognostications of an early death and became inordinately attached to this machine. It reacted to my moods. A bilious approach would provoke mule-like obstinacy and though I would kick the starter for hours it would remain inanimate. Happiness, induced by Sunday sunshine and freedom would bring a response of eagerness and burbling vivacity and we would roll along, friends, reluctant to turn back, anxious to explore together the next hill, the next horizon.

Flying, and my motor-bike, injected me with confidence. My inferiority complex almost vanished and boys became objects of scorn rather than envy. I held court with scores of them, patronizing one against the other, letting them bathe in my reflected glory as an 'ace' with queenly condescension. Only one little beast resisted and refused to become my liege. I cycled interminably past his home with passion and hatred in my heart. Unfanned, the flame soon expired and the courted became the despised courtier.

My life became a happy whirl of study and flying . . . and a waiting for Sunday. I learned the alchemy of Meteorology that produces the allies and enemies of the sky. Of the levels of pressure sporting in the desolate Arctic wastes that, later and thousands of miles away, would transform the sky from blue placidity to dark satanic fury. Of the counter-pressures, friends of pilots, that would restore serenity. I learned of the things that go up and down inside engines, though to this day I do not believe they do these remarkable things. The mysteries of Morse code were unravelled from dots and dashes. The stars became signposts to distant destinations and the quaint rotations of the sun and moon became a logical sequence upon which all life depended as I progressed from medium turns to steep turns and from gigantic bounces to tolerable arrivals. The mere sight of an aircraft sufficed to fill me with pride and not a little humility.

About this time, after sojourns in schools of varying quality though, in South Africa, identical curriculum, I managed to matriculate. So ended my formal education. I fully intended later to go to Oxford. My schooldays over, I devoted myself to flying.

After seventeen hours of dual flying, my instructor considered that I could probably get an aircraft into the air and down again without too catastrophic a result. My first solo! I was turned over to the Chief Flying Instructor for the flying test that precedes all first solo flights. He clambered into the Tiger Moth, plugged in the speaking tubes and sat motionless. After an exaggerated pre-flight inspection of the aircraft I climbed into the seat behind him. I examined carefully the back of his neck; it was inscrutable and he needed a hair-cut. I too sat motionless, considering this encouraging fallibility until a gentle 'Well?' erupted down the speaking tube.

We began badly. The engine would not start. With eyebrows eloquent the mechanic pushed and pulled at the propeller until both he and I were bathed in perspiration. The neck was still motionless and inscrutable. When I least expected it the engine sprang into unnecessarily hearty life, nearly decapitating the mechanic. Ghost-like my throttle closed as the Chief Instructor closed his (all controls are duplicated and interconnected on training aircraft). The mechanic, by now a confirmed misogynist, obeyed my signal and thankfully removed the chocks from in front of the wheels. Gingerly I opened the throttle and taxied to the down-wind boundary of the field.

'I want you to do three complete circuits and landings, please. And relax,' instructed the metallic voice.

'Yes sir,' I screamed down the tube. The neck winced involuntarily.

'Don't shout!'

'Yes sir,' I whispered.

'What?'

'Yes sir.'

'I'm not knighted . . . yet,' he answered.

Brooding over his heavy irony I stopped at right-angles to the take-off path and carefully went through the cockpit drill that precedes all flights. Petrol on and sufficient for the flight. Throttle friction nut adjusted to prevent the throttle from slipping back during the take-off. Trim-tabs set. Both magneto switches on. Mixture control fully rich. With a last look round the sky I turned into wind and opened the throttle firmly, at the same time easing the control column forward to lift the tail. At 60 m.p.h. the aircraft climbed gently. Tense and unsure I watched the airspeed indicator and tried to keep its elusive needle pointed steadily at 70 m.p.h. as we climbed straight ahead to 1,000 feet before I throttled back to cruising power and levelled off. Carefully I started the 180-degree turn that would bring us back parallel to the aerodrome. I turned too steeply and found myself too close to the field. I edged out hoping he would not notice, but an exaggerated look at the field by the head in front dispelled that hope. As the aerodrome passed under the port wing-tip I turned again through 90 degrees and prepared for landing. Throttling right back and trimming the aircraft for the gliding attitude I turned in at 70 m.p.h. and gradually flattened the angle of glide until we sailed over the leeward boundary at 20 feet or so flying level with the ground. As the speed dropped I eased the nose higher until we were in the three-point attitude and then, as the book says, the aircraft will sink gently to the ground. It didn't, and I waited in what I thought was the three-point attitude for anxious moments. A sinking sensation was followed by a distressingly hollow thud. I stopped without further incident, taxied back to the take-off point and awaited comments.

'Not bad. Try and make your circuit a little cleaner and don't level off so high on landing,' came the voice from in front.

I could have kissed him. With this shrewd praise my nerves vanished and I completed the next two circuits and landings with moderate success. After my third landing the Chief Instructor took over and, whilst taxi-ing back to the take-off point, issued instructions in a matter-of-fact voice.

'You can go solo. Do one circuit and landing and pick me up after you've landed. I'll wait here.' We stopped and he climbed out. I waved and swung into wind. I was astonished at the visibility. For twelve flying hours I had had to peer over and around the instructor's head a few inches in front of me. Now there was nothing but pregnant vacancy. Only then did I realize I was alone.

In the most complete solitude I have ever experienced I joined the sky. Looking down at the earth receding into a blur of green and brown I sang and handled the aircraft carelessly. At last there

13

was no instructor in front to comment acidly on the skidded turn or wayward airspeed. 'Look,' I cried. 'Everyone look up. It's me; Jackie Sorour. I'm flying, flying, flying.'

I waggled the wings and waltzed around the circuit in lyrical bliss. Even the aircraft seemed to respond to this magical moment.

'I'm flying, I'm flying.' I repeated the phrase, ecstatically aware, as one is rarely aware, of the moment at the moment. I knew that I could not deserve many more like it.

I landed smoothly and taxied back to pick up the Chief Instructor. He looked at my radiant face, smiled and held out his hand. 'Good show, nice landing. Take it up again for twenty minutes but don't lose sight of the airfield. I'll walk back.'

I shook hands, took off and drank more elixir.

After landing and receiving the congratulations of my fellow students I straddled my motor-bike and drove home furiously. To my intense disappointment the house was deserted. I sat fuming and fidgeting until my family returned, waited my moment and then calmly announced: 'I went solo today.'

3

WHILST PASSING THE FIRST MILESTONE, THAT OF GOING SOLO, and preparing for the second, my 'A' licence, a further project was passing through my mind. I dismissed it as firmly as I could whenever the thought overcame my natural reluctance. But the more I tried to banish it the more strongly it returned. My normal instincts of self-preservation were as ineffectual as Canute's demand of the sea. I wanted to try a parachute jump. That isn't true, I didn't want to. Nobody wants to do that. This was another obstacle of fear that by its very enormity of terror fascinated me as a doomed rabbit is fascinated by a snake.

During the following months as I prepared for my flying licence examinations I frequently glanced over the side of the Tiger Moth aircraft and looked at and through the emptiness beneath me. There flashed through my mind the image of my body falling through space, tumbling, tumbling to oblivion. I watched my body until it became a speck amongst the myriad of specks that made up the landscape. This recurring image brought violent attacks of vertigo and made me shrink, unnerved, into the cockpit, hating myself and the devil within that drove me to such idiocy.

Evidently I should explain why I had to jump. Ingenuously I have thought it simply the action of a coward. I had to prove to myself that I was not a coward; therefore I must jump. Later a more facile analysis by a flying comrade suggested that it was my innate sense of publicity. That so strong was my conceit and wish to be a celebrity, even at that tender age, I was prepared to go to the lengths of risking my life for public adulation. Another pseudo-psychiatric suggestion was that I wanted to be a boy and, therefore, this was simply another manifestation of frustrated masculinity. Now, in comparative maturity, I must confess the second theory rings true. (Though not for constant and international fame would I jump again.)

I waited patiently for my seventeenth birthday and practised interminably the various tortuous manœuvres on which I would be tested for my licence. 'Figures of 8' around two pylons, and dead-stick landings to within inches of a chalked circle in the middle of the airfield. The '8' was a test of flying accuracy. Two pylons had to be encircled at a constant height and airspeed with the evolution of the '8' to be as near perfect as possible. The flight path resembled a pair of spectacles, with the pylons in the centre of the lens. The cross-eyed effect of my earlier efforts caused a certain amount of unkind amusement but as the day neared I managed to give the impression of normal eyesight.

The flying test was arranged soon after I was seventeen. It was a sunny day, with people going their ways quite normally. I felt mild resentment that on such a day they could be so un-concerned.

The sealed barograph, an infernal contraption that traced on a chart any variations of height during my solo test manœuvres, was placed in the rear of the aeroplane. With this omniscient and incorruptible passenger and under the watchful eyes of the Chief Flying Instructor and fellow students I perspired my way through the test. I landed and accompanied the Chief Instructor, and the barograph, to his office. With ballot box tensity the seals were broken.

'Hum, what happened there?' asked the instructor, pointing to a sharp dip in the pen's spindly trace.

'A thermal current,' I lied hopefully.

'Some current!' he said as he continued examining the tell-tale trace. I examined him examining it and observed the analogy of the lines around his eyes and mouth. As they deepened, so my spirits sank sympathetically.

'I think it will do,' he observed finally. 'We'll send it to the Ministry. Now for the "Oral."'

Half an hour later, having survived the barrage of questions, I left his office. A week later my licence arrived.

The celebrations over, my thoughts returned to the parachute jump. Three months later I was still trying to obtain permission from the Ministry. Their replies were a masterpiece of prevarication not, under the circumstances, entirely blameworthy. Not to be outdone I decided to see the minister. I do not know who was the more astonished as I sat in his office in a vast leather chair, my legs dangling a few inches from the carpet: he at my audacity, I at my success in sitting in this exalted office. I peered over the desk and, strengthened by the knowledge that he had done the first parachute jump in South Africa, launched into what must have been a brilliantly persuasive soliloquy for within a few days I received official permission to jump.

My mother and I sat at home one serene Saturday evening. Idly she brushed aside her sewing and turned on the radio for the nine o'clock news.

'. . . particular crisis had passed. Hitler had declared himself

17

satisfied . . . At six o'clock tomorrow morning Miss Jackie Sorour, a young South African girl aged seventeen, will attempt a parachute jump from 5,000 feet over Swartkop aerodrome . . . Here are the sports results . . .'

I was dumbfounded and watched horrified as disbelief and incredulity passed across my mother's features.

'What on earth . . . Jackie, are you mad! How dare you! I forbid it.' She got up, a tiny tower of rage.

'I must do it now,' I appealed, alarmed at her anger. 'Everything's arranged.'

'The funeral as well?' she answered.

For the first time in my life my mother and I quarrelled bitterly. I felt ashamed at my deceit in not taking her into my confidence. However, the unfortunate announcement over the radio, made without my knowledge or consent, forced her compliance. She appreciated that I could not draw back now.

The next morning my mother drove me to the aerodrome. Under a thin cheerless drizzle the pavements glistened drably in the half-light of approaching dawn. The windscreen wiper clicked thumpily in unison with my heart.

As daybreak lifted the pallor of the low unseasonable clouds it revealed the airport road unusually heavy with traffic. The car-parks were full and cars had spilled on to the perimeter of the aerodrome; their owners sitting on the roofs placidly munching sandwiches. How I envied them. The faint lingering hope that I might escape the inevitable vanished with a thud into the pit of my stomach.

My mother stopped before the airport buildings and, rather importantly, opened the car doors for me. I stepped out into a blaze of flashes as press photographers jostled their way on to the front page.

The pilot, solemnly benevolent, strapped me in before we took off in a haze of waving handkerchiefs. As we climbed, climbed, climbed, the sun shone through the broken clouds giving dimension to the height.

'O.K.,' he shouted as we levelled off at five thousand feet. 'When you're ready.'

I undid the straps and cowered in the seat. 'What did you say?' shouted the pilot. I shook my head; I could hardly admit that I had sobbed: 'Oh Mum.'

Insane with fear I stood up on the seat and clambered out on to the lower wing. The slipstream screamed at my insolence and only the firm grasp of the pilot leaning out of his seat prevented me from being blown off unceremoniously. It suddenly occurred to me that sitting on the wing of an aircraft at 5,000 feet is a most extraordinary thing to do. I sat for long seconds gazing down at the mile of space beneath and the unfamiliar silhouette of the tail, usually unseen, perched inconsequentially on the end of the fuselage. Defying the fury of the wind I waved at the pilot. He waved back. I did it again; it seemed so funny with my legs dangling absurdly over the chasm beneath. The wind still struggled. 'Stop pushing,' I protested, 'I'll jump when I'm ready.'

The wind and the noise suddenly ceased and I knew I had jumped. Uselessly I splayed my arms to stop the sickening somersaults before plunging through a broken fragment of cloud. At the back of my mind was the thought that I had forgotten something. A thousand feet passed before I remembered and pulled the rip-cord. A brief flash of eternity passed before the sharp rupturing crack of silk proclaimed survival and the violence of

19

the last few moments gave way to a calm swinging gentleness.

Recovering I looked up into the huge umbrella of silk that flapped hollowly like sails in a moderate breeze, and began to enjoy the curious quality of floating through space, of altitude without noise. A bird passed; it circled and passed again. I am sure its features registered astonishment. Distantly I heard the drone of aircraft encircling my descent. One, I knew, had a newspaper camera man aboard. I waved and tried to appear composed.

The ground reached up with suddenness. I had missed the aerodrome. Angled hangars, loomed hugely; a telegraph wire pinged against my foot before a welcoming field slipped beneath my feet. I hit it, hard. A spasm of pain brought momentary unconsciousness. Then dimly, through the folds of collapsed silk I saw polo players approaching on horseback like an army of Pegasus. They helped me to one foot. The other was useless, the ankle broken.

4

THE ANKLE GROUNDED ME FOR THE NEXT SIX MONTHS. DURING that time I gathered a large circle of friends, including some of the South African Air Force. I envied the latter their dedication to flying and felt, by comparison, a dilettante. They and I were oblivious of the dedication to follow. That this peace-time practice of an art would flourish into a science of horror that would spray indiscriminate death; that would turn night into a holocaust of impersonal bestiality and enable crews to return, smiling insensibly, to their bacon and eggs.

But, I was carefree. My home became a free-house. My mother blossomed in the casual uniformed atmosphere and kept the refrigerator bursting with swiftly prepared delicacies. I went to my first ball with an air force cadet and hobbled awkwardly, though successfully, on one foot.

During the interim of plaster-casts and crutches I had secretly written to an aeronautical college in England for details of a residential flying course that would enable me to qualify for a professional 'B' licence. It would take a year and cost a thousand pounds, including fares. Poor Mother! That was a sizeable chunk from the debris of her marriages.

'But Mother, if I get a 'B' licence I can fly professionally. It's as good as a degree.' I had started my campaign to go to England.

21

'But your instructor told me you couldn't get a job as a pilot. They don't like women piloting passengers. I don't either!' This was the core of the argument that stretched interminably as my mother fought a determined rearguard action. A stream of eligible bachelors were inveigled to her support. The air-force cadets were given a cool reception at variance with their previous welcome. Our home became a maelstrom of sulks, counter-sulks and wilful obstinacy.

I BOARDED THE SHIP IN JUNE 1938. IT WAS AN ITALIAN SHIP, THE *Giulio Cesare*. My send-off from Pretoria was reminiscent of the kind loved by Hollywood directors when their small-town girl goes off to New York to make good. A cadet played an accordion as I danced around the station platform with all my friends. They cheered as I boarded the train and waved continuously as I disappeared in a flurry of steam and coal specks. My mother sat quietly and sadly in the corner of the compartment and sent a twinge of remorse through my heart at my thoughtless gaiety. We cuddled and cried as familiar landmarks clicked past the window.

I said good-bye to her at Johannesburg.

'Thank you Mother . . . for everything.'

'Now don't forget your promise. If there's a war, you return immediately.'

She disappeared, her face wracked as she fought back the tears. I waved to her on the platform until her tiny figure was lost. I continued, alone, to Cape Town.

The *Giulio Cesare* was an overture of sparkling white and expectancy. Faces registered extremes of emotion in the revealing sun. I edged my way up the gang-plank, threw a streamer amidst hundreds of others and watched it sadly as it fluttered into the oil-slicked ditch that sucked noisily between the ship and the quay. Pointlessly I waved to the upturned faces and nodded violently to nobody.

The purser, in impressive white and gold, steered me firmly through the gesticulating voyagers to the two nuns, an oasis of starched calm, who stood on the tourist-class boat deck. My chaperones. They were returning to the Emerald Isle and were to accompany me to London.

Slowly the ship wrenched me from South Africa. My roots dangled in suspended animation until, eight years later, they were transplanted in the mellow soil of Somerset.

I escaped my inseparable companions as the ship docked for a brief interlude at Dakar. Enchanted, I wandered alone through the monumental filth of the back streets. Filth meant difference, not poverty, misery and disease. I was oblivious of the tragic, conscious only of the foreign.

'It's about time we returned to the ship, miss.' I turned, astonished. A young steward, immaculate in sailor's civilian whites, grinned at me. 'Sorry,' he continued, 'Captain's orders. I mustn't let you out of my sight.' Both flattered and insulted by this attention I returned with him to the ship.

We docked at Marseilles and entrained for Paris, where we spent three days in an estimable, though dull, tour of the churches. Indefatigably the nuns and I explored dank crypts, penetrated stygian gloom in their devotion to God. He will forgive my frustrated preference for the frivolous. I noticed the northern twilight that stretches day into the domains of night and offers a siesta of darkening tranquility between work and play. The day, too, was different with gradations of colour unknown in sun-blinded South Africa.

The boat-train from Folkestone to London introduced me to the anarchy of the English countryside, its green luxuriant beauty a host of individual enterprise. Hedges and fences crawled bewilderingly. Oblongs jostled with squares, trees with wheat, dairy farms with slender tall chimneys. A perfection of chaos. A landscape of Lilliputian enchantment, with narrow roads curling inconsequentially through cool glens and dozing villages.

I was shocked at the straggling mass of chimney pots that heralded London. Short, slim, long, fat, they shot their filth into the polluted haze; even on this sunny temperate day. I was glad when these identical burrows were purged from my sight and replaced by the comparative dignity of warehouses and factories as we neared Victoria.

I said good-bye to the nuns and looked for 'Uncle' Jimmie, a friend of the family, who was to meet me. I sat on a bench on the platform innocent of the need to clear Customs where, of course, Uncle was waiting. The Customs shed emptied and no me. The platform emptied and no Uncle. We both waited independently, thinking unjust thoughts of each other. I sat for three hours. Pretoria was a long way away.

'Whasamattermiss?' I looked up and dashed a tear. The porter eyed me kindly.

'I was supposed to meet my uncle here. He hasn't turned up,' I answered woefully.

'Yore Awstryliyan aintcher?'

'No, South African.'

'Same fing.'

'I beg your pardon?' I queried, startled.

'Oh, you know.' I did not, of course. This was my first experience of that peculiar English idiosyncracy that considers

24

fluency a vice and inarticulation a virtue. 'Where yer going?' he continued.

'Witney Aeronautical College, near Oxford,' I replied.

'Coo! Kumon,' he summoned, picking up my small case and tartan travelling rug. 'We'll go to Enquiries.' We walked to the enquiry office.

'Lidy wantsago ter Oxford. Rite it down. Shees foren,' he explained. Later he put me in a taxi for Paddington Station with explicit orders to the driver to put me on the correct train. He refused my proffered tip, 'No fanksmiss. Spleasure,' and blushed at his kindness. I had learned of another English idiosyncracy: kindness to stray animals.

After a bewildering journey I found myself at Oxford. I felt crushed and insignificant in this illustrious city. Diffidently, and as instructed, I 'phoned the airport:

'Is that the aerodrome?'

'Yes,' exquisitely.

'I'm Miss Sorour from South Africa. Will you come and pick me up?'

'I'd love to, miss, but I'm on duty. May I pick you up some other time?'

'Is that Witney aerodrome?'

'I regret that it isn't. This is Royal Air Force, Brize Norton.'

Regretfully I replaced the receiver. The second call was more successful. A young gallant arrived, driving the college station-wagon and took me into protective custody. Thankfully I placed myself in his care and, sleepily and mono-syllabically, was carried along antiquity with ancient spires landmarking toy villages and graveyards nestling peacefully in the lengthening shadows.

Turning into a cobbled lane we stopped before a farmhouse.

With mews of sympathy I was welcomed and spoiled and tucked between welcoming sheets. I cried a little. Then, with a gentle reminder to God that I was here and not in Pretoria, I slept to the unfamiliar lullaby of crickets.

5

THE NEXT MORNING I AWAKENED LATE AND REFRESHED. A distant carpenter emphasized the quiet so strange to my urban-bred ears. Birds sang their solo to the accompaniment of nature's hum. The low baritone of a cow prompted the shrill answer of a cock. I washed and went downstairs.

'Good morning. Did you sleep well?' asked Mrs Hirons, my hostess. There being no accommodation for females at the school, it had been arranged that I would stay with Mrs Hirons and her family. It was a farmhouse without a farm. Oddly enough another South African girl was staying there, studying engineering. We did not become good friends. I had robbed her of her distinction of being the only girl at the school.

'Like a log,' I answered, looking for breakfast.

'Over here,' she pointed, anticipating my pangs.

Tall, elegantly slim and with the aquiline features of an aristocrat, she joined me at the table. I felt a little awed. It was weeks before I could emulate the example of the other students and call her 'Mum'. Her son John, equally imposing and of my age, was in the garden. 'Dad' too.

'Your uncle phoned last night . . .' she said.

'What happened to him?' I interpolated sharply.

'He waited for over three hours in the Customs shed at Victoria. Your luggage is still there.'

'Customs! What Customs?'

'Didn't you go through Customs?'

'No.'

'How did you get out of the station?'

'Just walked out,' I answered. She laughed. 'That explains everything. He saw your luggage in Customs and naturally assumed you were bound to come there. Poor man, he was terribly worried when he phoned last night. He asked me not to wake you.'

'What shall I do about my luggage?'

'Write to the Customs people at Victoria. They will clear it and send it on here.'

They did but in their diligent search for contraband pulled the rip-cord of my parachute. They enclosed a brief note of apology with the gigantic bundle of crushed silk.

I spent the following day, Sunday, exploring the countryside alone. In constant delight my eyes were filled with the quaint and the picturesque. I touched the hedges and crossed the stiles; discovered idling brooks wafting softly and coolly through magical pathways. Village vied with village in somnolent charm. As the sun lingered hugely on the horizon I walked home slowly, reluctant to end this enchantment.

Early the following morning the station-wagon arrived to take me to the college. I had dressed inconspicuously and wore a studious air.

I was disappointed at the school's insignificance. I had envisaged stone quadrangles, Norman towers and the rich cool green of carefully tended lawns. Instead I saw a cluster of nondescript buildings nestling on the boundary of a grass aerodrome. A hangar denoted aviation. Overhead a ubiquitous Tiger Moth droned and circled lazily. I turned resentfully to the driver. 'Is this it?' I asked.

'Is this what, miss?'

'The college.'

'Yes.'

'All of it?'

'Yes.'

Ruefully I recalled the glowing terms of the prospectus.

I was introduced to the Chief Flying Instructor. He was absurdly young. He was killed a year later whilst testing an exper-imental flying-wing aircraft. He introduced me to the other instructors and lecturers. The majority of the students were studying aeronautical engineering; only a dozen or so were taking the pilots' course. This was another disappointment. I had imag-ined a vast impersonal machine that spat out squads of trained pilots regularly and efficiently.

That evening at a cocktail party held in my honour in the club-house I met the other students. They were cosmopolitan in nationality and ambition. Shamefully I recall my patronage and condescension towards the coloured students from Africa and India. South African prejudice is too insidious and comprehensive to be banished in a day, or by the example of others. It has taken nearly a decade to purge the last lingering symptoms of this disease from my mind.

After a brief period of refresher flying with my instructor I was sent up solo to practise a few spins and stalls and to famil-iarize myself with the local landmarks. Uneasily I completed the spinning. Few pilots enjoy the unnatural contortions of spinning

29

with the aircraft pointing vertically at the gyrating landscape and groaning and heaving its resentment as the wind slaps sharply from unfamiliar angles. The stalls were a mild manœuvre in comparison. I then began my tour of the landmarks. Happily I sported with the clouds. Wisps of placid stratus carpeted respectfully the towering majesty of pompous cumulo-nimbus. Like a mosquito I buzzed insolently against their confined rage and darted off as they slapped at me with their turbulence when my audacity overcame prudence and I got too close.

I glanced at my watch: time to return. With a last defiant tilt at the clouds I turned back to the aerodrome. A twinge of anxiety tingled my spine when it failed to appear. I flew on, my head swivelling from side to side like a tennis spectator's.

Slowly and inexorably as the useless miles were spanned I became utterly lost. With growing anxiety I oscillated futilely over the bewildering similarity of the English countryside. Absurdly it occurred to me that some rascal had moved the aerodrome. Tacking errantly I followed likely paths until they disappeared into a vista of unfamiliarity. With maddening monotony the smug ground remained unmoved and refused to proffer the aerodrome. Almost babbling with fright and shame I jerked across the sky in aimless panic. Where is it? Where is it? Oh God, where is it? The cumulo-nimbus clouds had shaped into gigantic profiles that leered maliciously. The petrol gauge fed my fear. I had been up for three hours. I imagined the few remaining gallons of petrol swilling emptily in the tank. My calf muscles ached with tension; my hands slipped in sweat; my face was stiff. Only my eyes, searching the horizon like a coon, moved facilely. Fervently I offered penances to God if only He would show me the aerodrome, any aerodrome. The engine, oblivious of impending disaster, purred glibly and greedily sucked its own life's blood.

When I had been reduced to simpering vilification against fate, God optioned my penances and miraculously produced an aerodrome. A large hangar beckoning from the horizon, cut a swathe through the sky-line of calamity and offered sanctuary. Waggling my wings in an ecstacy of deliverance I dived crazily to refuge. The engine faltered as I finished my landing run and stopped altogether as I turned off the runway and taxied towards the Control Tower. The petrol tank was empty. With this last melodramatic gesture the aircraft rolled silently to a halt. Fortune smiled and moved on.

As I sat ruminating a car drove out:

'Where am I?' I asked.

'Royal Air Force, Brize Norton,' they answered.

They entertained me to tea. I telephoned Witney where two aircraft were searching for me and waited in the officers' mess for an instructor to fly me back.

6

THE MONTHS AT WITNEY PASSED BY PLEASANTLY AND FRUITFULLY.
My first 'love' was with an old man of twenty-four. A fellow
student, he made it quite clear that I was distinguished only by
his company. Meekly I accepted this analysis. There were only
two girls at the college. He had, of course, already discarded the
other one.

There was little to do to weld this quaint relationship other
than pastoral rambles and an occasional visit to Oxford. After
sundown we would walk together along the winding lanes to
the village and sit in a cool oak-shadowed arbour outside the
village pub. I would not go inside. He drank 'the usual', whatever
that was, and I sipped gigantic fizzy lemonades that provoked
hiccups all the way home. He would talk ever-increasing nonsense. Every night he got angry because I would not kiss him.

'Why not?'

'I don't want to.'

'But why don't you want to?'

I wished I had the temerity to tell him that the smell of hops
combined with my fortuitous hiccups was too much even for that
God-like profile. We would walk home in silence with the owls
hooting mockery and derision at his frustration. Or so I liked
to think. Sulkily he would try again before saying good-night.

Thwarted, he would amble off, muttering 'frigid iceberg' or similar unkind observations.

Finally he gave up.

The next affair was passed inarticulately. It was, of course, with John. We had blushes for breakfast and ers and ars for supper. The week-ends were passed in a comparatively brilliant series of monosyllables. His mother condoned our halting courting, knowing its artlessness. Still smarting from the dismal failure of my first love I resorted to high heels and a dash of lipstick in order to nurse this tender hot-house plant. The former provoked an uncontrolled guffaw; the latter, mild disapproval. I could talk only of flying; he of motor-bikes. We kissed once. My first kiss. We both slobbered a little and did not quite hit the mark. To my intense chagrin he did not try again. Our undying love died.

I seemed to spend my social hours in a stream of negatives. No, I don't smoke. No, I don't drink. No, I don't, don't, don't. I must have been exceedingly aggravating. Despite this I remained popular and found it difficult to preserve the hours necessary for studying. I danced well, despite my insistence that my partner should maintain the moat between us. I kept an anxious eye on the drawbridge and peremptorily pulled it higher whenever it slipped to my waist.

The ugly eruptions of Europe left me unconcerned. I was politically illiterate. Munich was less important than myself. I enjoyed the tense weeks of apprehension, the ill-informed arguments and the ominous warning of the nights cut with searchlight fingers as toy soldiers played with toy death.

I visited London during the weeks of suspense and swam on the edges of its hushed expectancy. Though the city had a solemn air, its people seemed to reflect the procrastination of the times.

Unconsciously I searched for those who knew the portent of that hour. Who knew what was to be fought and why it had to be fought. I returned to Witney knowing nothing.

My first personal contact with the flotsam thrown out by the tide of Europe's insanity was with a Jewish refugee. A young girl, she had left her parents in a concentration camp. She worked as a servant in a large county house.

We were introduced by a common acquaintance. I listened and appraised her curiously. She spoke English haltingly and lapsed frequently into German. She was my age but a hundred years older.

I invited her to tea in Oxford. She was late and looked a lonely figure as she came into the restaurant and stood near the entrance searching for me. I waved to her, she nodded in return and, looking neither right nor left, walked to my table.

'Tea and cakes?'

'Please.'

We searched for a subject. I gushed a little; she was taciturn.

'Joan told me about your parents. I'm sorry.'

'Thank you.'

'Do you hear from them?' 'Not directly.'

'I cannot understand . . . what have they done?'

'They are Jews,' she answered simply.

'Have they done anything else?' I asked stupidly.

'Isn't it enough?' she answered coolly.

I fidgeted in embarrassment; 'I didn't mean . . .'

'Not consciously, I know.' She made me uncomfortable.

'Look Helga, I like the Jews.'

'That's as bad as disliking them.'

She suddenly remembered an appointment. We shook hands

and parted. I had tried to run before I could walk, and had hurt her.

During that brilliant summer of 1939 I received a stream of letters from my mother who had suddenly shown a remarkable interest in current affairs. Her analysis of the European situation was worthy of a foreign correspondent. Her letters invariably ended: 'Therefore you must return to South Africa immediately.' I replied evasively, countering her accurate prognostications with highly inaccurate optimism, and remained in England.

Nineteen-thirty-nine became for me a race between my 'B' licence and the outbreak of war. As the shadows lengthened over Europe I crammed both flying and studies. Until the early hours of the morning a solitary light glowed at the farmhouse as I became dissipated with study.

Various incidents at the college foreshadowed its eventual demise. The Chief Flying Instructor left for his fateful test pilot appointment. A few students of military age left suddenly. Instructions were issued that under no circumstances were students to land at Royal Air Force aerodromes. Service officers appeared, inspected augustly, took notes and departed, leaving a conspiratorial air that bred rumour and counter-rumour.

My sole achievement during the months preceding the outbreak of war was the acquisition of an Assistant Instructor's endorsement on my original 'A' licence. This dubious accomplishment authorized me to pass on to unsuspecting pupils the undulating knowledge of flying that I had scraped together during a hundred and fifty hours in the air.

Owing to a shortage of instructors the college arranged for me to instruct the week-end students of the affiliated flying club. On week-days I was a meek pupil. On Sundays I was transformed into a swaggering veteran of the air and carried out manœuvres that would have terrified me on a Tuesday.

Early in September I was scheduled to take a pupil on his first cross-country flight. He was an Oxford undergraduate, so elegant and supercilious he managed to convey the impression that he was escorting me on this navigational exercise.

During that triangular flight, cruising smoothly at 3,000 feet, the backyards of poverty and the spacious grounds of affluence were strangely deserted. The roads, normally choked with cars heading for the sea, were empty. The entire nation were glued to their radio sets. We were alone in the sky; possibly the last aircraft to drone with peace, to pass by in the sky without terror for those beneath.

We flew steadily southwards until my pupil smiled at me in triumph as the golden sands of the south coast appeared sandwiched between the cool green of the Downs and the crystal blue of the English Channel. We were on course and on time. I ruefully recalled my first cross-country flight when I was neither on course nor on time. He turned through 90 degrees on to the new course and headed for the Isle of Wight that lay cradled in the caressing waves and sparkled brilliantly in the morning sun. The engine hummed unnoticed as a heart is unnoticed when it functions efficiently.

Below us liners cut their wake and swung in perfect parabolas into the docks; their smoke drifting idly towards us.

Feeling the necessity of behaving like an instructor I introduced a note of discord and commented sharply on our height:

'What height should we be?'

'Three thousand,' he answered.

'Well?' He opened the throttle and gained the necessary

200 feet. His face, reflected in the mirror, looked hurt. 'It's all right,' I weakened. 'You are doing very well.'

We circled the deserted beaches and set course for Reading.

Punctually Reading appeared. Overcoming my pique, he was making it appear much too easy, I congratulated him on his accuracy before we turned for home and war. We landed with a series of kangaroo bumps that restored my ego and taxied to the hangar where there was unusual activity. The aircraft were parked neatly in front of the operations hut. Familiar faces had an unfamiliarly grave countenance. We had returned to a different world. Had taken off in peace at nine-thirty and landed in war at noon.

PART TWO

WAR

We set off feeling very brave,
To blaze a Spitfire trail,
Across the sky o'er half the world,
With ne'er a thought of fail.

1940

7

THE FOLLOWING DAY THE COLLEGE CLOSED. IN AN END-OF-TERM atmosphere of excitement and bustle the others packed their bags and departed for fitting and adventurous destinations. The instructors for Royal Air Force squadrons; the late pupils for R.A.F. training schools. All flowed into tailored situations, except me. I wept with envy and jealousy as they left in taxis and private cars. I despised my body, my breasts, all the things that pronounced me woman and left me behind as solitary and desolate as a discarded mistress.

I was the last to depart, my destination commonplace Down-hill Farm, a mile or two away. I looked angrily at the sky as I walked home. It had become distant and aloof. A stage of valour for a male cast only. No female actress would tread those boards. Bitterness and gall brought on biliousness. An errand boy passed innocently by, one hand in his pocket and whistling cheerfully. You little fool, I thought bitterly, envying him the cross-bar, that symbol of freedom, of which he was so oblivious. I kicked a stone at him and his infuriating cheerfulness but he sailed by unharmed, intent on his next delivery. I arrived at the farm, ran past the astonished Mrs Hirons, threw myself on the bed and sobbed.

That evening in bed I thought of the Amazonian women who

41

were alleged to have cut off their breasts to enable them to sight their bows and arrows accurately. I looked malignantly at my breasts, symbols of weakness, rooted firmly on my chest and remembered Mr Hirons' cut-throat razor in the bathroom. Further speculation was interrupted by Mrs Hirons' call from the foot of the staircase: 'Phone-call, Jackie.'

It was a cable from my mother:

> *Pretoria, 3.9.39*
>
> *Return home immediately. Have contacted Union Castle Line here and made provisional reservation for soonest berth Southampton-Cape Town. Contact head office London immediately and confirm reservation. Acknowledge. Love Mother.*

I was furious and cabled accordingly:

> *Not returning South Africa. Cancel booking. Letter following. Jackie.*

and returned wrathfully to bed, potent with ambition and, though uncomfortably aware of who was paying the piper, determined not to return weakly to South Africa.

I awoke with my ambition a weak parody of the flame of the night before and sat down moodily to breakfast.

'Morning,' said Mrs Hirons, 'there's a letter for you in the hall.'

I got it, looked at its official envelope and skipped hurriedly back to the table to read it.

The Director-General of Civil Aviation
London, W.C.2
4th September, 1939

Miss D. T. Sorour,
Downhill Farm,
Bailey,
Oxfordshire
Dear Madam,

I am requested to enquire whether, in the present State of Emergency, you are prepared to offer your services in a civilian capacity as an ambulance or ferry pilot.

Would you kindly communicate your decision to the above office at your earliest convenience.

Yours faithfully, etc.

My affirmative reply was in the post within half an hour. I also fulfilled my promise and wrote:

Dear Mother,

Thank you for your cable. Did you get my reply? I have decided not to return to South Africa until the war is over. I have just received a letter asking me to stand by as a ferry or ambulance pilot. I can't let them down now.

I really cannot return at this moment. The war will be over in a few months, then I can return to Witney College and resume my studies for the 'B' licence. It's silly to pay the fare for my return to South Africa and then do it all over again in a few months' time.

It isn't dangerous, Mother. In fact, apart from the blackout and uniforms, you wouldn't know there is a war on. Mrs Hirons has kindly offered for me to stay here for the duration of the war and

43

to stay here during my leave and week-ends. So don't worry, I am
all right.

What about my allowance? I have £30 left in the bank.

Your loving daughter,

Jackie.

I waited confidently for the letter from the Ministry. The birds twittered with my joy, the sun beamed a glow of welcome in the sky. Too impatient to walk I ran everywhere and leaped up stairs in twos and threes. I forgave everybody. Grace and charity abounded. The world was full of hope and promise. The letter arrived.

14th September, 1939

Dear Madam,

With reference to our letter dated the 4th of September and your reply of the 5th, I am requested to thank you for your offer but to inform you that the services of women pilots are not now required.

It is suggested that you may find a suitable position in the Women's Royal Auxiliary Air Force.

Yours faithfully,

etc., etc.

You beasts! You rotten horrid beasts. This was the strongest epithet I could muster. Cads and beasts. Rotters. Inhuman fiends. In a passion of hatred and revolt against the tyranny of man I swore, like Lysistrata, to withhold my love until they should repent. I had not yet, nor never would, bestow my favours on these miserable creatures.

44

AFTER MY FURY AND MORTIFICATION HAD SUBSIDED TO manageable proportions I decided to find a 'suitable position in the Waafs.' The nearest recruiting station was at Oxford. They got to know me very well.

Within ten days I became a *de facto* member of the Waafs. The partial recognition was a result of my insistence in being enlisted before the Royal Air Force were quite ready for me. In harassed desperation the recruiting officer suggested that, if it were really quite impossible for me to wait until the next draft was prepared, perhaps I would like to help out temporarily as an orderly for Waaf officers stationed at a nearby aerodrome.

Reflecting ruefully on my present lowly state I reported, unsworn, undisciplined and improperly dressed, to the aerodrome. The recruiting officer had been unable to provide a complete uniform. As the bus approached the gates and the hangars and panorama of aviation unfolded dimly in the driving rain I felt a patriotic surge of emotion. Eagerly I lifted my bag, clutched my pass and swept imperiously through the gates.

'And where do you think you're going?' boomed a voice.

'To the Waaf officer in charge, please,' I answered, cowed by the formidable figure with legs apart that stood by the guardroom eyeing me with extreme disfavour.

'Authority?' he barked.

'Pardon, sir?' I stuttered, meekly.

'Where's your authority?' he repeated. 'And you call me sergeant, not sir.'

Completely unnerved I offered my pass. He glanced at it cursorily. 'Corporal,' he called, 'escort A.C.W.2 Sorour to the Adjutant. Not,' he added mincingly, 'to the Waaf officer in charge.'

Blushing crimson and glancing yearningly at the bus that was departing with a crash of gears I was escorted to the Adjutant. The corporal was taciturn and intent on flinging his arm violently in salute to distant figures. Determined to impress I threw a handful of fingers towards my right ear as an important-looking personage approached.

'Come here, you!' ordered the personage, in the rain.

Proudly I came.

'What am I?' he asked. I resisted the impulse to be facetious and looked carefully at the medals on his tunic and the badge on his sleeve. The rain dripped persistently on to both. I had not the remotest idea what he was.

'Don't know, sergeant sir,' I admitted apologetically.

'Don't know!' he bellowed.

'No, sir,' I answered contritely.

Heavily he brought up his right sleeve until it was within an inch of my shiny nose. 'That! young lady, is the badge of a warrant officer.' Irrelevantly I admired the richly embroidered badge. 'It's lovely,' I blurted out. The corporal grinned. The warrant officer did not.

'What's your name and number?' he asked ominously.

'Dolores Teresa Sorour. I haven't got a number,' I answered.

'Haven't got a number?' he asked incredulously.

'No, sir.'

'Why haven't you got a number?'

'Nobody gave me one,' I answered tearfully. He looked at me, looked at the corporal and beckoned assistance from the heavens.

'I'm taking her to the Adj.,' explained the corporal helpfully.

46

'Yes, yes,' answered the warrant officer wearily. 'Do that!' and he marched off in the rain.

The corporal and I walked on together past the hangars. 'What was he so annoyed about?' I asked.

'He's a warrant officer,' answered the corporal as though that explained everything.

'But . . .'

'You don't salute warrant officers.'

'Oh.'

'I should think he would be flattered,' I added, after a little thought.

The Adjutant was harassed. The corporal saluted smartly. I saluted.

'A.C.W.2 Sorour, sir,' explained the corporal apologetically.

'Full name?' asked the Adjutant, pen suspended above a form.

'Dolores Teresa Sorour.'

'Really!'

'Yes, sir.'

He wrote it down.

'Number?' he asked confidently. No, I thought, not again.

'I haven't got a number. Nobody gave me one,' I added quickly.

'Haven't got a number?' he exclaimed in a startled voice.

'No, sir,' I answered.

'Impossible,' he shouted. 'You must have a number.'

'No, sir, I haven't.'

'Corporal!'

'Sir?'

'Why hasn't she got a number?'

'Don't know, sir,' answered the corporal in a voice that disowned responsibility.

The Adjutant looked heavily at us both and then shuffled his fingers through the astronomical pile in his 'In' tray. The 'Out' tray was sadly empty.

'I haven't got time. Take her to the Queen Bee. Ask her to sort it out and 'phone me.' With this he waved an arm in dismissal and stretched wearily towards the 'In' tray.

The 'Queen Bee' proved to be the senior Waaf officer on the station. She was equally as harassed as the Adjutant but considerably kinder. I explained to her, before she asked about my number, that I was not yet really in the air force and was sent here to help out until the next draft at Oxford was ready.

'An enviable position,' she commented dryly.

I raised my eyebrows. 'Well,' she explained. 'This is in the nature of a trial. If you don't like it, you can leave. But,' she added confidently, 'I'm sure you will like us.'

I was appointed as personal batwoman to two Waaf officers who lived, unmarried, in married quarters on the outskirts of the aerodrome. My duties were all-embracing but could be defined as cook, housekeeper, char, valet and butt. I was quite unsuitable for any of these tasks except perhaps the last.

My mistresses were not unduly formidable, though I envied their tailored elegance and the thin pale blue stripe on their sleeves. I washed dishes and raked cold ashes in the grey light of dawn with all the self-pity and poignancy of Cinderella. My vision was limited to coagulated frying fat, wet coal, constant conflict with authority regarding my 'uniform' and, overhead, the tantalizing roar of aircraft. In bed, at night, my thoughts lingered over a burning effigy of the Director-General of Civil Aviation.

My first meal was, unfortunately, dinner. I found potatoes and a cabbage in the larder. I boiled both. Profusely. With brilliant enterprise I served the cabbage water as soup (I had rarely entered the kitchen in South Africa; neither I believe had my mother) and retired to the kitchen to prepare the second course.

'Sorour,' commanded a voice from the dining alcove.

'Ma'am?' I enquired.

'You have forgotten the salt.'

Relieved at so petty a reproof I brought it. They finished the soup. I served the cabbage and potatoes.

'Meat?' asked one, appraising dubiously the insipid combination of green and white.

'There wasn't any Ma'am,' I answered. They glanced eloquently at each other, looked with unspeakable disdain at their plates and then commenced poking with insulting fastidiousness at my dinner. I returned to the kitchen.

'You may serve the port,' ordered one as I collected the flatteringly empty plates.

'Pardon, Ma'am?'

'The port,' she repeated.

'Yes, Ma'am,' I answered confidently. Port, I wondered and repeated the word until it lost its meaning. Port, port, port. What's Port? I recalled the red sour-sweet liquid served during Holy Communion. Of course. Port wine. Amidst a sad and dusty collection of bottles I found one that held a similar coloured liquid. I poured two large tumblers full, put them on a rusty tin tray and walked carefully to the dining-room.

'Port, Ma'am,' I announced with dignity, whilst suppressing the impulse to giggle.

They stared at the tumblers and exercised their already

well-exercised eyebrows. 'Sorour. Those are not wine glasses.'

I returned along the well-beaten path to the kitchen, transferred, with moderate wastage, the liquid to more elegant glasses and tried again.

I watched them proudly as they sipped luxuriantly at the warm cosy-looking liquid. Suddenly, consternation shattered this idyllic scene and a fine spray of liquid burlesqued across the spotless linen tablecloth as one of the officers spat out the 'Port'. The other, mouthing horribly, retired hurriedly to the bathroom. On further investigation the port transpired to be vinegar.

My tears helped to soothe their ruffled feathers and brought an uneasy armistice. Dire threats of 'putting me on a charge' subsided to more general recriminations. I retired to the servants' bedroom. They washed their own dishes that night.

Fiasco followed fiasco for two interminable weeks before my orders arrived to report for recruit's training. My two officers, haggard looking, wished me a vehement farewell as I entrained for discipline. I had, however, learned something of the peculiarities of service life. So, no doubt, had my late mistresses.

8

I REPORTED TO THE WOMEN'S ROYAL AUXILIARY AIR FORCE recruits' training centre and was immediately absorbed into the slightly anarchic routine. Gaggles of highly individual females were to be seen entering the gates. A few weeks later, the processing completed, columns marched uniformly out again. I was canalized with moderate success. My service wardrobe was completed, thus eliminating the embarrassing necessity of appearing in a hybrid para-military pose. Also, at last, I received my service number from the orderly room clerk who, unaware of its significance, was surprised at my effusive thanks.

The barracks were solid two-storeyed edifices that served as an object lesson to the frivolously minded. Like guardians of Victorian sternness their stone floors, functional bathrooms and crisp no-nonsense beds cowed most of us to obedience more effectively than direct authority. Feminine giggles and squeals echoed hollowly in the long dormitory and reduced those responsible to self-conscious titters. A week or two was to pass before we could resist the silent intimidation of those walls, kick off our shoes and affix pinups to locker doors.

The next few days were spent in rooting out any lingering affection for anarchy or independence. We were numbered, ranked, and drilled until even our expressions became uniform.

Lectures on the omniscience of 'King's Regulations' and visits to the medical inspection room conveniently occupied any untoward spare time.

The final obstacle was the selection board who decided the future activities of those possessing special qualifications. Arming myself with my flying licence, log-book and correspondence from the Ministry including the letter that referred to my 'obtaining a suitable position with the Waafs' I presented myself to the board.

The interviewing room was sadistically long. Two unsmiling Waaf and three male officers appraised me stonily as I walked the miles from the door to the green baize table. I saluted awkwardly and stood to attention. I could feel my skirt trembling.

'You may sit down,' motioned the senior Waaf officer. I sat uneasily on the edge of the chair.

'You are a pilot,' accused one of the Waaf officers.

'Yes, Ma'am.'

'Have you your licence?'

I passed it across the desk.

'You realize there are no flying posts in the Waaf?' smugly interjected one of the men.

'Yes, sir.'

'Then why join the Waafs?' he asked truculently.

What sort of boards had he passed, I wondered, to ask such a stupid question.

'I love flying and the Waafs are closest to flying,' I answered.

'A negative approach,' he commented, scribbling a note on his pad.

'Tell us about your education,' suggested the one with pince-nez, sitting on the extreme right. I half turned to him and told them. They appeared totally unimpressed. There was an uncomfortable silence. I looked longingly out of the window. The sun shone on a sparrow perkily hopping from bush to bush; faintly its twittering penetrated into the room. My mind soared to distant places; to surf and palm trees and sea shells resting on glistening sands; where ships called twice a year.

'. . . prepared to volunteer for . . .'

'I beg your pardon,' I said, blushing at my insolence at begging the pardon of so august a committee.

'We need some girls for a highly secret operation. Are you prepared to volunteer for this job without knowing what it is?' repeated the chairman of the board. My mind soared again. This time to deeds of secret valour. Visions of Joan of Arc vied with those of Florence Nightingale. My tummy tightened with a vicarious thrill.

'Yes, sir,' I answered bravely, trying not to squeak.

The chairman glanced enquiringly at the others. Individually they stared at me then nodded to him.

'Then it is decided. You will receive posting instructions in the normal manner. You are aware of the Official Secrets Act?' he asked.

'Yes, sir.'

'That is all. You may go. Good morning.'

I got up, wriggled my skirt down, swung an improved salute and marched bravely out, my head in the air.

Orders were posted the following day for the entire draft. All but a dozen, including myself, were posted to training establishments. The dozen were to report the following day for further instructions; packed and ready to leave. We did so agog with excitement and with rumours virile and ripe.

We were shepherded into a train that crawled, backtracked and stopped throughout most of the night. I never did achieve a journey during the war on those trains that snorted imperiously to their destinations. Invariably I travelled, dirty and dishevelled, on those with insignificant priority that jarred to a halt with infuriating resignation in the blacked-out countryside and waited, their passengers cocooned in stale air, in the eerie silence broken only by an occasional tired grunt of steam or the creaking of metal.

We arrived 'somewhere in England' in the early hours of the morning. Escorts were changed and after marching along winding lanes with the smell of ozone wafting freshly in the breeze and bringing animation to our jaded faces, we came to a backwater jetty, mysterious and silent except for the brackish water sucking hollowly against three rowing boats moored nearby. A firm 'Quiet please' hushed our excited whispers. I looked primly at my colleagues. They did not appear suitable material for heroines. I could not see myself.

We rowed silently for half an hour. The waning moon played hide and seek in the trees as we disembarked at a tiny jetty that creaked protestingly and swayed alarmingly at the unaccustomed weight. We marched again until, passing through massive wrought-iron gates, the public lane gave way to the gentility of a gravelled drive and cultivated gardens. A blacked-out manor appeared, silhouetted eerily in the pale moonlight.

With our questions unanswered we were tumbled into bed.

9

DURING THE FOLLOWING FEW DAYS THE SUM TOTAL OF OUR knowledge of our future activities was the negative one of at least knowing what we were *not* going to do or be. The manor was a training school hedged and shrouded in secrecy that provoked even greater curiosity. It was not until the last day of the course, three weeks later, that the successful trainees at last discovered the great secret. Those unsuccessful were given short shrift and departed still not knowing. An unhappy fate indeed for those women. Garish posters caricaturing large mouths and black Homburged spies despoiled elegant panelled walls and warned of security.

The introductory talk given by the Commanding Officer resembled a speech by the prosecution in Kafka's *Trial*. 'I'm sorry girls, I cannot tell you what I'm talking to you about. But you mustn't talk about it either and that makes it easier for you.'

The large baronial hall was converted into a neat double row of cubicles that gave it the appearance of a beauty parlour. For three weeks we sat in pairs inside these mysterious blacked-out cubicles staring pop-eyed at a small screen illuminated with a wayward fluorescent green light that glowed eerily in the darkness and threw a deathly pallor on our faces. We fiddled and fussed with knobs, endeavouring to locate any green blobs of light that showed persistence or constancy among the bewildering variety of flashes and oscillating lines appearing on the screen. At the end of the working day we emerged from our cubicles eyes red-rimmed with strain and still echoing the elusive blobs. Every night the 'Riot Act' was solemnly read to us with dire warning against indiscreet talk.

The blobs of light were finally baptized as 'echoes'. The addition of a compass scale on the locating control failed to hint to us the nature of our work. By the third week those of us still remaining on the course could give the compass bearing and approximate distance of any echo appearing on the screen. Not, we thought, a particularly commendable achievement.

The monotony of our training, the secrecy and confinement – we were not permitted outside the manor grounds – brought boredom and restlessness. I might have been a submariner for all the relationship this bore to flying. The hot-house atmosphere bred turgid romance, for which the darkened cubicles were exploited unmercifully. Predatory females became peculiarly anxious to improve their echo spotting and emerged sans visible eye-strain.

On the last day of the course we gathered in the lecture hall for the unveiling ceremony. The Commanding Officer commiserated with us and thanked us for our patience. Our work was, of course, Radar Interception. The echoes would be, in the future, enemy aircraft approaching the coasts of Britain. We left the lecture rooms happily; the boredom and restlessness gone. Our work was simple but vital. Women rarely ask for more.

OUR FAREWELL PARTY LINGERED FAR INTO THE NIGHT AS CUBICLE-inspired romances jerked fitfully in the throes of rigor-mortis. I primly evaded the zero-hour attempts to storm my notorious unsusceptibility.

'Come on, Jackie; have a drink.'

'She thinks she's too good for us.'

'Just a little drink . . .'

'She's funny that way.'

'If she doesn't want to drink, why should she?'

'It's hot in here. Let's . . .'

'She's a Brylcreem girl. Officers only.'

'Let's dance. You do *dance? . . .*'

I stayed until the last cigarette was extinguished, the last drink quaffed and joined the also-rans on the terrace. We sucked the crisp coolness of the night into our jaded lungs and listened to the trees snoring softly in the gentle breeze. My eyes were drawn to the sky. To the stars that twinkled with remote unapproachable beauty. I was melancholy at the sky's infidelity as is a lover, discarded and miserable, who sees his ex-mistress continuing to smile and laugh with someone new. In those days of banishment I was comforted only by rain for, in my maudlin sentimentality, I imagined the sky to be weeping at my absence.

The next day we scattered to the coasts of Britain. Our destinations were various but identical. A small camp on high ground or on cliffs overlooking the shiftless seas. A lonely wooden hut nestling beneath and dwarfed by tall spindly masts towering with functional beauty into the skies. In these huts, isolated and stark, we grappled abstractedly with the enemy. Night and day we evoked evil spirits from the ether. Like spiritualists purging a malignant ectoplasm we hunted their echoes on our screens. Once spotted, their ethereal path was plotted, analysed and telephoned through to Central Control. Minutes later a new echo would appear on our screens as Royal Air Force fighters rose to intercept. With mounting tension and in silence broken only by the clipped voice of the plotter tell-taling Central Control the evasions of the enemy we would watch the silent drama unfolding on our screen. Sometimes the opposing echoes joined without equivocation in a perfect interception as the hunters found their foes. Or, slid past each other like strangers as the enemy skulked cleverly in the clouds. A violent *volte-face* of the enemy's echo would bring a smile to our faces and a jibe to our tongues on the few occasions that he turned and fled for home.

Anxiously we appraised the results of our work until the two echoes joined in combat in a single oscillating blur that told of *Tally-ho*, twisting evasion, screaming engines, the shrill rat-a-tat-tat of machine-guns or the throatier bark of cannon. We watched the eloquent echo as fathers, brothers and lovers fought on the razor edge of life or death and were silent if the echo, after battle, moved steadily eastwards towards enemy territory leaving behind a dying echo that remained stationary for a few tragic seconds before fading, as the life it represented faded into oblivion.

10

ON LEAVING THE TRAINING SCHOOL FOUR OTHER GIRLS AND myself were posted to a Radar station near Rye on the south coast of England. Our arrival caused considerable uplift in morale amongst the incommunicado male operators. The nearest town was seven miles away and shortage of trained personnel had virtually confined the men to camp. The air, for the first few days, was heavy with gallantries as claims were staked and counter-staked in the bid for feminine companionship. Initially, there being no suitable accommodation for Waafs in the camp, another Waaf and I were billeted with a bricklayer and his family.

We slipped easily into the unchanging routine of constant watch. Our period of duty was eight hours on and sixteen off with a team of four Waafs for each watch. One to operate the screen, one to fix the position of the echo and inform Central Control through a mouthpiece and earphones attached to the head, one to record events in a log and the fourth who acted as camp telephonist and tea-swindler. To relieve the eye-strain we alternated our duties every two hours. The hut, beneath the towering masts and situated for safety reasons 2 miles from the camp, was the first word in comfort. Completely blacked-out it creaked and groaned as the full fury of the biting wind struck from the English Channel. Inside we shivered in Balaclavas, greatcoats and scarves and interminably sipped stewed tea.

The girls were a sophisticated lot. Helen, with whom I was billeted, had come from New Zealand to study drama and had already obtained her L.R.A.M. which, she assured me, was a considerable achievement. She had remained in England to 'do her bit'. She did that, and more. Vera was a film extra. Obviously. Her hippy walk, long flaxen hair (despite orders to cut it), scarlet nails and lips, caricatured the severity of the uniform and brought agonized frustration to the faces of the airmen as she prowled around the camp. She was in constant conflict with the Queen Bee over her hair and unofficial silk stockings but somehow managed to retain both and her freedom.

My billet introduced me to a way of life that depressed me by its monotonous indigence. Our hosts lived a pinched existence that seemed peculiarly contrived. Their income was balanced so precariously with their cost of living that an involuntary expenditure, no matter how trivial – a broken cup to be replaced, shoes to be repaired – brought crisis. These crises though never sufficient to bring disaster, dripped at their happiness with the deadly monotony of ancient Chinese water torture. Our hostess, still young but once pretty, worked indefatigably and rarely complained. I felt guilty at adding to her burden until she told me that our rent was a 'Godsend'. This was a way of life unimaginable in South Africa where servants permit a wife the luxury of enjoying life and retaining her looks and a shock to me who envisaged the English as aristocratic scions, languishing in vast manors whilst not hunting, shooting and fishing.

This dreariness, the unkempt hair and slack figure increased my determination not to marry and, as a concomitant of my religion, not to court. It was not a difficult decision for I had failed to find the key to men that had presumably, judging by their anecdotes, been discovered by my colleagues. At this time I had been kissed once and that not with conspicuous success.

11

DURING THOSE LONG WINTER MONTHS IT WAS AN ESOTERIC experience to see daylight. The normal cycle of day, night and time had vanished and was replaced by a regime dominated by the eight-hour watch. We rarely quarrelled. Always hungry and sleepy, our off-duty moments were spent in cat-naps or searching for food in Rye.

Helen, who shared my watch, felt it her duty to acquaint me with some of the facts of life. Her approach to the problem was basic and elementary and made me grateful for the gloom of the Radar hut that concealed my agonized blushes. Embarrassment and frank disbelief vitiated her endeavours:

'But people don't do that all the time?'

'Of course they do!'

'Even kings and queens?'

'Of course.'

'Do you?'

'Next question, please.'

'Does Joan?'

'I'll say.'

'And Peggy and Pat?'

'Pat does. Not sure about Peggy.'

The next day, at noon-time breakfast, I looked carefully at Pat as she munched placidly at her toast. She looked perfectly normal. Her eyes were tired but so were mine. That afternoon I went with Joan into town. She bought some lingerie that, I thought, was far too exotic and extravagant (we both earned eighteen shillings a week) and I some fruit. Later we relaxed in an olde worlde café that served dainty teas for two-and-six. She was twenty and languidly self-possessed. I brought up the subject tortuously: 'Are you meeting him tonight?'

'Who?' she answered casually.

I was aghast. Was there more than one?

'Your boy-friend.'

'I'm meeting someone tonight, yes. Why?'

'Is that the one who . . .' I broke off in confusion.

'No,' she answered, misconstruing my question. 'You haven't met him. He's in the army camp at Brooklands.'

'Do you like him?'

'So-so.'

'Helen told me yesterday about sex.'

She turned startled eyes towards me. 'You're joking!'

'Joking what?'

'You know as well as she does.'

'I know where babies come from,' I answered proudly.

'Who's talking about babies?'

'We are.'

'Oh no we're not,' she answered emphatically. 'Didn't your mother tell you about it?' she continued, looking at me directly for the first time during our talk.

'A little,' I replied, 'but she seems to have left out a great deal.'

'And nothing's happened in the Waafs?'

'No. Of course not.'

'Extraordinary. Haven't you been out with a man at all?'

'Not since I joined the Waafs.'

'And before?'

I blushed again. 'Yes, at college. We kissed, once.'

'Is that all?' she asked incredulously. I nodded silently in reply wondering why *I* should feel so ashamed. Slowly she reddened and looked curiously at me. 'You are normal?' she asked.

'Perfectly. Thank you very much,' I answered tartly, annoyed at the reversal of roles that had made me the subject of the inquisition.

'No,' she explained. 'You don't like girls?'

'Of course I do.'

'No, I mean you don't like them that way?'

'What are you talking about?'

'How old are you?'

'Nineteen.'

'Nineteen,' she mused. 'You're a Catholic aren't you?'

'Yes.'

'So am I.'

I was horrified. 'But you can't be!'

'Why not?'

'It's impossible,' I expostulated. 'Catholics don't do that sort of thing.'

'You haven't read Graham Greene,' she replied enigmatically.

'Who's he?'

'A Catholic's Catholic.' The bill arrived. 'Are you "on" tomorrow?' she asked as we counted out the shillings.

'Yes, second shift. Why?'

'We Catholics must stick together,' she laughed. 'Come on, let's go.' I got up regretfully, still ignorant.

A few days later I received a message to report to the Queen Bee at my own convenience. The implication of reporting at my own convenience brought a tremor of conscience.

She gambited circuitously. We liked her even though she was terribly old; rumour suggested thirty. How was I? Fine. How was the work and various other questions that seemed insufficiently important to warrant an interview. I waited and wondered.

'Joan came to see me.'

'Yes, Ma'am,' I replied politely, wondering what Joan had to do with me.

'About you,' she added.

'Oh.'

'She told me about your talk.' I was furious.

'Don't be angry. I'm here to help you. She was quite right in coming to me about you.'

She helped me. Ruthlessly and for over an hour she filled in the gaps left by my mother, experience and Helen. She assumed, correctly, that I knew nothing and left nothing to my ignorant imagination. Abstractions like love, infatuation and infidelity were dissected and explained, before the earthier physical manifestations of sex were shaded in with the skill of an artist. Page upon page was turned over like a medical blow-up that, on the first page, shows the complete body and then, with each succeeding page, reveals this and that until finally with the last page the skeleton is left distressingly bare.

As she explained certain things hitherto closed books opened magically. Coolly, ignoring my wriggling discomfort, she stripped my ignorance until I felt naked before her, then, gently and deftly, she covered me with the protective coat of knowledge. Finally she relaxed the objective expression on her face and

65

lighted a cigarette. She had spoken without passion, almost clinically. I longed to ask her: Had she? Did she? Perhaps, I thought ingenuously, they learn these things at the officers' school. I giggled. 'Ladies, today we will discuss Sex.'

In conclusion she used an inelegant expression elegantly:

'You haven't been having me on?'

'No, Ma'am.'

'It isn't unnatural you know.' Dubiously I nodded my head. 'Not with the right one,' she continued, with a distant look that answered my earlier curiosity.

She stood up in a gesture of dismissal and held out her hand:

'Take care of yourself, Jackie. I'm always here.'

The first thing I saw when I left her office was an airman. I looked at him curiously. He caught my look, preened and winked. I blushed, shuddered and fled.

12

By now France had fallen and Britain was alone. Desperately, vulnerably alone. A few pilots and one man's oratory stood between her and defeat. On our Radar screens, day and night, the opening thrusts, like the tuning of an orchestra, prepared us for the climax to come. Life had become a maniacal symphony that grew in a gradual crescendo of wailing sirens, crashing bombs, the distant crump of anti-aircraft fire and the scream of dying aircraft. In this mighty moment of history I, as all others, became submerged in the will to live. Rationing, falling masonry, broken nights and hideously impersonal death became the foundation on which Britain stood and transformed road-sweepers, housewives, shop assistants and business men into heroic comrades of those who fought in the skies.

The petty problems of life were swept away in the determination to resist. I was staggered by the spirit of this nation that hitherto had seemed flaccid, even bored. Housewives became masters of enterprise filling the marrow of the nation's backbone with a magician's skill at producing something from nothing. Civilian dress was the uniform of countless unassuming heroes.

I can remember little of those days. The early morning watch was the worst. Pale, eyes sore from lack of sleep, we stared at the screen with heads drooping until a change in the echoes gal-vanized us into action:

'Hello, Stanmore. Echo; Echo. I'll give you the bearing in a moment.'

'O.K., Rye. Distance?'

'About 125 miles. Large echo, two or more aircraft.'

At Stanmore Central Control the Waafs standing around the huge plotting table and connected to the Radar stations by direct telephone would move symbols on to the table representing the information we passed to them.

'Stanmore. Hostile. Bearing 112.'

'O.K., Rye. Definite? No other stations reported yet.'

'Certain. Large formation . . . splitting up! Bearing 108. Moving fast. Distance 118 miles.'

'I.F.F.?'

'No. Definitely hostile. Bearing 100. Ninety-eight miles.'

'O.K. Confirmed. Hastings have picked it up. Keep passing bearings.'

'O.K.'

'We're sending fighters. Watch for them.'

'O.K. Bearing 100. Ninety miles.' By this time new echoes would appear on our screen; echoes with certain characteristics that identified them as Royal Air Force aircraft. Tensely we would watch as the two echoes merged.

'Stanmore. Echoes merged. Bearing 097. Distance 60 miles.'

'O.K. Thank you.'

'Stanmore. Scattering. Bearing 110, 095. Distance 65.' We watched and wondered as the battle was fought.

'Stanmore. Screens clear.'

'Roger. Stand by.'

The next day we would receive a laconic intelligence report similar to the following:

'Twenty-six hostile aircraft headed for London. Successful interception by fighter aircraft. Four enemy aircraft shot down. One probably shot down over the English Channel. Three damaged. Bombs jettisoned over wide area. Slight casualties. One of our aircraft missing.'

13

'Jackie.'

'Yes?'

'Queen Bee wants you.'

Oh dear, I thought, more sex! 'What for?'

'Don't know. She wants you right away.'

I cleaned my buttons, brushed my hair the regulation one inch above the collar and reported to her office.

'Yes, Ma'am?'

'Morning, Jackie. Sit down.'

I sat.

'You are to report to Hatfield.'

'Yes, Ma'am . . . What!'

'Air Transport Auxiliary, Hatfield Aerodrome.' Please, God. Please. Can it be? I sat motionless. 'For a flying test.' The office spun, my hands trembled.

'Does it mean I'll fly?' I asked stupidly.

'Of course.'

'And leave the Waafs?'

'Yes.' At last it registered. The months of misery vanished. I wanted to leave the office and shout and run and jump.

'Happy?'

'I can't believe it.'

'You've got to pass the test first.'

'God couldn't be that cruel.'

'What?'

'Fail me.'

'Well,' she answered dubiously, 'don't build too many castles. How long is it since you've flown?'

'About nine months.'

'Hum, that's a long time . . . I think we could spare you for a forty-eight-hour pass before you report to Hatfield, if you want to do some studying.'

I smiled gratefully. 'No thank you, Ma'am. I have my books here with me.'

'Well then, good luck. Come and see me before you go.'

I saluted, walked smartly out of her office and hopped, skipped and jumped past the astonished Orderly Room clerks.

The Air Transport Auxiliary, brainchild of Gerald d'Erlanger, was formed in September 1939. In those early days its duties were not strictly defined but it was felt that use could be made of pilots who were either beyond military age or unfit for operational flying for general communications work.

Civil pilots were circularized and from the many replies thirty pilots, all male, were selected and formed the nucleus of a civil organization that by the war's end employed 650 pilots and had ferried over 300,000 aircraft from factories and maintenance units to Royal Air Force and Fleet Air Arm squadrons.

As the first few months of the war progressed and the factories produced a steadily increasing flow of aircraft it was a propitious moment for attacking the prejudice against women pilots. Service pilots were too busy on vital operational flying to be spared for ferrying. There were a hundred women pilots in

Britain wasting their priceless experience in domestic chores. Some wrote, others interviewed. The influential, and there were many, pulled strings but to all their advances they received a polite 'No'. It was not in the national interest to trust vital aircraft to the whims and fancies of feminine pulchritude.

A spokesman was needed; perhaps I should say a spokeswoman. She appeared in the person of Miss Pauline Gower. Her name was internationally renowned, her influence in flying circles formidable. It would have taken a courageous person to resist the cogency and urgency of her arguments.

Within a few weeks her victory was complete and she was charged with the responsibility of recruiting a small number of women pilots to form the first all-women A.T.A. ferry pool at Hatfield.

A few days later I reported to Hatfield Aerodrome. The suspense of the last few days had reduced me to numb anticipation of failure. I knew that had I taken the flying test immediately after my days at Witney I would have passed. But now. Even the saffron yellow Tiger Moth training aircraft busily taking off and landing and following each other around the aerodrome circuit like a brood of chicks had lost their familiar look and taxied by like strangers. I had forgotten the vast spread of aerodromes and was awed by the verdant turf, as smooth and resting to the eye as a billiards table, reaching to the horizon. Only the windsock waved to me in welcome.

Luck, cunning, industry and circumstance had contrived this crossroad. I knew succinctly what it meant to me. Success and fulfilment. Failure and uselessness. As usual when I wanted something I prayed.

With lips fingering a mental rosary, uniform neatly pressed, buttons gleaming and hair a compromise between officialdom and chic I penetrated the security guards and R.A.F. police guarding the main gates. One of the latter escorted me to the tiny offices of the Air Transport Auxiliary perched insignificantly behind de Havilland's hangars and workshops. Overhead the occasional business-like rumble of experimental fighter aircraft dominated the twittering of the Tiger Moths.

As we walked, the smell, the passing show, and the cacophony of aviation sent crystal shivers along my nerves and calmed them as though with cocaine.

'Come in.' The R.A.F. policeman left me with an encouraging smile that contrasted strangely with his scarlet brassard and white blancoed belt. I entered the office as vulnerable as a snowflake. A smile and I might win. A frown and I would melt into oblivion.

She smiled: 'Miss Sorour?'

'Yes, Ma'am,' I answered envying and admiring the trim picture smiling so confidently. The A.T.A. at that time possessed only a few dozen pilots, eight of whom were women. Here was one. One of the eight. To me she was one of the most distinguished women living. She wore navy-coloured tunic and slacks. Her shoulders bore two rich gold stripes. On her left breast she wore wings embroidered in gold thread with the letters ATA in the centre. I confess without shame that here was the height of my ambition. Patiently for years I had courted flying. Its glamour, its adventure, but above all for its elusive mysticism and solitude. Before me I could see a union that I must achieve. To have flying and to wear it modestly on my breast. The infatuation that I possessed for flying in those earlier days was nurtured greatly by vanity. Today, without wings and other florid insignia, I catch the bus from the aerodrome, vanish into the incognito of my

73

fellow passengers and relive the contentment that the last flight has brought. Modesty, the modesty of one who loves not too wisely and knows that one is not entirely loved in return has overcome that earlier vanity and conceit.

Deftly she weighed me up. Hours, types, qualifications, and the last significant question: 'When did you last fly?' My answer brought pursed lips and a 'Hum' that shattered my newly acquired confidence.

We climbed into a Tiger Moth parked at the edge of the apron. I was clumsy and awkward. She slipped neatly into the front seat and sat patiently waiting as I fumbled frenziedly for the elusive straps and gadgetry. Her voice trilled absurdly through the speaking tube:

'Carry on and do three circuits and landings. Keep a good look-out. There is an R.A.F. elementary training school here as well as de Havillands.'

The first take-off, circuit of the aerodrome and landing was shocking. I taxied back to the take-off point grimly aware that none of the landings I had seen today at this *ab initio* training school was quite as putrid as my recent effort. I tried again; there was a decided improvement. I took off on the final circuit knowing that the score was even. A bad one and I was finished. Carefully I climbed the Tiger Moth to 1,000 feet and throttled smoothly back to cruising power. I watched the altimeter like a lynx and nursed the slippery Turn and Bank indicator that was eager to point waywardly to perdition. Turning again on to the cross-wind leg I knew I had a chance. Slowly I closed the throttle and trimmed for the glide. 60 m.p.h. 61, 59, 62. No! It must be 60. That's it. Nicely. 60. 60; stay there! I had judged it perfectly. The aerodrome was set correctly beneath the nose. Easy, easy.

Over the fence, level out. Slipstream sighing its swan-song. Back on the control column. Not too much! Back, back. This is it. I waited for a tortured second; the result now beyond my control. If I had judged it correctly we would sink gently and without a bounce on to the grass skimming beneath the wheels. Please, please, I begged, let it be a good landing.

It was, and I was in the Air Transport Auxiliary.

14

I RETURNED TRIUMPHANTLY TO RYE, MY FACE WREATHED IN A fixed grin, to await further orders. Already I could imagine the gentle burden of gold stripes on my shoulders and wings on my breast. In the mirror my reflection was transformed from drab Waaf blue into a neat figure clad in trim navy blue, silk stockings and flattering forage cap. I made friends of enemies, gave things away and spent my last few pounds in the bank in anticipation of the fabulous salary I was to earn in the A.T.A. The airmen saluted my success in beer; the Waafs in chatter.

A few days after my return we were paraded for formal inspection by a senior Waaf staff officer. Motionless but for our skirts flapping gently in the wind we stood in a thin blue line. In deference to the occasion our hair was severely correct, our buttons brilliant. The more timid wore official issue underwear though how these could be inspected defied the imagination.

I glanced out of the corner of my eyes and saw that the inspecting party were still at the beginning of the file. My shoes were covered with a thin film of dust. Hurriedly I stood on one leg and rubbed the shoes against my calves. With mob psychology those surrounding me stood like cranes and repeated my example. There was a suppressed giggle and I felt an insane desire to laugh.

A dirty look from our Commanding Officer brought self-control and immobility.

The inspecting party walked along the line in spasmodic progress, stopping here and there to ask pompous questions and receive inaudible replies. To my dismay they ground to a halt in front of me. I stared vacantly into the past hoping my vacuous expression would deter questions. My officer smiled proudly. 'This is A.C.W.2 Sorour, Ma'am. She is leaving us shortly to be a ferry pilot.'

I preened.

'Humph,' coldly. 'Who said so?'

'Er . . . the A.T.A.,' answered the officer, in confusion.

'What's that?'

'The Air Transport Auxiliary,' I chirped impertinently and was immediately frozen to silence by imperial hauteur.

'I'm not letting my girls go. We are too short of operators. And the raids are getting worse. I will see that she stays here.'

They moved on. The C.O. anxiously looked back at me. Her sympathy broke down military discipline and I could feel, as though it were another face, the tears slowly brim over and trickle down my cheeks. They tickled in their shameful progress and I wanted to brush them away, but I kept my arms to my sides and stood stiffly to attention. Two minutes passed. Three, as I tasted utter defeat. I knew that I could faint. I wanted to faint; merciful oblivion. Faintly I heard Helen's 'The bitch!' and Joan's 'The bloody old cow!' and grunts of sympathy from the others. I did not want their sympathy. I hated them. I hated God with a hate heaving heavily within me like a sullen sea ready to break into white- capped anger. Please dismiss us, I begged silently. Let me go . . . Let me go!

'Parade dismissed.'

I ran. Ran from the parade ground, out of the gates. Ran until my heart was too busy pumping blood to think of breaking.

THE WEEKS PASSED WEARILY. MECHANICALLY I CONTINUED MY work and tried to retrace my footsteps. But my feet would not, could not fit the footprints of old. The camp was colourless; my comrades dull. Even the echoes failed to stimulate.

The weeks became months. There seemed little I could do but carry on. I was so insignificant that rebellion would be futile. New operators arrived, making our duties less arduous. Our work became routine. On Tuesday nights I wrote to my mother. Dispirited letters that saddened her but loosened the tight grip of hate holding my heart. It was three months before I could pray with humility; even then, there remained a small dark corner of reserve against Him that I should be treated so.

'Going to the dance tonight, Jackie?' asked Helen one morning as we sat drinking tea in the Naafi canteen.

'What dance?'

'Brooklands have invited us.' This was an Army depot five miles along the coast.

'No, I don't think so.' It was Tuesday. 'I must write some letters.'

'Come on, Jackie,' she protested. 'It'll do you good. The Army are sending transport.'

'Who else is going?' I parried.

'All of us not on duty. Officers as well. Transport is coming at eight o'clock.'

'All right,' I begrudged. Anything was better than an empty, silent barrack room.

The camouflaged lorries arrived in convoy promptly at eight o'clock, their raucous horns shattering the calm and bringing derisive whistles from the airmen. Clumsily we climbed aboard assisted by a profusion of willing hands and drove out of camp, horns blaring triumphantly. I felt like a prize cow going to market as I sat near the tail-board and watched the landscape passing by as though we were in a tunnel. Early, restless searchlights, weak in the twilight, flexed their fingers of light in preparation for the dark offensive hours to come. Near the coast anti-aircraft guns, like pencils of steel, swung, rose and fell, and then became still, their muzzles pointing steeply to the sky, reminding us of those on watch. Over all the landscape, gradually vanishing with the day, an ominous calm held.

Arriving at the Army depot we pushed our way through musty blackout curtains and blinked in a brilliantly lit drill hall. Long wooden tables, covered with coarse, spotless tablecloths lined one side of the hall and bore, with evident unease, their burden of beer and lemonade. Spindly, austere chairs lined the other wall. At the far end a motley crew unpacked musical instruments, arranged their unwieldy music stands and rendered extempore snatches of popular melodies. Khaki mixed readily with blue, an officer made a brief, self-conscious speech of welcome and the dance was on.

I danced, refused beer, drank too many lemonades and finally subsided on a chair in the corner, concealed almost entirely by the heavy folds of the blackout curtain. The lights were dimmed and groups merged in animated conversation. I felt gauche and un-pretty.

'What on earth are you doing there?' I looked up and, despite myself, looked again at the khaki blur topped by undisciplined blond hair. The face, clear and untroubled, looked down enquiringly. 'Dance?' he asked. We danced. Once, twice. A waltz, inevitably, and a tango. He was handsome, I noticed lugubriously. He'll leave me shortly, I thought. My back ached in the effort to keep my cheek from his shoulder.

'Another?'

'Thank you.' It was another waltz. Suddenly there was tension in his arms. I lifted my head and heard the thin whistle that, in a brief second, became a maniacal shriek piercing our ears with menace and our hearts with fear. The dreamy waltz continued defiantly though couples had frozen. Mercifully the scream ended in a reverberating crump. The dance hall quivered slightly from the blast and resettled undisturbed. The music continued absurdly.

'That was close,' he murmured, as the dance ended. In the silence left by the band the enemy bomber cruised insolently overhead. A nuisance raider, dropping his bombs singly and haphazardly. I pictured the pilot encased by night; his face reflecting the dim glow of his instruments. His engines deliberately unsynchronized to confuse the anti-aircraft sound detectors. 'That won't confuse Radar,' I commented smugly.

'What?'

'Sorry, I was thinking aloud.'

'Drink?'

'Yes please.'

'Beer?'

'No thank you; lemon squash.' He left me to get the drinks and my thoughts returned to the German overhead. Still circling. Tense, anxious, nerves vulnerable, supremely aware of his body. Looking down at the carpet of unbroken blackness. Wondering why the anti-aircraft guns were not firing at him; perhaps Royal

Air Force night fighters shared the sky. Precariously balanced in the air, as though on the tip of a pencil. Wishing he could drop his bombs in one stick and dive steeply for home, away from the oppressive, impersonal night.

'My name's Reg.' I took the squash. I looked over at Helen surrounded by attentive khaki. She caught my eye, winked hugely and nodded approvingly. 'You dance beautifully,' he continued. He did not, but it did not matter. I went to the converted Ladies' Room, returned and still spoke hardly a word; but still he stayed, easily changing the conversation when my gaucheries brought still-birth to a score of openings.

The crash of cymbals heralded the National Anthem and the end of the dance. We stood stiffly to attention, avoiding each other's eyes. Suddenly, again, heads cocked in an attitude of listening. The menacing whistle screamed again, closer, as we waited for someone to make the first move. The Anthem was a feeble tinkling compared with the banshee howl of the bomb. I watched the band conductor's arm as he quickened his beat, faster, faster. It was a race between the shortened version of the Anthem and annihilation.

'. . . our King.' We dived to the floor. I grovelled and smelled the polished parquet flooring. Reg covered me with an arm. An eternity passed before the scream of the bomb ended in an absurd little thud. We got up sheepishly. Reg took his arm away, grinned. 'It was a dud.' I felt sorry for the German crew still circling obdurately overhead. Watching, waiting for the blue flash, the red aftermath. The justification of their night of fear . . . and nothing but mocking darkness.

The lorries returned to Rye heavily laden with merged khaki and blue. I wondered what colour resulted from this combination.

Reg's thighs pressed close to mine as we sat on hard benches in the friendly darkness. A left-hand bend threw me against him, a right-hand away from him. I began to like left-hand bends. Trailing behind, I saw the dim horizontal slits of the masked headlights of the others. Snatches of ribald songs reached us faintly.

Reg's fingers searched for mine. Hurriedly I sat on my hands. He riposted cleverly and put his arm around my shoulder. I wriggled his arm away and released one hand. He held it. I was glad of the darkness; the conspiratorial cloak that concealed my unsophistication. The drive appeared much shorter. We bounded through the camp gates and jerked to a halt. I knew that something had to happen. Nothing would be too many anti-climaxes for one night.

The German plane had gone. Uneasy armistice reigned in the sky. The stars twinkled imperviously as we stood together, apart from the good-nights of the others. He drew me to him, gently at first, but firmly when I stiffened against him. I wanted him to kiss me.

Unkissed, I wrenched myself from his arms.

'What's the matter?' he asked.

'Nothing. I – we've only just met . . .' I muttered, angry with myself. He looked over at the others, intent in each other's arms. Please understand, I begged silently. Please don't sulk. Please ask to see me again.

'Goodnight,' and he had gone. The lorries drove out of the gates. I watched and listened until their engines faded into the horizon leaving an accusing, offended silence.

An arm reached around my waist. 'Well?' its owner asked. It

was Helen. 'You're a dark horse,' she continued. 'The beau of the ball and you monopolized him all night.'

'What did you think of him?'

'Um-um,' she answered. 'When?' she added confidently.

'When what?'

'When are you seeing him again?'

'I'm not.'

There was a pointed silence before she spoke again: 'Jackie, you're a clot!'

I lay awake a long time after my comrades had fallen asleep before wryly concluding that she was right.

15

JULY THE FIFTEENTH, 1940, DAWNED UNOBTRUSIVELY AS I WENT to bed, bleary-eyed and haggard from a night on watch, unaware that this was to be one of the most momentous days of my life. I awoke grudgingly as a hand violently shook my shoulder. It was Helen. 'Wake up, wake up, Jackie. The Queen Bee wants you.'

'What for? I've been on watch all night . . . what's the time?'

'Eleven o'clock. She wants you immediately,' replied Helen, ruthlessly pulling the warm blankets from my bed. Drearily I got up, searching my conscience for a clue to this peremptory summons, decided my buttons were clean enough and reported to the C.O.'s office. Her face beamed as I entered and saluted. 'Jackie,' she cried getting up from her desk, 'I've got wonderful news. Your orders have come through. You are to report to A.T.A.' I shook my head unbelievingly. Oh no, not again, I thought warily. The C.O. laughed at the disbelief written on my face. 'It's true, Jackie. Look,' she said, showing me the orders. 'A.C.W.2 Sorour, D.T., seconded for flying duties with the Air Transport Auxiliary w.e.f. 29.7.40. To report to Hatfield Ferry Pool, A.T.A., 30.7.40. Discharge to be carried out in accordance with special instructions, etc., etc.' The words danced before my eyes. The Queen Bee put her arms around me, her eyes glistening despite the neat blue rings on her sleeves. I walked back to my empty billet, sat on the rumpled bed and sobbed. Shortly afterwards Helen came in. Her face wreathed in consternation when she saw me weeping copiously. 'What's the matter, Jackie?' she asked anxiously. 'Bad news?'

I shook my head, unable to speak and suddenly burst out laughing. Helen looked at me in astonishment. 'I'm leaving,' I cried. 'I'm going to the A.T.A.'

She grabbed me around the waist and danced with me the length of the billet until we collapsed on to a bed. 'That's wonderful,' she cried. 'This calls for a celebration.'

I cabled my mother, not forgetting in the bliss of the moment, a hint for further funds. I had to buy civilian clothes. Impulsively I phoned Reg and invited him to the party we were throwing in Rye the following evening.

The party was a roaring success though, as the others staggered out of the pub into the blackout, its inspiration was forgotten by all except Reg. We waited, to the tune of an expurgated version of *Eskimo Nell* and *Bless 'em All*, for the bus back to camp.

'Perhaps', suggested Reg, 'we should have a private celebration.' Flattered and happy I agreed to meet him the following day.

It was my day off and I spent the morning fussing with my hair, pressing my uniform into some semblance of elegance and viewing myself, with considerable dubiety, in the mirror. He was waiting patiently by the camp gates, the sun glinting sharply from the badges and insignia on his uniform. We met shyly, both inordinately interested in our feet or the distant hills.

'Rye?' he suggested as the single-decker bus approached the request stop outside the gates. I nodded. The bus was empty and we sat, by mutual consent, in the back. He got out a pipe. I liked that. I scratched at the blackout material that was firmly pasted to the window and tried to lift a corner to relieve the gloom. I felt embarrassed as he paid the fare; it was a small proprietary gesture and I was not yet ready to accept it. I could feel my body. What was worse, I was conscious of his. He cleared his mouth as though to speak but then put his pipe back in his mouth. I became absorbed in the anachronistic advertisements. The bus stopped arbitrarily, waited hopefully for a passenger, gave up and, with a pompous ping of the starting bell, moved on.

'I have two weeks' leave next week. I want you to come home and meet my mother,' he announced baldly and put the pipe back.

I reared like a startled horse. 'I don't know where I shall be . . . whether I can get a pass.'

'We can write,' he answered, the possessive echoing ominously through the empty bus. Had I admitted, implied so much during our last meeting? Surely not. I wished I had the authority to rebuke this impertinence but I knew any protest would have manifested itself as an absurd little squeak.

We went to the pictures. It was a Noël Coward film, packed with controlled middle-class sentiment that brought an uncontrolled flood of tears. I went hurriedly to the Ladies' Room to repair the ravages as the lights went up. I looked at myself in the mirror; even the bloom of youth had been mastered by the tears. I looked like an old hag. I left the back way and caught the bus back to camp.

An hour later I was called uneasily to the phone.

'What happened to you?'

'I . . . er got lost in the crowd,' I lied weakly, carefully working out the penance.

'I'm still in Rye. Is there a bus?'

'From where?' I answered.

'From the camp here,' he replied firmly.

'Yes, at seven-thirty . . .'

'I'll meet you at the bus station at eight-fifteen,' he ordered, replacing the receiver before I could reply.

I had a brilliant idea. I took Helen. I peeped at his face as we met him in the Square. He was livid but riposted cleverly with a heavy show of gallantry towards Helen. Over fish and chips he ignored me. His master stroke was in contriving to sit next to Helen in the bus on the way back to camp.

I was putty in his hands when he arranged the next rendezvous.

16

I arrived at Hatfield with the diffidence and misgivings of one entering the portals of a new boarding school. The A.T.A. building, still insignificant, was in an elegant uproar. Women sat with awe-inspiring confidence on the edge of tables or slouched past in the narrow corridor, parachutes slung over their shoulders. I apologized profusely, like a slave strewing flowers for her patriarchal mistress, and asked for the Commandant's office. A disdainful finger pointed to an office at the end of the corridor. I knocked timidly. Waited and knocked again, wondering whether I should enter. I opened the door and looked in like a mouse, ready to flee at a harsh word.

'Come in. Come in,' smiled the slim, attractively uniformed figure sitting at the desk.

'Commander Gower?' I ventured, intimidated by the three gold stripes glistening on her shoulder epaulette.

'Yes.'

'I'm Miss Sorour. I er . . .'

She got up from the desk and, after a moment of searching for it, shook my hand. 'I've been expecting you.' Here was praise indeed. Miss Pauline Gower, pioneer holder of many international records, and now Commandant of the Women's Section of the A.T.A., was expecting me!

'Sit down, Miss . . .'

'Sorour.'

'We can't call you that. Sounds much too tragic. What other names . . .'

'Jackie,' I whispered.

'Please?'

'Jackie,' I shouted. She blinked and grinned.

'You mustn't be shy. We are all newcomers here. How old are you?'

'Twenty,' I murmured apologetically.

'That makes you the youngest,' she commented, idly glancing through my papers. 'You are from South Africa?' she added curiously. 'What are you doing in Britain at this time?'

'Doing my bit,' I mumbled.

Noticing my inarticulate embarrassment she gracefully changed the subject. 'You can get a billet in Hatfield. The Adjutant has a list. You are awfully young,' she added musingly. 'We must arrange that you get back here after each day's flying. I don't want you wandering around strange hotels.'

I sat absorbed as she chatted casually about my new life, accepting me as though I were a veteran of epoch-making flights instead of a very, very green fledgling. 'You can take care of yourself?' she asked suddenly.

'Oh yes, Ma'am,' I lied.

'Pauline, not Ma'am,' she said. 'I'll arrange for one of the pilots to check you out today. I'd like to do it myself, but,' she pointed to the mass of papers strewn untidily over her desk. 'You will start ferrying tomorrow. There are four Tiger Moths to go to Scotland. We fly only light aircraft at the moment, but,' she added

89

with a glint of battle in her eyes, 'we'll be flying the heavier stuff soon if I have any say in the matter.'

I nodded ineloquently. Gosh! Scotland was a long way away.

'Go and see the Adjutant. She will soon put you right about pay and things. By the way,' she added parenthetically, 'our uniform allowance hasn't yet been confirmed. Can you afford to buy one? You'll get the cash back later.'

'Yes . . . Pauline,' I answered, thankful for my foresight in requesting funds from South Africa.

'Good. Get one as soon as possible . . . Good luck. Pop in any time.'

I went to the crew-room to find the colleague who was to give me a brief refresher flight on the Tiger Moth. There were four or five women lounging on chairs and tables. One was laughing uproariously as I entered. I looked at her dumbfounded as I recognized the face that had inspired me during my brief flying career and had flitted on the world's headlines for a decade. Idiotically I rushed to her and gushed: 'Miss Johnson, may I have your autograph?' She stared at me, astonished. There was a painful silence. Oh God, I wished the floor would open up and devour me. How could I have behaved so inanely. Suddenly she grinned: 'My dear child. I'll swap it for yours.'

17

EXTREME YOUTH, IGNORANCE OF WHAT IS AND WHAT IS NOT done in England and lack of sophisticated veneer did little to endear me to those members of the A.T.A. who still regarded it in its early days as an exclusive flying club. Though I was not entirely plebeian, my habit of considering myself firmly attached to the bottom of the social scale or class or whatever euphemism is used to describe the ugly, slippery ladder that plagues social intercourse in Britain, irritated some of the pilots beyond measure and invariably brought an expression to their faces, whenever I entered the crew-room, that suggested mice had taken temporary residence beneath their noses.

Because of this the first professional flight of my career was spectacularly successful, though perhaps an unfortunate one.

The four Tiger Moth aircraft were to be collected from a factory aerodrome near Cowley and delivered to Lossiemouth, Scotland. In those pioneering days maps were scarce, frequently we navigated with the assistance of pages torn from school albums and geographical magazines, and it was decided that the one available complete set of maps should be given to the most experienced pilot who would lead the formation, the remainder following in Indian file fashion. The leader selected was, to my dismay, also the leader of the snob group and a skilled exponent of the glassy stare. Consequently I was far too intimidated to ask questions and took off from Cowley totally ignorant of the route and where we were to land for refuelling.

With eyes glued to the formation, already callously heading for the North, I made a horrifying take-off and clawed anxiously for height like a duckling paddling furiously after its mother. With engine at full blast I caught them up and shot past the leader as I tried, too late, to reduce speed. She glanced at me disdainfully as I sailed by. 'Sorry' I mimed apologetically and eventually settled down at the tail of the formation, content to be out of sight of the others. Obediently I followed them through the thick industrial haze over the Midlands, landed when they landed and faithfully mirrored their every manœuvre. It was a day of low cloud, racing scud and heavy showers that irresistibly forced us lower as we flew steadily northwards. By the time we had crossed where I imagined the Scottish border to be I, being lower than the other three aircraft in order to avoid their slipstream, was blithely skimming over heather and gorse, confident that the leader's prowess would get us through. Gradually, as visibility decreased in the driving rain, the leader vanished, then number two, until finally I intently followed the dim silhouette of number three who, I hoped, was following number two, etcetera. For an uncomfortable moment I lost her too, but an unexpected lifting of the clouds, like the curtain of a theatre, revealed the three aircraft landing at an airfield. Hastily I landed after them and, stiff with cold and blissfully anticipating a hot mug of tea, taxied to the parking ramp.

I had just cleared the landing area when to my astonishment the three Tiger Moths loomed out of the mist and took off again as though pursued by satyrs. Must be the wrong aerodrome I decided with a chuckle, pleased that the leader had made such a gaffe. Swinging round violently and with safety straps undone I scrambled after them.

Resuming my position at the tail of the formation I glanced up at the needle-type petrol gauge perched on the upper wing. The little red-painted float nestled comfortably at the bottom of the glass stem. I opened up and signalled frantically that I was dangerously low on petrol. The leader gave me a startled look and veered away violently as though my aircraft showed symptoms of a contagious disease. Determinedly I stuck to her as she twisted and turned trying to be rid of me. At last, when it occurred to me that this was taking social distinction too far, she slackened speed, dropped her nose and pointed peremptorily to an airfield that had appeared out of the mist and which I correctly assumed to be Lossiemouth. Ignoring protocol and dispensing with the conventional circuit of the field, I landed down wind, wondering why a pilot of her experience should cut things so fine. I switched off and preparing an apology for having landed first walked over to the leader as she climbed out of her machine.

'Sorry, I was nearly out of petrol . . .'

'And who the bloody hell are you?' asked a wrathful, heavily moustached visage emerging from the helmet.

I pulled off my helmet.

'Good God. It's a woman!'

Over steaming mugs of tea the mystery was solved. My A.T.A. colleagues had remained at the previous refuelling halt and I had inadvertently joined an R.A.F. formation. It was entirely fortuitous that they also were bound for Lossiemouth.

The next day I returned by train to Hatfield. My erstwhile colleagues, stranded by bad weather, returned a week later.

After a month of more orthodox delivery flights the day arrived when I had arranged to collect my uniform from Moss Brothers, purveyors of uniforms on credit to impecunious officers. In the svelte luxury of their show-rooms I tried it on. It was magnificent.

'I'll keep it on,' I remarked, admiring myself in the mirror. Navy blue, severely cut, black buttons, a crisp gold stripe on each epaulette, rich gold-embroidered wings on the left breast and an absurd little forage cap that seemed to transform my face. Quite suddenly I realized that I was not bad looking. The nice little thing from Pretoria looked as cute as a button. Twinkling with this remarkable discovery I walked along the Strand through the lunch-time bustle of office workers and servicemen. For the first time in my life heads turned as I walked along the street. The greatest compliment of all came when women also turned. It was a wonderful day.

18

DESPITE MY UNWAVERING GOOD SPIRITS AND CHEERFULNESS I must have been an irritating companion in those days for though I had spent over two years in England I had not yet learned that any hint of non-conformity in dress, speech or thought created an uncomfortable atmosphere and was the monopoly of bad types. That was another discovery; that England was populated by good and bad types. By an extraordinary coincidence the good types invariably spoke with a lozenge in their mouths; the bad types with a dialect. I was 'not-bad' for my accent was South African, and consequently could not be analysed with that remarkable perspicacity with which the English place a person swiftly and surely by his accent—and react accordingly. Time and time again I watched the reaction of my colleagues when being introduced to newcomers. If the accent was right, i.e. slightly inarticulate and affected, there was a meeting of minds and a graceful acceptance of the newcomer. If however it was natural and given individuality by a dialect, then a certain amount of coolness and brevity was discernible. If the dialect was, God forbid, Cockney, patronage and condescension reared like a cobra's head.

The first few months in A.T.A., months of groping for values and opinions that would bolster the newly acquired confidence I got from my job, seem a child-like memory as I sit here, fifteen years later, trying to select personal milestones from the dominating theme of war.

Outwardly there were no longer any problems. It was evident even to the most ill-informed, that the war would not be over by Christmas. I knew what I would be doing tomorrow, next month, next year. Also, my flying had reached a stage where accidents would be caused not by inexperience but by carelessness. And I was much too frightened to be careless.

Inwardly I was peculiarly ill-equipped for a period when abstractions like Democracy, Truth and Right, had become daily fare. God it seemed, according to the newspapers, was unequivocally on the side of the Allies. I wondered about this as I travelled through London at night. A London of darkness shattered by the flash of death, the scream of agony, the sobbing of despair and a reckoning at dawn in the debris of fallen masonry. This was a very different God from the one my grandmother used to talk about with a soft look in her eyes.

Two texts dominated my theosophical reflections: 'An eye for an eye' and 'Thou shalt turn the other cheek'. The Church and the Allied leaders trumpeted with enviable single-mindedness the first text. Those favouring the second languished in Brixton gaol.

CASUALTIES IN THE A.T.A. WERE INFREQUENT BUT NOT sufficiently infrequent to let us forget that one could take off never to land again. In an age when casualty rolls number millions it is perhaps petty to remember those of the A.T.A. who died. Merely a few score. But they were my comrades.

Most of them died victims of the weather, particularly in winter when the British sky is as trustworthy as a rabid dog. Though there were definite minima of actual and anticipated cloud base and visibility in which we were expected to fly, the urgency and the dogma of individual responsibility resulted in a press-on spirit particularly when priority deliveries were scheduled. Radio communication, the most powerful weapon in flying's unceasing battle against weather, was denied us for security reasons. Once in the air we were on our own: *ex-communique*.

On the 4th January, 1941, H.M.S. *Hazlemere* patrolled the Thames Estuary off Herne Bay. The Captain, Lieutenant-Commander Fletcher, R.N., muffled in a duffle coat, stood on the bridge as his ship ploughed through the heavy seas. It was a dull patrol. Only sea-gulls, mewing plaintively, shared the dismal rain-lashed scene.

That same afternoon I took off from South Wales with a

twin-engined Oxford aircraft bound for Kidlington. Simultaneously Amy Johnson took off from Blackpool, also bound for Kidlington.

The weather that harassed H.M.S. *Hazlemere* lay like a blanket over the Southern Counties. Drizzle and low cloud were forecast for most of the route to Kidlington but with a promise of improvement. Reluctantly I headed into the curtain of rain and, a few hundred feet above the ground, searched hopefully for the promised improvement. It was non-existent. I should have turned back but valleys beckoned invitingly like tunnels. I shot into one and peered ahead for the circle of success, but the trap had sprung. The other end of the narrow valley was blocked with a wall of cloud. I rammed open the throttles, pulled the control column back and climbed steeply. With unnerving suddenness the ground vanished as the clouds swirled around the Oxford in a cold embrace and forced me to climb on instruments. Inexpertly, I had not flown on instruments for months, I tried to keep the angle of climb constant. Suddenly at 4,000 feet the clouds splintered into bright wintry sunshine; beneath me the clouds stretched to all horizons like a soft woollen blanket. Desperately lonely and frightened, I searched for a gap. There was none. Whilst I stayed above I was safe. Like a spotlight the sun cast a shadow of the Oxford on the top of the clouds and circled it with a halo of rainbow hue. I had the odd thought that I was the shadow and the shadow was me. Curiously I watched it to see what it was going to do next; silly thing, it was going round in circles. I looked back at the radio equipment. A closed book. Mockingly it kept its secrets of aerodromes open to the skies.

The petrol gauge drooped inexorably. I had to go down. I glanced at the maps and headed south-west away from the hills and balloon barrages lurking in the cloud. Reluctantly I throttled back, put the nose down. The clouds embraced me like water around a stone. I descended slowly. Two thousand feet. Fifteen hundred. One thousand. Six hundred. It's no good, prompted experience, get back. Ignoring the urgent warning I eased lower with the altimeter ticking off the altitude like a devilish clock. If I were lucky I would be over the hill-less sea. If not, I had not long to live. Suddenly the clouds broke, revealing, just beneath, the grey, sullen waters of the Bristol Channel. I pulled off my helmet and wiped the sweat from my face and hands before, sandwiched in the narrow gap between sea and cloud, turning towards the Somerset coast faintly visible to the east.

I looked at the petrol gauge. Twenty minutes left to find an aerodrome. Absently I worked out the little problem. Twenty times sixty. Two sixes are twelve. Add two noughts. That's it, one thousand two hundred seconds before I wrecked the aeroplane and paid the penalty for not turning back. But, unfairly, all the luck in the sky was with me that day. Soon after crossing the coast an aerodrome blossomed out of the ground like a flower from a desert. Pulling the Oxford round in a tight circuit I landed on the glistening rain-soaked runway. Switching off I waved cockily to the duty pilot sheltering in the Control Tower.

Next day on returning to Hatfield I learned that Amy Johnson was dead.

She had been caught in the same way; had been forced to climb above the clouds. More experienced and with a greater understanding of the risk, she had realized it was foolhardy to attempt a descent through cloud and had taken the only decision left to her. To bale out by parachute. It was the right decision but a tragic one, for in her desperate search for a gap in the clouds she had drifted over the Thames Estuary.

The crew of H.M.S. *Hazlemere* saw her drop from the clouds and plunge into the icy, storm-tossed waters. They launched a lifeboat but failed to close the gap. Lieutenant-Commander Fletcher, watching from the bridge, saw that the lifeboat would be too late to reach the figure struggling desperately in the water. Unhesitatingly he dived overboard and swam towards the victim, now recognizable as a woman. They were seen to join, but despite the frenzied efforts of the lifeboat crew, they both perished.

The paths of a gallant officer and a brilliant woman pilot had crossed.

20

THE EXPERIMENTAL FERRY POOL AT HATFIELD, THE FIRST TO BE staffed entirely by women pilots proved, despite gloomy masculine prognostications, to be an unqualified success. Inevitably the time came, as larger and more complex aircraft poured from the factories, when the authorities were faced with the decision of whether to continue imposing restrictions on the type of aircraft ferried by women. Pressure of events forced the issue and women pilots were, subject to their C.O.'s discretion and a brief period of training, permitted to fly 'anything, anywhere'.

We were given brief training at the R.A.F. Central Flying School and introduced to the mysteries of hydraulics, retractable undercarriages, flaps, constant speed airscrews and scores of other refinements made imperative by the struggle for air superiority. At the end of the course we were promoted first officers and had the delightful task of sewing another thin gold stripe to our epaulettes. I must admit that for the first few weeks we pushed and pulled knobs and controls with parrot-like obedience and with only the haziest idea of what went on at the other end.

Despite the efforts of the ferry pool commander I led a nomadic life of one-night stops in hotels or fitful sleep in the luggage racks of all-night trains with a disreputable macintosh to disguise my uniform when I subjected it to the indignity of climbing into the luggage rack.

A typical day started by reporting to the pool at 8 a.m. to collect the ferry-chits and board the milk-run aircraft that set off each morning on a round-robin flight dropping off pilots at their first collecting point. From there the pilot would start the day's programme; usually two or three flights, e.g. a Wellington from aerodrome A to aerodrome B. A Hurricane from B to C and a Hudson bomber from C to D and then a dreary train journey with parachute, helmet and maps, back to base and bed. I was still young enough to enjoy every minute of every day and rushed to the aerodrome each morning with a gay vivacity that must have been irritating to the elders.

The operational planning, a formidable chess-like problem, shuffling aircraft and pilots over the entire British Isles, was controlled by Central Operations at Andover. Such were the magnitude and complexity of A.T.A.'s operations that at the peak of the war over two hundred A.T.A. taxi aeroplanes were being used to return pilots to their ferry-pools at the end of the day and thus end time-wasting train travel.

DURING THE SUMMER OF 1941, BY WHICH TIME I HAD FERRIED most of the non-operational types of aircraft and an occasional Hurricane, there was one aircraft, the most illustrious of all, which I longed to fly. Yet the prospect of so doing filled me with trepidation. Like a man who knows a visit to the dentist is inevitable but, when the pain eases, puts off the evil day, I scanned the delivery chits each morning, wanting yet fearing to see: Spitfire.

*

102

IN AUGUST THE EVOKING NAME STARED AT ME FROM THE FERRY-chit: Spitfire. From: Cowley; To: Tern Hill. Pilot: D. T. Sorour. As nonchalantly as possible I climbed aboard the taxi aircraft and was dropped off at Cowley.

The Spitfire, a machine with the simplicity of features of a beautiful woman, stood outside the hangar basking as proudly as a thoroughbred in the warm sunshine. I clambered into the cockpit as warily as a rider mounting a highly spirited stallion and sat gazing absently at the instruments. It seemed the most natural thing in the world to be sitting there in the cockpit, as though my entire life had led to this moment.

I started up inexpertly and felt the power coursing through the Spitfire's frame and registering on the instruments. A little awed but stimulated by the urgent throb of the Merlin engine that seemed to tremble with eagerness to be free in its own element, I taxied cautiously to the down-wind end of the field. The brakes were touchy and recalling the warning of my colleagues I used them sparingly. The Spitfire is notoriously nose heavy on the ground.

A few second later I found myself soaring through the air in a machine that made poetry of flight. Carefully I familiarized myself with the controls as the ground fell away at fantastic speed and felt exhilarated by the eager, sensitive response. Singing with joy and relief I dived and climbed and spiralled around the broken clouds, before turning on to course.

I landed uneventfully at Tern Hill, a fighter squadron base, and climbed out with spurious nonchalance as fighter pilots, sun-ning on the grass and awaiting the call to battle, waved and wolf-whistled in welcome. With an easy *camaraderie* I waved back, for after all I was, almost, one of them.

*

As the summer closed, a new women's ferry pool was established at Hamble aerodrome near the south coast. A few of us from Hatfield, relative veterans, were transferred to form the nucleus of the new pool to which new women pilots, fresh from A.T.A. training schools, were added.

There was an immediate scramble for billets on our arrival at the new pool. We collected our billeting slips and rode off on bicycles like locusts about to descend on unsuspecting pastures. After numerous enquiries and false trails I cycled along a glade, thick with fallen leaves from the overhanging trees, that followed the winding unassuming River Hamble. My billeting slip showed only the name of the house. Picturesque bungalows, their backs to the river, peeped cosily through the rust-tinted trees. One in particular caught my eye with its neat tiny drive and mellow air. Wish that was it, I sighed wistfully as I looked at the name plate. With a second look I slammed on the only brake that worked, the front one, skidded, parted company with my bicycle and sat on the wet leaves gazing at the name plate just above my head: Creek Cottage. Hastily I got up and tried to make myself presentable, but it was too late.

'You wouldn't be coming to stay with us, would you?' enquired the elderly gentleman eyeing me from the drive with a mixture of amusement and concern.

'Yes,' I admitted.

'Come in. We have been expecting you,' he invited kindly, 'though not quite like that,' he added with a grin, taking my bicycle and wheeling it along the drive.

Surreptitiously I examined the bungalow. It was a gem of story-book charm that so often rewards those who explore unpromising bye-ways in England. A garden, carelessly elegant, spread to the water's edge where, in a small boat-house a motor-boat and a dinghy, promising idyllic summer evenings, were moored in the still waters of the lock. My hosts welcomed me warmly and quickly dispelled my qualms that they might resent their imposed guest. The Greenhills, though retired, took me to their home as naturally as though I were their own daughter. Now that peace has returned to that quiet glade on Hamble River may they have back the happiness they gave to me.

I spent a day exploring the tiny river and the garden and adding my own personality to the bedroom overlooking the river banks, before reporting for duty. By then some semblance of order had emerged from the packing cases and chaos at the aerodrome and we plunged into a heavy backlog of work. It was five days, every night spent in different though similarly dreary hotels, before I returned, dirty and exhausted, to Hamble and climbed out of the taxi aircraft.

'Hi, Jackie,' greeted the operations officer. 'We had a phone call from a Mr Greenhill. He wanted to know if you were all right . . .'

21

MEANWHILE REG COURTED ME WITH A CLINICAL TENACITY that boded ill for my independence. Every day I received a letter until his agonizingly cramped writing became as familiar as my own characterless scrawl. I was paddling on the banks of a river that threatened to suck me reluctantly into midstream and on into the estuary of marriage. After meeting his parents in Taunton I left exhausted, following a week of nervous politeness and appraisal with the feeling that I was walking up a descending escalator. There seemed to be something peculiarly unexciting about Reg and me. As though we were following a path across a plain instead of exploring the foothills of a majestic mountain.

With the fulfilment of my job and the easy comradeship of war I was no longer blindly flattered by his attentions and met him in Taunton and Hamble with an equanimity impossible six months before. But he remained a yard-stick against which others were compared and found wanting.

Often, during the winter of 1941–42 when the night sky over the southern ports became a battlefield, I sat in the cosy oasis of Creek Cottage discussing with my proxy-mother, Mrs Greenhill, the prospect of marriage.

'But I don't want to get married.'

'You will have to, some day.'

'Why?'

'Why! . . . You want children, a home . . .'

'I want flying . . . I cannot have both.'

Interminably and inconclusively we discussed and probed. Reg, with a delicacy of perception that belied his more stolid qualities, waited patiently. It was a long wait.

In the spring of 1942 Reg telephoned me at Hamble soon after completing an O.C.T.U. course at Aldershot. 'It's India,' he confirmed casually. 'Two weeks' embarkation leave starting tomorrow. Can you get leave?'

'I think so,' I answered.

'Right. Come down to Taunton as soon as you can get away.'

'Did you get your commission?'

'Yes, darling. It's Lieutenant Moggridge now.'

I packed a toothbrush, ferried a Fleet Air Arm Albacore to Bristol and hitch-hiked on to Taunton. On the army lorry that carried me the last few miles to Taunton I itemized the reasons why we should not get married. I knew what I was in for. It seemed silly to answer simply: I don't want to get married. A man departing for two years in the grim Far-Eastern theatre deserved more rational reasons for going un-wedded.

Nature partisaned his cause. The weather was idyllic, the days balmy, the nights mellow and making nonsense of my obstinacy. Reg was cunning. During the day when we played tennis or lounged in sweet-smelling fields listening to the put-put of distant tractors, he wore a martyred air. At tea each cup was punctuated with a sigh. It was during the evening calm that his campaign took a more tactical turn. In the garden under the insidious influence of the stars and with his arms around me as

107

we sat in the swinging hammock I became equivocal. Perhaps, maybe. My resistance was at a perilous ebb by the tenth day. If I could last out one more day it would be too late to arrange the ceremony.

On the twelfth day he admitted defeat. 'You have no objections to an engagement?' he asked ironically during lunch.

'None whatever,' I replied. We kissed formally and then not so formally.

We bought the ring in the High Street. In the jewellery shop I wondered that assistants carried on business as usual, working from nine to five, with Thursday afternoons and Sundays off. It seemed grossly unfair that history should pass them by and leave them trailing in a wash of ration books and petty monotony. I felt guilty as the assistant glanced enviously at our uniforms and mechanically quoted prices as we pondered over the rings. I chose an inexpensive zircon that sat unobtrusively on my finger. It had to be small. I always wore gauntlets when flying.

We had tea in a quaint shoppe. I fidgeted with my left hand like an inexperienced actress. 'Take your glove off,' grinned Reg. I obeyed and stared at my hand as though it were a stranger's.

Reg's departure for India left me curiously un-distraught. There was a gap in my life but it was the gap of an extracted tooth. An emptiness without feeling or pain, noticed only when in idleness one feels for it.

22

TRYING TO EVOKE MEMORIES OF WAR IS LIKE WRITING THE epitaph of a dead friend. As with the friend one remembers only the virtues. The epitaph becomes a eulogy and another generation is weaned on the glories of war.

There was John. I met him a year after Reg had left for India. Cadaverously good looking and frustrated he had, to him, the ignominious task of towing targets at an aerial gunnery school; a menial and unexciting job allotted usually to pilots who had misbehaved. He wanted to fly Spitfires in a fighter squadron and met me with sour malice when I landed at his aerodrome with a coveted Spitfire to refuel. He was duty pilot on that day, responsible for arriving and departing aircraft. The weather was bad and, after an introduction spiced with irony about my sex and phallic-symbolled Spitfires, he invited me to a dance to be held that evening in the officers' mess. I accepted and telephoned Hamble that I was staying overnight.

He drank too much at the dance with a feverish boyish defiance. He later confided that he did not like whisky and beer made him sick. He became cheeky and I did not mind. He made the most outrageous suggestions and I did not mind that either. Then he became maudlin. His technique was admirable. I guided him to the porch like a tug nudging a transatlantic liner into harbour.

'Where are you going?' he asked.

'To get you some coffee,' I replied firmly.

'Dowant coffee. Wanna fly Spits. Sit down.'

'You'll fly them. I'm sure you will.'

'Huh. Whatdo-you-knowaboutit. Bloody . . .'

'Stop swearing.'

'Jesus . . . Spitfires and piety. Cocktails for two.'

I could not be angry with him. 'Somebody has to train the pilots,' I suggested soothingly.

'Oh. Reasonable. I hate reasonable people.'

'Why don't you say something?' he added, after a moment's silence.

'Because you want me to be unreasonable,' I promptly replied.

'Beautiful Spits,' he observed irrelevantly. He was sitting down, head on knees, when I brought the coffee. He grimaced and drank it quickly.

'Well?' I prompted.

'I think,' he said suddenly but as though continuing a conversation, 'we all want to know how we would react to danger. It must be a satisfying thing to know one isn't a coward.'

'Is that all?' I prompted.

'Pretty well,' he replied.

'Isn't that rather selfish?'

'You want me to say things about Democracy and Truth and King and Country . . .'

'Well?'

'Sorry. No go. That gives me a pain. All I remember of democracy is derelict coal-mines in South Wales, the Dole and a hunger march to Hyde Park.'

'Are you a Socialist or a Communist or something?'

110

'That's right, dammit,' he answered angrily, 'pigeon-hole me.'

'Sorry.'

'I've been a nonentity all my life,' he continued. 'Ten Weights for fourpence. Fifty-shilling suits.' He looked wryly down at his officer's uniform and his wings. 'Now I'm an official gentleman and an incipient hero. *I'm* not fighting for the good old days. I want to fight because I shall enjoy returning to the airfield with the guns empty and mechanics patting me on the back saying "Good show, sir." I want to sew medals on my tunic and see people look at me and nudge each other when I walk into a restaurant.'

Bloodshot and sheepish, he saw me off early the following morning. I promised to answer his letters.

His letters, alternating between hilarious idiocy and gloomy despair, reflected faithfully the progress towards his ambition of being a fighter pilot. Frequently they lay in the post-box next to the air-letters from India, posing a neat little problem in loyalty. I had carefully told each of the other, though there was not much to tell Reg about John. Two short visits to Hamble, a dozen letters and sporadic telephone calls. There was more to tell John about Reg.

A few weeks later I collected the ferry-chits from the operations officer and scanned the day's programme as pilots banged open their lockers and greeted each other with a cheerfulness born of the clear blue sky and the promise of a perfect day. The first chit ordered me to collect a Miles Master from John's aerodrome and ferry it to the Midlands. I grabbed my parachute and helmet and climbed into the taxi aircraft already ticking over on the tarmac. It was a short flight and I was dropped off within twenty minutes of taking off.

The aircraft was waiting for me. I signed the chits before looking for John. He was not in the Control Tower or the mess. Anxiously I phoned his Flight Commander. 'He's flying,' he answered.

I took off and headed for the practice firing range a few miles to the south. The speck on the horizon grew larger until I could recognize it as a Master with a target drogue trailing behind. Keeping well clear I watched his monotonous progress back and forth as another aircraft positioned itself for a practice attack. After three or four attacks the attacking aircraft broke off and headed back to base. Gleefully I positioned myself in what I hoped was the correct position and made an attack on unsuspecting John. Instead of breaking off the attack with a violent downward dive I carried on, pulled up close to him and waved. He gave me a startled look and violently waved me off. I shook my head and pulled off my helmet.

'It's me,' I mimed. He peered at me as I tucked in closer until a few feet separated us. Suddenly his face broke into a delighted grin and he blew me a kiss. We flew parallel with each other. He pointed down. I shook my head and pointed to the north. He held up ten fingers, pointed to himself and then down again. I shook my head. He pleaded with his hands held in the attitude of prayer. 'I can't,' I shouted idiotically, 'I must go.'

To my astonishment I blew him a kiss before waggling my wings in farewell and peeling off sharply to the north. As I looked back he resumed his monotonous beat as another aircraft positioned itself for an attack.

A week later a telegram arrived at Creek Cottage:
Posted. Fighters. Weeks leave. Can I see you. John.

Since the kiss I had been stricken with remorse. In itself it was nothing. In its impulse it had revealed, like the brief flash of a lighthouse, the reefs and rocks that stood between Reg and me. I had determined not to see John again but this laconic cable, hinting an appointment with death, entreated partiality. Not the cold neutrality of a prude. I wavered but the decision was taken firmly out of my hands for returning the same evening from the aerodrome I found John, flanked by the Greenhills, calmly sitting in the lounge.

'Hello,' he greeted casually, 'I was just passing by.'

I tried to be angry at his audacity but his bland refusal to take up the cudgels soon reduced me to impotence. He studied carefully a new portrait that had recently arrived from India. 'Reg?' he asked.

'Yes,' I answered.

'Hum. Brown job,' he commented idly, replacing the portrait on the writing desk. The Greenhills laughed.

'And what's the matter with a brown job?' I asked irascibly.

He raised his eyebrows. 'Oh, nothing,' he hurriedly assured me.

'Thank you very much!'

'Well, what shall we do?' he asked, imperturbably.

'Do? When?'

'Tonight. And tomorrow and tomorrow and tomorrow. I have to report to the O.T.U. on Thursday.'

'Spitfires?'

'Yes,' he answered jubilantly. He looked much younger. The top button of his uniform was already undone.

'I cannot get leave. There's a priority flap on at the moment,' I said.

'That's all right. I'll fly with you. It is allowed?'

'I'm not sure,' I answered uncertainly.

113

He flew with me on the second day and sat quietly in the back seat as we took off in a Miles Master. Conscious of his scrutiny (pilots are almost pathologically intolerant of other pilots' abilities) I flew with excessive care.

'Nice take-off,' he commented. Hands busy I nodded acknowledgement before throttling back to cruising power.

Gradually as we flew steadily across a sky mellow with soft clouds and shafts of sunlight I felt a mood of exalted surrender. Linked by the engine's incidental music – John, the sky, the green chequered fields – the knowledge of life's inconstancy in war built up a confederacy of such profound intimacy in the cramped cockpit I felt myself beyond body; as though I had stepped into a poet's unwritten soul. Into a world of metaphor and image whose ecstasy defies man's alphabet.

Distantly I heard his voice.

'Don't you do any aerobatics?' he shouted.

'Not allowed to,' I shouted back.

'Who's to know? May I?'

I held up both hands to signal that he was in control and tightened my straps. He started with a barrel roll to the left then, to emphasize his versatility, a slow roll to the right.

'You try,' he shouted.

I took over and tried a roll to the right. It was appalling.

'Not bad,' he shouted. 'Use more top rudder going in and coming out. Try it again.'

I nodded and tried again. It was a good one.

'Very nice. I've got her,' he shouted, and flicked the Master over on its back and held it inverted whilst the dust and dirt showered into my eyes from the bottom of the cockpit. 'Enough,' I begged, hanging uncomfortably upside down from my straps.

He rolled the aircraft back to level flight and handed the controls back to me.

We returned to Hamble in the taxi aircraft as the sun lingered on the horizon and painted peaceful hues in the evening sky; a moment of armistice before darkness and death prowled again.

There was an unwritten agreement between John and me not to discuss what we were doing. Where we were going. What would happen at the end of the four days. It was a life within a life. A short story developing with classical precision. He did not kiss me, nor touch my hand. His eyes only were his advocate.

He called for me on the last evening, driving a disreputable car that he had borrowed from someone in the mess at Hamble. We were going to a dance in Southampton and he had insisted that I wear a dress. I looked at myself in the mirror. The trim uniform had vanished leaving a distressingly plain reflection. I was perversely content. The *denouement* would gather the loose ends of the story and end it as neatly as a Bach fugue.

He looked up from the evening paper as I entered the lounge. Coolly his eyes dropped to my ankles and then slowly rose as I hesitated in the doorway. It was a long time before his eyes finally reached mine.

'What's the matter, Jackie?' he asked carefully. 'Did you think it was the uniform?' I nodded. 'It wasn't,' he said simply.

The car made it a perfect evening. 'Do you want to drive?' he asked as we drove back from the dance, the masked headlights almost extinguished by the oppressive blackout.

'I don't drive,' I admitted.

'That's a funny thing. You fly and you can't drive.'

We watched the dotted white line slipping beneath us and the play of searchlights on the horizon. The dimly lit instrument panel surrounded us with a conspiratorial glow.

'I must teach you one day,' he said suddenly.

'What?'

'Driving.'

'Um.'

'You will marry me?' he continued.

'Yes,' I answered.

He covered my hand with his and carried on through the blackout to Creek Cottage. Somehow it seemed superfluous to do anything else.

During the weeks that followed I seemed to develop three different personalities. There was one that was reckless and indomitable when I was with John. A second that read Reg's frantic cables from India with remorse and equivocation and a third, neutral, that looked at the other two with scornful disdain. I did not like myself very much. I lied to John, to Reg and to myself. I was too cowardly to hurt any of the trio and too unsophisticated to enjoy the role of *femme fatale*.

The little buff envelope arrived whilst the Greenhills and I were listening to the news on the radio.

'It's for you, Jackie,' said Mrs Greenhill, handing me the telegram.

'You open it,' I said in the sudden cold silence, broken only by the unemotional voice of the news announcer. Please God, I begged silently as she fumbled with the seal, don't let it be Reg.

'It's John,' she said, passing me the telegram. 'Missing in action.'

I phoned his squadron. They were polite but could add little to the telegram. His formation had been jumped by an overwhelming force of German fighters. In the ensuing scramble he had vanished. No one had seen him go down. They would let me know if they heard anything further.

I carried on flying in a sky suddenly unfriendly. Each flight evoked John. Each cloud was like a gravestone; silent and reproachful. Each time the landing wheels touched, skimmed over the surface and finally settled on the runway I remembered that John had not landed. At night, in bed, I convinced myself that there had been an empty space in the telegram until my decision had irrevocably written the name of John. That I had wished him dead that Reg might live. Guilt played havoc with commonsense and for weeks I reported to the aerodrome and ferried aircraft with the slinking furtiveness of a criminal.

Six weeks elapsed before I was reprieved. Weeks of reasoned argument from Mrs Greenhill who knew all. Of phone calls to his squadron who already were beginning to forget him. I refused to answer Reg's bewildered unhappy letters. It was in this mood that I returned to Hamble after ferrying a sluggish heavy Walrus amphibious aircraft. Dispirited and tired I slouched into the mess for a cup of coffee. Dropping my parachute and helmet on the floor I got the coffee and slumped into one of the deep leather armchairs that were dotted around the mess.

'Hi,' greeted the figure sitting in the chair next to mine.

'Hi,' I answered mechanically, intent on balancing my coffee. He got up and, grinning like a Cheshire cat, stood in front of me.

'John. John!'

He had lost weight and looked drawn and haggard. That evening in Creek Cottage he told me his story, reluctantly.

'What happened?' I asked.

He shrugged disinterestedly, got up and sat next to me on the settee. 'What happened?' I insisted.

He smiled wryly. 'I caught it too soon. We were at 20,000 when they jumped us. We broke up. I got on the tail of a 109 and pumped everything I had into him. Funny thing,' he mused, 'I was enjoying it; enjoying trying to kill him.' He lapsed into silence for a moment and then continued: 'But he wouldn't go down. Then someone blew *me* out of the sky. Own fault. I didn't see him. I caught fire and got out quick. You did a jump once didn't you?' he asked parenthetically.

'Yes.'

'You must be crazy. Anyway I got down all right and walked home.'

'From Germany?'

'Yes. I was captured but jumped off the train on the way to prison camp. Got to Holland. The underground did the rest.'

I looked at the top button of his tunic. It was done up. He caught my eye and grinned, bringing a lustre to his tired eyes. 'I don't want to be a hero any more,' he said.

I lied to him for two months, until he was fit and well and wore the blue and white ribbon of the Distinguished Flying Cross before I told him.

23

DURING THE EARLY SPRING OF 1944 THE A.T.A. WAS ALMOST overwhelmed by a flood of aircraft pouring from the factories. Every available pilot was called to cope with the heavy programme of priority and super-priority delivery flights. Rumours of a big show were rife as, from dawn to dusk, we criss-crossed the skies with an armada of fighters, bombers and troop-transports freshly painted with dramatic black and white markings.

As we flew over the southern ports we could see something was going on. Rivers and creeks were stuffed with landing craft. New balloon barrages sprouted like cabbages over harbours crammed with shipping and supplies. Puzzling structures, subsequently renowned as 'Pluto' and 'Mulberry' added to the crop of rumours.

On June 1st all leave was cancelled, long stretches of coastline were declared prohibited areas and all aircrew subjected to a belated security check. By then even the most unsophisticated agreed that it must be the invasion.

A sudden lull proclaimed the end of preparations, the moment of decision. Most of us guessed that the lull was the eve of history. Lost by the sudden inactivity and the strange quiet that settled on the aerodrome the pilots moped around the operations room trying to cadge flights, or played tennis desultorily in the shadow of the hangar.

'Jackie!'

'Yes?'

'Ops want you right away.'

I dropped the racquet and ran.

'Tempest to New Church,' greeted the operations officer. 'Priority, they are waiting for it. Pick it up at Aston Down. I'll arrange for the taxi aircraft to pick you up later at New Church.'

'Roger. I'll go and change.'

'Where?'

'Creek Cottage.'

'No time for that. Off you go.'

'I can't go like this,' I protested, indicating my white tennis shorts, plimsolls and sweatshirt.

'GO!'

I found another pilot, jumped into the stand-by Auster aircraft and took off hurriedly for Aston Down where the Tempest fighter, its deceptively simple lines cloaking with an air of innocence the most formidable fighter in the skies, stood parked near the Control Tower.

By the time I had completed the handing-over formalities a large crowd had gathered. A hundred hands helped me on with my parachute and there was a delighted roar of 'Ride her cowboy' as I thankfully hid my legs in the slim cockpit.

The roar subsided to a speculative hum as I got out the Tempest pilot's notes and refreshed my memory before starting up. Heads shook disapprovingly at this cavalier treatment of the mighty Tempest. Enjoying the effect, I propped the book up against the windscreen and pretended to read whilst starting up and taxi-ing with important blips of the throttle to the take-off position. They were still standing in front of the hangar as I shot into the air like a startled faun and set course for New Church.

A few minutes later I glanced idly to the east where the English Channel glistened in the warm sunshine like a limpid lake and beyond, faintly visible in the heat haze, the French coast waited and challenged. To the north, balloon barrages swayed like drunken elephants at a carnival. Content with speed, power and solitude, it was some seconds before I appreciated the possible menace of the speck that detached itself from the enemy coast and headed towards me. I sat up and watched it warily. Must be one of ours, I reassured myself hopefully, waggling my wings in a timid gesture of friendship as it loomed closer. No answering waggle untied the tight knot in my stomach. It was too late to run for it. With a show of bravado I turned towards it but it ignored me and continued steadily on its course. I was mildly insulted before it shot past in front of me showing fully its hideous black silhouette. It was a Buzz-bomb. Impulsively I opened the throttle, turned steeply and, bobbing violently in its wake as it sped through the air with the soulless determination of a torpedo, chased after it. There was nothing I could do except perhaps topple it with a wing-tip. The Tempest's guns were empty. Urging on the Tempest I stared fascinated and repelled as the macabre gaunt parody of an aircraft headed insolently for the distant haze that pin-pointed London. It was uncanny; my legs were clammy with goose-pimples.

Suddenly, shooting puffs of black smoke from the stovepipe exhaust, it slowed down, dropped a wing and began its menacing gliding turn to oblivion. It circled lazily like a scavenger picking its prey before plunging with inhuman robot hate into a tiny

121

picturesque hamlet. Sickened I circled the stricken cottages, cut through the bitter pall of dust rising slowly in the peaceful afternoon sun and turned back on to course.

Unnerved by this sombre glimpse of the future I made a shaky landing at New Church. It was a relief to hear the warm wolf calls of welcome and see the startled scurry of naked airmen disturbed from their afternoon sun-bath as I pulled off my helmet and emerged from the cockpit.

Shortly afterwards a squadron of Typhoon fighter-bombers returning from an offensive sweep over the French Channel ports taxied in and switched off, their wings stained by cannon smoke. In a moment I was surrounded by nervously chattering pilots, clad in saffron-coloured Mae-Wests, describing the results of the sweep. One of their aircraft had failed to return. Shot down by ground fire. There was shock and fear and drunken excitement in their eyes. May God forgive me but I was almost glad that one of them had died. There was still some humanity in war when one risked life to kill. When the limitations of flesh and fear mar the scientists' robot perfection.

24

THE INVASION, THE STEADY CREEP OF ALLIED FORCES TOWARDS Berlin, Reg's impending return from India and frequent flashes of irritation from my fellow pilots in the A.T.A.: 'Oh grow up, Jackie,' were a nagging reminder that the roundabout of flying, ingenuousness and *naiveté* on which I had ridden as contentedly and aimlessly as a butterfly since the early days of the war would soon grind to a halt.

My reaction was typically perverse. To genuine innocence and ignorance I defiantly added a breathtaking pious pseudo-saintliness that would have made a nun of Assisi a harlot by comparison. I met all casual references to sex and sensibility with a blank stare and determined misunderstanding, saw smut where there was none and ruined many a good joke by ostentatiously not seeing the point. Thus I determined to counter maturity and evil, which I misguidedly assumed to be the same thing, by being totally immature.

It was unfortunate that casual acquaintances found me quaint and refreshing thus encouraging the growth of this exotic off-shoot in my character (though, when flying, I always left St. Dolores Teresa in the crew-room with a secret, though unad-mitted, sigh of relief).

Looking back it is difficult to understand how I survived the fury of my colleagues during this period of immaculate virtue. Even the priest, incognito on the other side of the confessional grille, implied that I was being very tiresome when my only admitted sin was the wish that the war would never end. To please him I confessed imaginary sins and smugly enjoyed fulfilling undeserved penances.

It was in this mood that Reg found me on his return from the Far East during the closing months of summer. It had been a full day with a touch of tension that lifted it out of routine. In the morning I ferried a replacement bomber uneventfully from Dunsfold to Kirkbride in Scotland. Over lunch in the mess I met the engineer who was to accompany me on the return ferry-flight in a dilapidated aircraft, a Mitchell, destined for the graveyard. The ferry-chit was endorsed in red ink with the curt statement: ONE LANDING ONLY, the laconic warning used in the A.T.A. when a machine was on its last legs.

We approached the Mitchell dubiously. It looked very sad and tired in the driving rain. Rows of bombs neatly painted on the nose under an exotic though faded Varga girl testified to its honourable career.

We climbed aboard, cleared the debris from the cockpit, started up and, with the rain alternately dripping and pouring in thin streams as the aircraft lurched heavily on each wheel, taxied to the take-off point.

'Going to the dance tonight?' shouted the engineer, referring to an invitation received at Hamble from the officers of a nearby American army camp. I nodded absently as a forbidding black squall threatened from the north turning, like a cloud of locusts, day into twilight. At that moment a red flare shot high into the sky from the Control Tower and hovered brightly in the darkening gloom. 'The dance,' urged the engineer as I hesitated whether to obey the order, implicit in the flare and the approaching squall, to cancel the flight and return to the hangars. A vision of couples dancing and the thought of spending another night away from the comforts of Creek Cottage guided my hands to the throttles.

Carefully looking away from the Control Tower we accelerated down the rain-thrashed runway and disappeared over the hills as another flare mottled the sky with an angry red glow. Grinning like truant schoolchildren we levelled out just beneath the clouds and headed out towards the sea where no hills lurked.

As we neared Dunsfold the starboard engine as though suddenly struck by the absurdity of contributing to its own demise coughed and began to vibrate alarmingly.

'Feather it,' I shouted, opening up the port engine to maximum power and adjusting the trim. The engineer reached up, pressed the large red feathering button and watched the starboard propeller slowly jerk to' a halt, its blades knifing the slipstream. 'O.K. She's feathered.' I checked the maps. We had ten minutes to go.

'Is she holding?' shouted the engineer, anxiously scanning the instruments. I nodded. The altimeter held steadily at 800, the air-speed indicator at 140.

'What about alternating?' shouted the engineer, wriggling and fidgeting in his seat.

'No. Dunsfold is the nearest. We'll be there in five minutes. Watch out for it.'

'There it is,' he shouted, pointing straight ahead at the runway shining like black glass in the rain. I nodded and circled warily.

One engine meant that, once the undercarriage and flaps were down on the final approach, there was no room for error.

The engineer, his hand suspended over the undercarriage lever waited tensely as I lined up the Mitchell and began the final approach to the runway beckoning encouragingly through the misty curtain of rain. 'Have you done a single-engined landing before?' he shouted anxiously.

'No . . .' I replied. Without comment he tightened his safety straps.

'Now?' he anticipated, his hand fidgeting with the lever.

'No! We'll undershoot. Hold it,' I shouted, kicking the rudders as the Mitchell drifted and crabbed sluggishly in the gusty cross-wind.

'O.K.,' I shouted about a mile from the end of the runway, 'undercarriage down.'

With a gesture of relief he threw the lever forward. The nose dropped immediately as the undercarriage unfolded like the legs of a bird. I compensated for the increased drag with a touch of throttle and trim as the runway appeared to sway in the wind like the landing deck of an aircraft carrier. The engineer's hand now hovered over the flap lever.

'Half flap,' I ordered.

'Half flap down,' he acknowledged, selecting the lever half-way.

'Full flap.'

'Full flaps down,' he replied.

As the flaps came fully down we sank like a lift and waited, committed. We were a little high but the wheels touched, bounced and settled safely. The engineer grinned hugely and clenched his hands happily above his head as we rolled to the end of the runway. I switched off the gallant port engine, as the crash wagon clanged out to meet us, and looked at the maps clutched in my hand. They were shaking like an aspen tree.

'You all right?' shouted the crash crew as the engineer slid back the side panel and poked his head through.

'Sure,' he shouted, with a grin. 'The pilot was a lady.'

I felt a childish glow of pleasure at the surprised and impressed glances. A single-engine landing occurred a dozen times a day in the air force. But it was my first and I had pulled it off in an unfamiliar aircraft.

The dance inevitably turned out to be an anti-climax and as our foursome returned to Creek Cottage for good-night coffee my thoughts still lingered on the Mitchell rather than the jitter-bugging marathon of the last four hours. I was surprised to see a faint crack of light edging the blackout curtains. The Greenhills usually retired early. We got out of the car and crept quietly into the lounge. As I blinked the blackout from my eyes Reg, bronzed and thinner, rose from the easy-chair and the clutter of pipe cleaners and magazines that tokened a long wait. I remember little of what happened in the shy haze of welcome except that the others were curtly dismissed and I was firmly kissed.

25

THE NEXT FEW WEEKS AS THE LEAVES TURNED AUBURN AND the sun moved imperceptibly south were weeks of supreme illogicality. A sort of mad-hatter's tea party during which I was transformed from an eminently Victorian product, prudish and priggish, into an impatient fiancée eager to be dominated by man and marriage. I have tried to avoid saying what must be and is the answer, for it is such a simpering banality. I fell in love. It is not a banality to do so but to write so.

There was little left from our past relationship. The past two impressionable years had changed us both. At first we searched for the things that had committed us to each other two years before. But we had discarded those unconscious mannerisms; forgotten also the conscious ones used to attract.

As his tan faded and his pipe became as familiar as my own hands, the shy curiosity of getting to know another who had the privilege of intimate friendship but who was as a stranger, was slowly transformed into feelings that gave an almost gross significance to perceptions and experience. Flying north was flying away from him. Like a horse returning to the stable I was discontent until the compass once again swung south. A flower, an ode, a falling leaf, everything had a link, however tenuous, with him.

It did not occur to me that my experience was commonplace. I thought I had made a unique discovery and walked and flew constantly astonished that I could achieve such an avalanche of happiness. The erstwhile embarrassed glimpses in the bathroom mirror became speculative and curious appraisals to find outward symptoms of the extraordinary things going on inside.

I shed the cloak of gross piety as easily and naturally as a snake sheds its skin, much, I suspect, to the relief of my comrades.

He listened patiently as the last lingering weeds still clung to the soil of the past. As I drifted between independence and the desire for domination, between fear of man and hope of mysterious pleasures. There were many buts. He ticked most of them off and placed the remainder in the pending tray. Only the years to come could solve those.

'Well?' he prompted one evening as we dozed by the fire at Creek Cottage.

'Easter,' I suggested.

'No. Earlier. January.'

'That's very soon.'

'We *did* meet in 1940.'

'It doesn't give us much time.'

'For what?'

'I have to make a wedding dress and . . .'

'We can get married in a registry office.'

'Oh no we won't!'

'I'll marry you in church if you make it January.'

'All right.'

We sat unmoving, moved by the enormity of the decision. I tried to sit up. 'I stay in the A.T.A. of course?'

'Of course. We can't build a home until after the war.'

'It will be just like it is now,' I observed contentedly, 'except that we will be married.'

'Well,' he leered, 'not exactly.'

I blushed.

'There's just one thing.'

'Yes?'

'I want to see South Africa again before we get married.'

'How?'

'Hitch-hike.'

'You're crazy!'

'Thank you.'

'Sorry, but it is a bit far-fetched. Must be 10,000 miles to Pretoria and back.'

'Twelve thousand,' I corrected.

The following morning I cabled my mother the announcement of the marriage. She riposted with a cable that she was seriously ill. I had a shrewd suspicion that her cable was prompted by the impending nuptials but nevertheless, to Reg's dismay, I arranged compassionate leave from the A.T.A., obtained an impressive 'To whom it may concern' letter from South Africa House, and ferried an aircraft to Lyneham, headquarters of Royal Air Force Transport Command.

After a mild brush with red-tape I was soon on my way to Malta as second-pilot of a squat Liberator bomber. Sitting at the controls as the landscape changed from England's dull grey to the brilliance of the Mediterranean I enjoyed patronizing the top-brass and V.I.P.s who came up from the rear to have a look at the works. From Malta I worked my way as an 'air-hostess' to service-men as far as Cairo, where I was bogged down with an apparently insoluble problem. I had no Yellow Fever certificate and it took ten days before an inoculation became valid. Two precious days passed before I came to the reluctant conclusion that the medical services were incorruptible and forged the thing myself with an impressive flourish.

Eleven days after leaving England I arrived in Pretoria to find my mother moderately ill but indulgently so. Her tragic greetings of 'My child' were rebuffed with a crisp matronly approach that soon had her out of bed on to a less maudlin field of battle regarding my future. She was shocked by my pallid appearance and stuffed me with milk and fresh fruit as though I were the supposed invalid.

She had ten days to change my mind. Ten days in which she dangled lusty carrots: a car, a flat, even an aeroplane, in front of my nose. When these failed a thin stream of bachelors, considerably depleted since 1938, again paid court. But hers was a hopeless cause.

It was a bizarre experience to be so suddenly engulfed in a forgotten world of rich food, naked lights and untroubled skies. I felt an alien in my own land, a nun bewildered in a tempting garden. It was too much. My destiny was with an austere island still grappling with a mortal foe.

I returned to Taunton four days before the wedding.

Reg greeted me with almost comical relief, his mother with gentle resignation. She was too conscious of my domestic ignorance and the mortal danger threatening her eldest son to be serenely in favour of my return.

As we drove away from the church I felt numb and embarrassed. The swish of chiffon, the white ribbon fluttering from the car's mascot and the sly grins of the passers-by made me feel like a harlot. Peering through a veil was a singular experience after a decade of peering through goggles. I took a quick look at Reg sitting beside me and felt a wave of encouragement that he too wore the stiff mask of shyness. We held hands and stared absently at the back of the imperturbable chauffeur's head. I wondered whether he had had as many weddings as I had flying hours. I asked Reg but he was not very interested.

The lingerie, smuggled in from South Africa, was shameless. Whilst Reg waited downstairs and shepherded away the last lingering guests I slipped it on and stared at myself in the mirror. 'Jezebel', I muttered, shocked at the reflection. 'Just like Mother to buy something like this.' It had not yet occurred to me that the delicious anticipatory tremor of body and soul was legitimate. That the quaint ceremony in church had turned evil into good.

When deciding the date for our marriage I omitted to take a certain matter into consideration. Consequently our brief honeymoon was so in name only. He was convinced that I had contrived it so. I replied unkindly that I thought that that was why he married me. I thought the honeymoon delightful and returned from Brighton's bracing breezes with a glow on my cheeks and at peace with the world. Reg bore the pangs of unfulfilled desire with tolerable good humour though with a glint that boded ill for my future immaculate state of grace.

The circumstance of war smiled benevolently on our marriage and, by keeping us homeless, sheltered it from the series of calamities that might have been had I been wrenched from flying and pitchforked into domesticity.

It is difficult to be dull when uniforms meet; when first officer's stripes rest fleetingly on captain's pips. We knew little of each other's work. I flew, he was in the Army. There was no overlapping here and that added to each other's desirability. He tried to explain the difference between a regiment and a platoon. I, what made an aeroplane fly. Years later we are still trying. Our rendezvous were not the casual peck after a tiring day but the fruit of absence, cables and trunk-calls. We spent the few weekends and leaves that were synchronized in Taunton or Creek Cottage where holes in his socks and a missing button were still his own problem and we retained the status of life's guest. Thus our marriage was a continuation of courtship and not the plunge into physical familiarity and domestic responsibility that I had feared.

Few could have had so gentle an introduction to marriage. Few perhaps needed it as much as I.

26

The cool nip of dawn still lingered under an unblemished sky as we sat waiting in the crew-room for the day's ferrying programme. It was a small programme, but I had the plum. A Mosquito fighter-bomber to Aldergrove near Belfast, via Chester. Resisting the offer of swops, few aircraft could compete with the exhilarating Mosquito, I joined the other pilots in the taxi Anson that dropped me off a few minutes later at Odiham aerodrome.

Whilst waiting for the Mosquito to be finally checked over I drew a dog-leg to Aldershot on my maps, scribbled a note for Reg and tied it firmly to a stone. I had dispensed with the refinement of a handkerchief parachute since I had landed in a Hurricane under the eyes of a very senior A.T.A. officer with Reg's note fluttering brazenly from the tail.

Over Aldershot I announced my arrival in the usual manner with a blip of throttles and a wild pass at nought feet across the barracks. No drill this morning I speculated, puzzled by a large mass of upturned faces, white against the well-groomed officers' mess lawn. They waved encouragingly. Assuming they wanted a show I obliged. Reg I knew would be stubbornly inside. He had told me a score of times that it was useless to show off over the camp as he would not watch anyway. It was too dangerous. With a final pass that, according to Reg's Colonel, blew the blasted chimney off the blasted cookhouse, I dropped the note on the lawn, blipped a rebellious farewell to Reg and headed for Chester to refuel.

At Hawarden aerodrome I was greeted with blissful faces. The propellers had barely twitched to a halt before a labourer jumped on the wing, pulled me out of the cockpit and danced a wild jig surrounded by his comrades. The smell of beer, intense in the sunshine, was overpowering. I was accustomed to an occasional riotous welcome but what was this?

'What's going on?' I gasped giddily.

'Do ye no ken?' he grinned broadly.

'Is it Peace?'

'Aye, it is, lassie. It's all o'er. Ye can go back to ye bairns noo,' he shouted, kissing me with a rich smack firmly on the lips. I was still being kissed by weather-beaten faces, like whiskered beer bottles, when the aircrew pick-up van arrived. Not to be outdone, they kissed me too.

The officers' mess where I drove for a quick lunch seethed like a football stadium. Sergeants, arm-in-arm with officers, swayed blissfully in a sea of spilling pewter tankards. They spotted me hovering in the entrance and with a roar seized me, hoisted me on to the mantelshelf, thrust a crescent of cheese and an enormous tankard of beer in my hands and on their knees, salaamed with drunken grace. In the corner a radio ineffectually blared the details of surrender. No one listened in the intoxicating miasma of victory.

Choosing a moment when a seething mass fell to the floor and had beer gaily poured over them I hopped down, scuttled through the French windows, already stripped of blackout, and walked quickly to the hangars where the Mosquito was being refuelled.

'How long?' I asked the refuelling crew.

'Ten minutes,' they answered cheerfully. 'Got to check the oil and coolant yet, Miss.'

'Please hurry,' I urged.

They grinned easily. 'What's the matter, Miss? The war's over . . .'

'They may cancel the flight,' I explained.

'Keen type,' they chorused. 'They won't want it now.'

The words echoed significantly as I headed out over the Irish Sea. They won't want it now. It's all over. No more Tempests and Spits and Lanes. No more Wings and stripes, excitement and fun. No more of not caring or knowing what day it is. No more of this, I continued miserably, glancing out at the oil-slicked Merlin engines. Glumly I checked the instruments. They were normal, like a cow placidly munching cud on the way to the abattoir. Perhaps, I comforted myself, they will let us ferry planes to the Far East. No they won't, sneered better judgement, that and the Continent are men's prerogative. Mechanically I carried on across the Irish Sea, noticing with a jaundiced eye that it had suddenly lost the sinister threat of no-man's-land and was transformed into a placid highway where ferry-steamers would soon chug peacefully over the unmarked graves of gallant seamen. The sky, annoyingly impervious to my mood, wore a cloak of pale blue flecked with sun-bleached cumulus clouds like gentle cherubs as though nature, too, welcomed the return of peace.

The sky was lonely as the Mosquito gracefully consumed what might be its last flight. It was as though I were hitched to a suicide. A little drunk with self-pity I gave the rudder a violent kick to induce revolt in this inanimate thing. The Mosquito lurched, grunted and stabilized easily back to course.

The coastline beckoning from the horizon, usually a welcome sight after a sea-crossing, left me cold. It was like a signpost to genteel retirement. At Aldergrove aerodrome, a major base in Coastal Command's contribution to the Battle of the Atlantic, I dived steeply and shot viciously over the runways. Pulling up in a vertical climb that left me trembling with fright I stall turned, dived back again far too low and shot between the hangars. For ten minutes I flew like a maniac until exhilaration purged the bitter taste of gall. Feeling much better I did a meretricious side-slipping landing and taxied to the ramp.

'You want to be careful, Miss,' observed the anxious-looking mechanic as he took my parachute. 'You only just missed the hangars. The O.C. flying wants to see you. He's hopping mad,' he added warningly.

I did not care twopence for the O.C. flying or anyone else at that moment but acquiesced meekly as he delivered his thoroughly deserved reprimand.

Returning to Hamble the following day, to the anticipated decline and fall of the A.T.A. I was relieved to find my melancholy mood premature. No decision had yet been made. It was some weeks before the cracks that were to reduce it to dust first appeared. A few outlying ferry pools were closed down. Some of their pilots, replete with flying, were released. The remainder drifted and lingered like spectators loathe to leave the cricket field when rain stops play.

The indecision was ended after three months by the experiments at Hiroshima and Nagasaki, and Japan's acknowledgement of their success. It would be hollow mockery in 1957 to describe those events as Victory and Defeat.

A.T.A., with few mourners, died with the autumn, despite efforts to find a square hole for it in the paroxysm of peace. As the leaves curled and dropped from the trees, so familiar faces disappeared and ferry pools faded away. Hamble was one of the first to go. Evading a pressing invitation to return to civilian life I contrived a transfer to Prestwick pool and continued the lugubrious task of delivering aircraft to the disposal aerodromes where they waited silently like tombstones for the ignominious hammer. Old ones honoured with the trophies and scars of battle seemed content. New ones, stillborn from the factories, wore a resentful air like children arriving too late for a party.

It was during this period of decline that I discovered I was carrying an unauthorized passenger. A surreptitious visit in civilian clothes to a private doctor confirmed that I was a third of the way to motherhood.

The next few months developed into a race between the final demise of the A.T.A. and my waistline. Being one of the pioneers of the A.T.A. I was obstinately determined to be with it to the last flight. I developed an eagle eye for the insignia of a medical officer and on spotting one would hold in my stomach. My female colleagues, sworn to secrecy, were almost indiscreetly helpful and winced whenever I slung a heavy parachute over my shoulder and climbed in and out of fighters and bombers. Later, as I let out the first tucks in my skirts and slacks we swopped flights whenever I was scheduled for the more formidably massive aircraft, particularly the heavy, sluggish Walrus, apocryphally notorious for producing miscarriages. By such subterfuge I remained flying. Reg's letters from Germany where he was stationed with the

Occupation Forces were burdened with care about his embryonic child being subjected to the indignities of flying. I replied tartly that he or she would probably be a pilot anyway, and what better pre-natal environment.

In November I was posted to White Waltham, for demobilization. It was a poignant moment as the last pool closed down writing *finis* to a great war-spawned organization, but by fortuitous timing I was not sorry. The kicks and assertions going on inside me were becoming insistent. For the first time in my life I was glad to be on the ground.

Turning at the door and content to be Mrs Moggridge, I announced my condition. My last memory of A.T.A. is the look of startled incredulity on the faces of the men-folk as I drove away in a taxi.

Dolores Teresa Sorour, born 1 March, 1920. She became Jackie in her teens, refusing to answer to any other name.

Jackie's beloved grandmother Helen Sarkis. 'Old-fashioned and strong willed', but Jackie adored her.

Jackie and her mother Veronica in South Africa c.1937.

Preparing for her parachute jump, in front of the de Havilland Moth, at Swartkop
Aerodrome. They had no suits small enough to fit a 17-year-old girl – only
men jumped out of planes in those days – so Jackie's tiny frame was completely

'I saw polo players approaching on horseback like an army of Pegasus.' Jackie, the
first South African woman to perform a solo parachute jump, is carried back to the
aerodrome with a broken ankle.

Jackie on her beloved motorbike 'Jill' in Pretoria. Years later, Jackie would name her first daughter after this bike.

Jackie and Reg pose for the camera in July 1942 during a precious week's leave spent together.

Jackie poses with fellow Air Transport Auxiliary (ATA) pilot Hazel Raines on the wing of a Spitfire. Photo taken at RAF Brize Norton in 1943.

The women of No. 15 Ferry Pool relax in the sunshine between duties.

RIGHT 'To you darling with love Jackie. March 1943. In the Anson, taken at 2000 ft.' A photograph sent to Reg during one of many periods of separation.

BELOW The full team of No. 15 Ferry Pool, Jackie can be seen to the left of the propeller.

PAGE 2

Occupation...... *Ferry Pilot*

Place of Birth...... *Pretoria, South Africa*

Date of Birth...... *1st March 1920*

Home Address...... *"Creek Cottage" Satchell Lane*
Hamble, Southampton

Photograph and Signature

National Registration Identity Card.

E.E.W 665 742

'I want to see South Africa again before we get married.' Jackie managed to obtain this work permit in order to see her family again before settling down to married life.

Jackie with her extended family, Matatiele, December 1944. Clockwise from left: Jackie's Uncle, her youngest brother Eddie, her baby sister Rosemary, Jackie, her mother Veronica, her aunt Mary, two cousins, her brother Laurence and three more cousins. The two sisters (Veronica and Mary) married two brothers, making the family very close.

Jackie and Reg were married on 12 January, 1945 at St George's Catholic Church in Taunton. Here they are pictured with their bridesmaids, Sally Malthouse (left) and Barbara Gill (right).

Jackie was straight back to work following the wedding. Here she is in her favourite aeroplane, a Spitfire. As she was only 5ft 2in., Jackie always carried a cushion with her in order to reach the controls.

ABOVE Jackie and Jill, 1949.

RIGHT Jackie continued to encourage other women to fly. Here she is with the Women's Junior Air Corps (WJAC) in the early 1950s.

'Graduation photo, Wings at Wellesbourne!' Jackie is the only female face in a class full of men – something she was very used to by now. They are posing in front of an Airspeed Oxford.

Jackie finally gets her full Wings, 25 August, 1953, at Royal Air Force Wellesbourne.

Jackie in the cockpit of a jet, taken during her campaign to become the first woman to break the sound barrier.

ABOVE 'I was happier than I had been for years.' A photograph of Jackie taken during the Spitfire trips to Burma,

LEFT 'Ferrying Spitfires at Bahrain in Persian Gulf, 120 degrees in shade!'

BELOW Last arrival in Burma, having delivered all the Spitfires, 1955.

Jackie working as an airline captain for Channel Airways in the late 1950s. She wasn't allowed to use the tannoy in case passengers took fright at being flown by a woman.

Jackie and a colleague pose with a de Havilland Dragon Rapide, September 1956. It was in such an aircraft that Jackie had her first flight, aged fifteen.

Jackie as local celebrity: interviewed by Richard Dimbleby for *Down Your Way*, with Jill proudly looking on.

Jackie at Weston-super-Mare, 1967, where she piloted pleasure flights.

The ATA's forty year reunion, 14 August, 1985. Jackie is crouching at the front.

Jackie and Carolyn Grace prepare for Jackie's last flight in Spitfire ML407, 29 April, 1994.

PART THREE

POST-WAR

'You're out' they say when war is won,
'We know of all the work you've done';
But men must work and women weep,
And women say yes like a lot of sheep.

1945

27

'FIFTY-SIX POTATOES, PLEASE.'

'Pardon, madam?'

'Fifty-six potatoes!'

'Excuse me, madam, why fifty-six?'

'That's what the cook-book says. I've added it up. Fifty-six potatoes for meals for a week for two persons.'

'Yes, madam.'

'And they must be the same size.'

'You must be Mrs Moggridge!'

He humoured me, carefully selected and counted fifty-six potatoes. I put them on my bike and rode home. We had just moved in to a grace and favour house owned by my father-in-law. Though ugly and one of four in a dismal row I liked it. Situated on the Ilminster Road two miles from Taunton's moderately bustling centre it faced a Constable landscape and backed distant forests. Every night over supper we agreed it was only a temporary arrangement until we built our own home. A simple thing surely for Messrs. Moggridge & Sons, Building Contractors. As I sit, years later, typing this book, the same landscape dulled by familiarity stares obdurately back at me and the forests at the back are hidden by council houses that anger by their intrusion but comfort by their example of social progress.

My daughter, weighing six and a quarter pounds (though why that should interest puzzles me) and none the worse for having a few hundred flying hours to her credit, arrived punctually in the nursing home. The nurses hurriedly assured me that all new-born babies are equally monstrous. With her arrival came a King's Commendation for valuable services in the air. It seems that I had ferried more aeroplanes than anyone else, male or female, in the A.T.A. I looked wryly at the crisp parchment scroll disappointingly signed by the new Prime Minister, Atlee, whose autograph for all his virtues lacked the collector's appeal of Churchill's, and then down at the terracotta coloured bundle nuzzled at my breast. Was one to end the other? Reg had just paid a flying visit from Germany, exhibited hopelessly subjective sentiments about his daughter and returned to Germany happy and content with the acorns of his new life.

Reg was demobilized shortly after I left the nursing home and returned without equivocation to the family business. Following his urbane example I put away my uniform and log-books and, for the first few months, enjoyed painting and wallpapering, choosing utility furniture and uttering the absurd but enchanting goo-goos of mother-baby language. Her helpless dependence invoked a discipline that smothered revolt and nostalgia whenever dishes were damned with faint praise, the weekly wash – sans washing machine – overflowed the dirty-linen basket or aircraft passed overhead.

Once a viable routine was established it was not long before I succumbed to the temptation to scan through my flying log-books, and step back into memories of war. In the peace of the afternoon, the housewife's armistice between lunch and dinner, I recalled the smell of hot oil and glycol, the thunder of the

Lancaster, the lyrical Spitfire and a getting up in the morning with one eye on the sky. I knew there were many others with the same temptation, whose station in peace mocked their achievements in war. Most of them had the courage to turn back to the factory bench, the brief-case or the pen and recall the old days only over a mug of beer. I could not, or would not. I was happy with the trilogy that most women desire – a husband, a baby, a home – but the stimulant was lacking that would bring peaks to the foothills of dull content. Being a wife, a mother and a housewife was too constant an occupation. Even heaven must be dull without a brief relative glimpse of hell.

There is an abandoned aerodrome near Taunton. It was my opiate. When tears of maudlin self-pity welled I rode there on my bike and walked along the silent runways already crumbling at the edges and cracked with weeds. The gaunt wooden huts became filled with the potent bustle of aircrew, the runway trembled with the surge of accelerating bombers and the air was filled with the ghosts of those who did not return. For many hours I relived Hatfield, Hamble and Creek Cottage. But the drug was ephemeral. The trilogy insufficient.

'Reg,' I blurted one evening as he pored over plans and estimates for other people's homes.

'Uh-huh.'

'I want to do some flying.'

He looked up and grinned ruefully. 'I thought it would come sooner or later. How? You haven't got a licence.'

'I can get a "B" licence easily enough. My A.T.A. experience will exempt me from most of the examinations.'

'Then what?'

'Nothing much,' I prevaricated. 'Just to know I've got the licence and can fly if I want to. That's all.'

'All right,' he sighed. 'If that's what you want, go ahead.'

Within a few weeks I received my first professional licence. I carried it with me everywhere, next to the ration books. It was not quite so bad then when an aircraft glinted sharply in the sun, or hummed overhead at night.

Once or twice a month I collected the small hoard of sixpences and shillings appropriated from the household budget, sneaked off to Exeter Flying Club and for an hour hired a Tiger Moth or Auster. It was enough at first. To hide behind a cloud, to have my fingers curled around a control column instead of kneading dough. To share solitude with the sky and sorrow for those who know it not. But, soon, the flimsy innocuous club aircraft, toys compared with the Tempests and Typhoons of the war, and the aimless circling of the aerodrome, began to pall.

'Reg.'

'Uh-huh.'

'Do you mind if I get a job?'

'What on earth for?'

'Just a little flying job . . . you know . . . part-time.'

'Oh, I see!'

'It's silly now that I've got a licence not to use it and the money would be useful for Jill's schooling.'

'What sort of flying?'

'I don't know yet. I thought of answering some of the jobs advertised in *Flight* and *The Aeroplane*.'

He frowned dubiously. I loved him for not saying where my place was. 'What about Jill and the housekeeping?' he asked.

146

'It wouldn't interfere with that. Mother could take care of Jill on the days when I'm flying.'

'And I have lunch in town?' he said wryly.

I nodded eagerly.

'All right,' he decided, unconsciously repeating himself. 'If that's what you want, go ahead.'

The aeronautical journals were crammed with vacancies for pilots. I wrote only to the illustrious firms and waited confidently for a flood of replies. I got the replies but they were monotonously identical in content: Dear Madam, We regret to inform you that, owing to passenger psychology, it is not our policy at present to employ women pilots. However we have placed your name on our files and will communicate with you if etc., etc.

In desperation I put an advertisement in one of the journals: *Woman pilot 'B' licence, 2500 hours. 70 types including Single, Twin and Multi-engined. Seeks Flying Post.*

I received one reply. It was from a company marketing a new type of flying overall who hoped I would be interested in the enclosed brochure.

'So this is what I flew in the war for,' I said bitterly. 'To make the world free . . . if you're a man.'

'That's nonsense and you know it,' answered Reg. 'You flew in the war because you love flying and,' he added with a grin 'either the passengers have freedom from fear or . . .'

'Oh shut up. I suppose you agree with these stupid letters.'

'Yes,' he answered honestly. 'More or less. I don't know much about flying but I'd be frightened to death if I sat in a passenger's seat and saw a luscious blonde mince up to the pilot's seat.'

'Prejudice,' I shouted furiously.

'Agreed,' he admitted, 'but the reaction of a normal passenger, male *or* female.'

'You of all people,' I spluttered. 'Judas!'

He smiled at my fury. 'Look, darling,' he soothed. 'I think I've been fair. I've let you try to get a flying job but, prejudice or not, passengers will never accept a woman up in front. You've got to face up to it. The war's over. Give it up. You'll only make yourself miserable.'

'I won't. I'll get a flying job if it kills me.'

'That's all right. As long as it doesn't kill anyone else.'

'Pshaw!'

28

I CONTINUED ANSWERING ADVERTISEMENTS BUT EVERY FLICKER of hope died by return post. It was a disheartening period. Now I am partially reconciled to the rebuffs of prejudice but in those earlier days I felt sick with humiliation and envy whenever an aircraft droned by in the sky.

A few weeks later Reg passed a letter across the breakfast table. 'Sorry,' he apologized. 'It was addressed to *Mr* Moggridge.'

'It's a job,' I shouted triumphantly, passing the letter back to him.

'Not quite,' he corrected, scanning the letter. 'It's an invitation for lunch to discuss a job.'

'Same thing,' I asserted confidently.

He shook his head. 'Not when the letter was addressed to me. They don't realize you are a woman.'

'I'm going anyway,' I said. 'What shall I wear?'

I boarded the express to London wearing a charcoal-grey costume and modest shoes. In accordance with the instructions in the letter I located a small luncheon club in London and asked for Mr . . . 'He is expecting me,' I added untruthfully. A few moments later a small middle-aged man with the paunchy loose look of a publican hesitantly approached me. 'Mr . . .?' I asked. He nodded warily. 'I am Mrs Moggridge.'

'Er. Howdoyoudo,' he welcomed. 'Your husband?'

'There has been a misunderstanding,' I explained. 'I wrote to you for the flying post.'

'But you are a woman,' he frowned.

'Yes,' I said brightly. He cast a surreptitious glance at my legs. I wished I had worn high heels.

Over lunch I told him about myself. He was impressed though his lips still pursed. Then he told me about himself. I did not purse my lips though I was equally doubtful about him. There was something flushed about him as though his heart or his conscience were working under pressure.

'I operate a small freight run to the Continent,' he explained over the mock-turtle soup. 'Urgent aircraft spares and valuable small bulk cargo. Doing quite well,' he added proudly, sipping his half-bottle of wine.

'What type of aircraft?'

'Austers and a Proctor,' he answered.

I was surprised. 'You can't carry much freight on those,' I said.

'No,' he agreed. 'But it isn't the bulk that matters. It's the value and urgency of the cargo that justifies the expense of air-freight.'

'Or perishables,' I added trying to be sagacious.

'That's right,' he nodded, pleased with my attention.

He ordered another bottle of wine with the cutlets and an orangeade for me. I could see he was in an ambiguous frame of mind, trying to balance my virtues as a woman against my potential as a pilot. To help him decide I slipped out to the Ladies' Room and added a further layer of lipstick and a touch of mascara.

'I want only a part-time pilot,' he continued over the cheese and brandy, 'to stand by and fly whenever required.'

'But that suits me admirably,' I replied with a beaming smile.

'Do you think you can manage Austers?' he asked tactlessly.

I refused to be insulted and passed him my flying log-books. He grinned sheepishly as he scanned through them. After three more Napoleon brandies he became jovial and offered me the job. 'Seven pounds ten for each return trip, plus expenses. You should average about two flights a week.'

I accepted promptly.

'Good,' he smiled. 'A toast,' and touched his glass to mine. 'You won't have to worry about Income Tax,' he said as we rose to go.

I danced in the empty train compartment back to Taunton. It was not the job I would have chosen. Austers were insipid aircraft but at last I had stepped on the professional ladder.

After a month during which I had completed six flights without incident I sat in the airport lounge waiting for minor repairs before setting out on another flight when in walked an ex-A.T.A. pilot now resplendent in the uniform of a well-known air charter company.

'Hello, Jackie,' he welcomed, 'still flying?'

I nodded and we talked about old times.

'What are you doing now?' he asked later.

'I'm with . . .' I answered proudly.

The smile dropped from his face. 'Crikey, Jackie!' he ejaculated. 'I hope you know what you are doing.'

'What's the matter with them?' I protested. 'They are treating me splendidly.'

'I'm not surprised,' he said with a cynical laugh. 'But I'm surprised at you,' he added.

'What is it? What are you talking about?' I asked irritably.

'Smuggling.'

'Nonsense.'

He shrugged his shoulders. 'No proof of course, but it's common knowledge.'

'Holy Mother of Mary,' I whispered. 'I've done six trips already.' There was silence at the awful implication.

'You didn't know?'

'Please,' I protested.

'Then you had better get out quickly,' he advised. 'Or, better still, go and see the Customs.'

I shook my head.

'Why not?' he insisted.

'It's too much like Judas.'

He shrugged again. 'It's your funeral. The Customs won't believe your story unless you tell them now.'

Like a criminal I glanced furtively at the uniformed airport police and sank deeply into the armchair until the tannoy announced the departure of his flight.

'Here's my card, Jackie,' he said, getting up. 'Maybe we can convince the Customs of your innocence if the whole thing blows up. But,' he warned, 'don't fly for them again.'

I nodded feebly and shook hands from the depths of the armchair. Enviously I watched his confident, open stride past the uniformed officials and waited for the bustle of the departing flight to distract them before sneaking out of the passengers' exit.

Retreating to Taunton I wrote a letter of resignation without giving any explanation, told Reg vaguely that the job had fallen through and waited in agonizing suspense for the imperious knock of authority at the door.

A week passed. Two. Three. Four, before the epilogue to my life of crime was rather sadly written. Picking up the evening paper I read a small news item that a plane had been lost over the Channel. The pilot was my ex-employer. As a result of his death the company was disbanded and I, I deduced, was safe.

29

'Now what?' asked Reg suspiciously some months later as I opened a large O.H.M.S. envelope.

'I was thinking of joining the air force,' I replied, meekly.

'Oh. Is that all,' he said heavily.

'Yes, dear.'

'Which?'

'Which what?'

'Which air force?'

'The Royal Air Force Volunteer Reserve of course.'

'What's the matter, wouldn't the Russians have you?' he said, referring to my partisanship for the only air force in the world that has operational women pilots.

'Don't be silly, Reg. I'm serious.'

'I'm sure you are,' he brooded.

I left it at that for the time being, drove to R.A.F.V.R. Western Command headquarters, near Bristol and met the Commanding Officer of the Reserve Unit. He was intrigued by my suggestion that I should join his unit but was genuinely flummoxed what to do with me, an occupational disease with the R.A.F. as far as I am concerned. We had tea in the officers' mess whilst he looked through the files and regulations to decide whether he could have a female in his unit and, if so, what sort of specimen she should be. He scratched his head, admitted defeat and suggested I return home until he had investigated further.

He wrote to me later stating that the Royal Air Force Volunteer Reserve would be delighted for me to join them under a new policy of recruiting experienced women pilots. I would hold a temporary non-commissioned rank of airwoman until I qualified as Pilot Class IV.

The R.A.F.V.R. consisted primarily of ex-R.A.F. personnel who had reserve commitments, voluntary or otherwise, and a small number of experienced pilots and ground crew voluntarily recruited direct from civilian life. They were, broadly speaking, civilians except when attending lectures and flying training. Thus being a member of the R.A.F.V.R. conferred many of the privileges of the R.A.F. with negligible sacrifice of civilian freedom.

Distributed throughout the country were a dozen or so flying schools where V.R. pilots during their spare time reported for flying training and lectures. Each pilot was expected to complete a minimum of forty hours' flying annually, usually over the week-ends and to attend evening lectures twice a week.

In this way, and at comparatively little expense, a reserve of pilots was maintained in what may be described as the third line air force whose worth in an emergency would be incalculable.

The highlight of the year was the two weeks' compulsory attendance at an annual summer camp. Each R.A.F.V.R. unit seconded its members in batches of six or so to a regular R.A.F. station where they received the full impact of service life. During this period they lived on the station, wore uniform and were expected to conceal civilian decadence.

I was pleasantly surprised to discover that I would also receive a salary, flying pay and out-of-pocket expenses totalling approximately one hundred pounds per annum for the privilege and pleasure of flying His Majesty's aircraft.

I was all set.

'Reg,' I said as he sat at his desk.

'No!'

I let fall a poignant tear. Just one in the brooding silence. I turned my face to the window so that he could see it, but he was oblivious. I sniffled loudly and squeezed out another tear from the other eye. 'You go to the Territorials,' I sniffed, as he looked up.

'That's different,' he replied with masculine logic. Contriving an avalanche of tears I made great play with a pathetic wisp of handkerchief. 'All right; all right,' he grunted as he got up to go to the Territorials. 'Stop weeping. If you must, you must.'

The following week I 'signed on'. There was little ceremony at my return to the fold but in the weeks that followed the administration of the week-end air force sagged dangerously with the stress of absorbing a female into masculine prerogatives. Inevitably I had trouble in getting a number. After considerable correspondence my old Waaf number was resurrected, found wanting and discarded. A brand-new one was triumphantly produced only to be snatched away when it proved to be of masculine gender. I am convinced there is a secret vault somewhere in the depths of the Air Ministry where millions of numbers stacked in silent rows are guarded by sinister, taciturn men determined to guard the sacrosanctity of their charges. Eventually I got a number so astronomical I had difficulty in memorizing it. My uniform – slacks and battle dress – was also of masculine gender. With buttons in the wrong place.

I was attached to the R.A.F.V.R. flying school at Filton aerodrome, near Bristol, for flying training and lectures based on a syllabus designed to fill in the gaps left by civil flying. It was a small unit with five ubiquitous Tiger Moths, a strength of fifty or sixty pilots, of which I was the only woman, and tiny administrative offices.

My first flight in the R.A.F.V.R. was not auspicious. Though there was no resentment at my presence with the V.R. school – on the contrary my new comrades thought I added a touch of piquancy – I was determined to be a paragon of tact. Thus, clad in inelegant Waaf battledress, I approached my first flight with the Royal Air Force with diffidence and humility.

The Chief Instructor sitting warily in the front seat of the Tiger Moth asked me to carry out a take-off, circuit and landing. I did so. His praise was effusive. 'Very nice, very nice,' he coaxed as I did a second. 'Do another one like that and I'll let you go solo.' I did so and went solo with the instructor wishing me a dramatic good luck. After I landed the instructor met me with my flying log-book in his hands. 'You might have told me you had nearly three thousand hours,' he commented irascibly. 'Trying to make a fool of me?'

During my first year with the V.R. I qualified for preliminary Wings. Not, I should make it clear, the full Wings worn by qualified R.A.F. pilots. Though I had many thousands of hours I was not considered the equal, rightly so, of the air force pilot with three hundred hours who has completed the fully integrated and comprehensive R.A.F. flying training course. My background and experience had too many serious limitations – no night flying, Jet flying, formation flying, gunnery, advanced aerobatics, instrument flying and familiarity with radio equipment – for me to be considered a fully competent pilot.

Jill presented no problem. Reg and I were rarely on duty simultaneously. If our week-end duties clashed I took Jill with me to the aerodrome, where she explored hangars and cockpits and soon possessed the privileges of squadron talisman. Once I suggested that Reg take her to the Territorials but apparently they do not do that sort of thing in the Army.

She also accompanied me when, in addition to the V.R. I got a job as part-time pilot with a flying club. On Bank Holidays and week-ends when I was not scheduled to fly with the V.R. I took passengers on short joy-ride flights, the joy being confined to the passengers and, occasionally, carried out private charter flights for gentlemen in loud tweeds to point-to-point and race meetings. It was a tepid occupation but it kept Jill in shoes and me away from Mrs Beeton.

30

DURING THE WAR I HAD NO OPPORTUNITY OF NIGHT FLYING
for all A.T.A. ferry-flights were conducted during daylight. On
a few flights when I deliberately dawdled in order to descend
with the sun the mild flirtation with the darkening sky merely
increased my envy of those who, in Bomber Command, thun-
dered into the night; even though their destinations were the
pitiless skies over Germany.

It was therefore something of an occasion when I received
orders to report for night-flying training and in the evening drove
to the aerodrome past others destined for the pub or the cinema
to whom the darkening sky held no significance.

The pupils and the two instructors who were to give us our
first night-flying lesson had a late supper of the traditional bacon
and eggs in the mess and drove out to the aerodrome when day
had long gone. The aerodrome, no longer familiar, presented a
night-scape of shadow broken only by the flickering flame of
goose-neck flares outlining the runway. Around the perimeter
of the aerodrome further lights twinkled guidance for taxi-ing.
Flanking the runway stood the flying control van, a converted
truck with a perspex dome that glowed eerily and outlined the
head of the control pilot standing inside.

I felt nervous and tense. My day experience seemed peculiarly irrelevant to a setting that had dismissed the guiding horizon and substituted a small cluster of instruments. Instruments that had to be coaxed and guided until they indicated that the aircraft is following a normal course and not plunging to the ground or pointing to the stars; ultimately the same thing.

The stars shone brightly, promising a sky untrammelled by cloud. All the pupils were subdued; the instructors omnipotent.

I climbed clumsily into the cockpit, knocking against protuberances that hid themselves in the darkness. The instruments gleaming fluorescently in the shaded cockpit lights, indicated information that had acquired a more urgent significance in the darkness. A car passed distantly, the gear change registering clearly in the silence of the night. Momentarily I envied the driver his destination.

The confident voice of the instructor echoing through the speaking tube left me wondering at his nonchalance as he instructed me to sit back and gather impressions whilst he did a circuit and landing. I felt most impressionable. My eyes but not my mind noticed the familiar movement of the controls as he prepared for starting. Petrol on, throttle slightly open; 'Contact,' he shouted to the dim figure waiting to swing the propeller. The engine coughed into action, spitting meteoric sparks as though clearing its throat before subsiding into a steady blue flame that licked and curled from the exhaust. With a wave of his hand we taxied towards the runway with sharp, crackling blips of the throttle. Confidently I assumed we were taking a logical path through the bewildering taxi-ing lights.

Lining up between the two parallel rows of goose-neck flares the instructor flashed our recognition signal on the navigation lights. An answering steady green from the perspex dome signalled the all clear. 'All set?' asked the instructor nonchalantly. I nodded stupidly at the dim silhouette in the front seat before grabbing the speaking tube and answering: 'Yes, sir.'

Snorting flame we charged at the windmill of night. The wheels bumped and jarred interminably as we accelerated and the tiny islands of light flashed by on either side. With the detachment of a passenger I counted them . . . three . . . four . . . five before, like a tube train leaving a brilliantly lit station, we soared into a tunnel of darkness. The flares dropped away and were left behind as the midnight blue enveloped us in welcome. Mechanically I looked ahead for the horizon. But there was nothing except the instructor's head bent intently forward over the instruments as we climbed like a submarine into the sea of night.

The haze of lights of a city gradually approached as we climbed and became a sparkling star that looked like a snow-flake under a microscope. The arteries of life, illuminated by street lamps, radiated from the brilliant core and curved through the darkness to other communities glowing like fireflies on the horizon. We climbed steadily to 2,000 feet before levelling out. I regretted the obtrusive roar of the engine. Without that reminding cacophony I could have imagined true flight and fulfilled the childish dream of joining the pixies, the fairies, the birds.

'Jackie!'

'Sir?'

'Did you fall asleep? Take OVER!' I grabbed the controls and continued the gentle turn to the left started by the instructor. It was easier than I had anticipated. I relaxed and enjoyed the carnival of fight beneath.

'O.K. I've got her,' shouted the instructor through the speaking tube. 'Well do a landing.'

Below, the runway twinkled like illuminated parallel bars and seemed suspended in mid-air. I felt that if we landed on it we would drop through to the bowels of the earth. It was small, too small. I was glad of the confident silhouette in front as he flashed the navigation lights. Immediately an answering green beam of light from the control van searched waveringly for a moment before glinting sharply in our eyes. Regretfully I watched as the instructor throttled back, lost height and turned towards the runway. Cutting the throttle we glided in a shower of sparks towards the nickering flares that outlined the runway and swayed, rose and fell as though determined to evade us. With a dying swish of slipstream we touched down with a heavy un-instructor-like thud, rumbled the length of the runway and taxied back to the flying control van.

'O.K., Jackie. Try a circuit and landing.'

I did so. It was tolerable.

'Another,' he ordered encouragingly from the front seat. I obeyed and made a perfect landing. Nothing to it, I thought cockily until he climbed out of the front seat, leaving an eloquent void and said: 'Right. Off you go. Try one on your own.'

I looked up at the sky. It was black. Very black. It had, I decided as I taxied to the beginning of the runway, got very much darker since the last landing. Beyond the perimeter of the aerodrome I could see cosily lit homes where people listened to the radio and faintly heard my exhaust. I envied them as the green light flashed and I was committed to the sky.

A few moments later I was a thousand feet above and no longer envying them. Fear forgotten for night-flying was no longer an unknown. In the slim cockpit the instrument lights glowed with the intimacy of a camp fire. The stars twinkled a welcome. The buffeting of the slipstream that snatched at my helmet and goggles as I looked down was like the roll of drums that highlights a spectacular achievement.

It was another first. My first solo flight at night. I felt the old thrill of achievement and felt content that every step, every decision, every yea or nay had brought me to the night sky over Bristol.

The landing was poor; but what did it matter?

Driving home I put the car away. It was late, nearly four o'clock, but I searched for Reg's pen, found my log-book and entered in the night-flying column: 1 hour dual and 30 minutes solo, before going to bed.

31

CONTRASTING WITH THE SLOW BUT SURE PROGRESS OF TRAINING in the R.A.F.V.R. my civilian life, despite the love of husband and daughter, freewheeled listlessly. Whether I am to be censured for being discontent, despite such gifts, I do not know; nor really, do I care. It was as frustrating for me not to fly constantly as it is for a woman yearning for a home and family to be a spinster. I knew that flying would not be enough without Reg and Jill. But, equally, Reg and Jill were not enough without flying. It is a man's right to recognize and admit this by having his career and returning to his family in the evening and week-ends. I do not recognize that this is not also a woman's right.

During the two weeks' annual summer camp with the R.A.F. I had a tantalizing glimpse of what might have been. For fourteen days and fourteen nights the only thing I scrubbed was my teeth. The evenings were spent in hangar-talk in the mess and not in darning socks. And the days were spent on the aerodrome or in the skies building memories which must last a year. The other V.R. pilots, released for two weeks from their civilian duties as test or airline pilots chatted with easy familiarity about their jobs. The virtues of prototype Jet aircraft were argued. The impious merits of ground hostesses at Tokio, Montevideo and Reykjavik were discussed with reminiscent anecdotes. And the R.A.F. pilots listened without envy. For, at the end of their careers in the R.A.F., they would step into civil aviation and roam the open skies for another ten, twenty, thirty years. Next week, whilst the test pilots hovered on the sound barrier, the airline pilots set course for exotic latitudes, and R.A.F. pilots engraved the skies with vapour trails, I would be back at Taunton, washing dishes and ironing shirts.

Perhaps the reader detects a note of pique. So be it. I was qualified, had the experience and, through my husband's gentle understanding, the domestic freedom, to roam the world in airliners. To greet dawn over the desert, sunset over the ocean and know summer when winter is at home. But wings clipped, in toy aircraft, I flitted meekly in England's back-yard skies.

As the months drifted by I lost that cheerful anticipation of a million corners around which fun lurked. Not a chink of light showed through the curtain of understandable prejudice, that prevented me from following my natural highway. Again and again I had charged at it with a lance of optimism and bounced off, the lance bent but not irreparably. Now the lance had been straightened out so many times it was in danger of breaking off altogether.

But corners did turn up unexpectedly. One was the stage. 'You dance very well. Why don't you join the Opera Society?' suggested a girlfriend who had for months stoically offered a shoulder for me to weep on. 'I can get you an audition,' she encouraged as I hesitated.

At her insistence and with Reg's cautious assent I went for an audition with the Taunton Operatic Society and was given a microscopic singing and dancing part as a soubrette in *Vagabond King* then under rehearsal.

After a month of rehearsals where the mysteries of acoustics, the vagaries of spotlights and the inhibitions of the newest member of the cast were overcome, the show was on. Clad in black tights, red sequins and raw nerves I contributed my might before packed houses mercifully hidden by the glare of footlights, and did sufficiently well to secure larger parts in subsequent shows.

Inevitably the V.R. pilots at Filton heard of these post-flying activities and invaded the theatre one evening to see a great deal more of Pilot Class IV Moggridge, D.T., R.A.F.V.R., than they had had the opportunity of seeing before. I assume the whistles were a verdict of approval but I felt rather like the person who dreams that he walks the High Street without trousers. 'It's nothing,' soothed Reg during the interval. 'It's just like wearing a swim-suit on the beach.'

Later, after ballet lessons with an epicene Russian teacher who insisted that I should give up singing because it spoiled my posture, and singing lessons with an Italian professor who insisted that I give up ballet because it spoiled my breathing, I appeared in professional pantomime. The press notices were flattering and prompted a producer to sign me up with a touring company as leading dancer and singer in a revue. But the reaalys and deaarlings of the professional theatre were too much for me. After one successful short tour and a comfortable scrap-book of provincial press notices I returned home and confined myself to the Taunton Operatic Society. Grease-paint, I decided, was no substitute for vapour trails.

The next corner was totally unexpected. After a year with the R.A.F.V.R. I was promoted to commissioned rank as Pilot Officer. Once again I collected a uniform from Moss Bros. A sleek elegant affair of worsted and patch pockets; a pleasant change after the itchy flannel of Pilot Class IV. The thin pale-blue stripe on my sleeves was almost infinitesimal but now *I* would be addressed as Ma'am though it was some weeks before I could divest myself of the habit of still being intimidated by other officers and addressing them as 'Sir'. I regret to confess that, in fact, I was rarely addressed as Ma'am by the other ranks. They were almost as stricken as I with the comic absurdity of my transformation into a gentlewoman officer. In some endeavour to remove the anomaly I was dispatched on an officers' course for three weeks shortly after I was Gazetted and learned something of the totems and taboos of military etiquette.

Being commissioned, apart from feeding my vanity, improving my appearance in uniform and giving me the delightful pleasure of signing P/O after my name, altered very little the routine of my life. In the V.R. it was rather like being promoted Minister without Portfolio. I wore the trappings of authority but had no one over whom it could be exercised. Not that I cared to. I am not the type who gives orders with equanimity.

32

WE WERE PUTTING UP THE 1952 CHRISTMAS DECORATIONS. REG exuded an air of seasonal goodwill.

'Reg.'

'Uh-huh,' answered Reg absently from the top of the ladder.

'What do you think about going through the Sound Barrier?'

The ladder shook dangerously as he looked down at me.

'Apropos what?' he asked, warily.

'It hasn't been done by a woman yet.'

'So?'

'Well. It would be nice if an Englishwoman were the first woman . . .'

'Admirable patriotism. You mean it would be nice for you if you were the first.'

'The publicity might help me to get a job,' I urged, passing him the end of a streamer.

'You haven't flown Jets,' he countered. I waited until he had a drawing-pin in his mouth before confessing that I had written to V.P. Headquarters for permission to fly Jet aircraft at an R.A.F. station.

'Do you think you can do it?' he asked.

'Of course. Just a question of getting hold of the right air-craft.'

'Have you told the air force?'

'Not yet. I want to get some more Jet time in first.'

He sat on top of the ladder, looking at his watch. I got the tears ready.

'It's Christmas,' he observed irrelevantly. 'All right. Go ahead; but take it easy.'

After a few weeks of training with the R.A.F. on an 'old boy' basis I did a few hours solo flying on a Meteor Jet aircraft. What followed is best told by the following letters selected from a vast file of correspondence dealing with that period:

To: Officer Commanding,

R.A.F., Pucklechurch.   *13th March, 1953*

Dear Sir,

Thank you for your kindness in obtaining permission for me to fly in a Meteor at Merryfield.

I would be grateful if you would help me again by applying to the Air Ministry for permission and facilities making it possible for me to achieve a faster-than-sound women's international speed record before this is achieved by Madame Auriol of France who is backed by the French Government or Miss Jacqueline Cochrane of America.

          Yours etc.

Royal Air Force,

Pucklechurch.   *8th April, 1953*

Dear P/O Moggridge,

With reference to your letter dated 28th March, with the details concerning your recent interview at the Air Ministry, the Air Officer Commanding is pleased to know that your request to realize your ambition to fly faster than sound received sympathetic consideration, but notes that the Air Council are unable to help you at the present.

Under the circumstances, it is considered that no useful purpose could be served by your continuing to fly as a passenger in two-seater Jet aircraft. The question of your qualifying for 'Wings' and an 'Instrument Ticket' will be dealt with as a separate issue in due course.

Yours etc.

The Secretary of State for Air,
Air Ministry,
Whitehall.   *23rd April, 1953*

Dear Mrs Moggridge,

The Secretary of State for Air wishes me to thank you for your letter of the 16th April in which you request that you should be given assistance to enable you to fly faster than sound.

He admires greatly the spirit which has prompted you to make this suggestion, which is typical of the Women's Royal Air Force Volunteer Reserve.

He wishes me, however, to point out that whilst you have a great deal of general flying experience, before you could apply this experience to Jet aircraft, a great deal of further flying training would be necessary.*

Furthermore, as you are no doubt aware, aircraft capable of flying faster than sound are not yet in general use in the R.A.F. in this country, and aircraft belonging to civil firms do not normally come under the control of the Secretary of State for Air.

He very much regrets therefore that for this reason, among

---

*Rubbish (J.M.).

others, it is not possible for him to arrange for you to undertake this enterprise. He trusts that you will still enjoy the flying facilities which the Women's Royal Air Force Volunteer Reserve performs, and he is sure that you and other pilots of the W.R.A.F.V.R. will continue to be a source of inspiration to the young women of this country.

Yours etc.

Jill Moggridge,
'La Retraite' Boarding School,
Burnham-on-Sea.   *10th May, 1953*
Dear Mummy,

Hurry up and go threw [sic] *the sound barrier. My friends keep asking me why you have not done it yet. We have prayers for you every day and you still have not done it yet.*

Love etc.

Henry Tony Skace,
Veterans Administration,
252-7th Avenue,
New York City.   *12th May, 1953*
Dear Aviatrix,

Hi! Have just read in a mag that you are going through the Sound Barrier. I sketch as a hobby. Will you please sign and return enclosed drawing of 'Lovely (sic) and Talented you.' You are a terrific gal. Sure hope you accomplish all your ambitions!

I am an ex G.I., Bomb Disposal, U.S. Army, Patton's Third. Now with U.S. Govt.

Hoping you favour me,

Your admirer etc.

Air Ministry,
London, W.C.2.   *May, 1953*
Madam,

I am commanded by the Air Council to reply to the letter you
wrote to His Royal Highness The Duke of Edinburgh on the 25th
April, regarding your desire to be given facilities to fly an aeroplane
at faster than the speed of sound. I am to say that the Council
appreciate highly the spirit that prompts you to make this request,
and to express regret that, for the reasons recently explained by the
Secretary of State for Air, it is not possible to grant you the facilities.

Yours etc.

ON THE 28TH MAY, 1953, MISS JACQUELINE COCHRANE OF THE
U.S.A., whom I briefly met when she was attached to the Air
Transport Auxiliary for a few months during the war, was the
first woman to exceed the speed of sound. She achieved this and
other speed records in a British (Canadian) built Sabre Jet aircraft.
Madame Auriol, of France, has since also achieved speeds faster
than sound but, to date, this has not yet been accomplished by a
British woman.

33

AFTER THE MELANCHOLY AFFAIR OF THE SOUND BARRIER – I
had a shrewd suspicion of what the Air Ministry thought of 'that
Moggridge woman' – I thought it more prudent to lie low for a
few months and be content with 'being a source of inspiration
to the young women of this country' before pressing the Air
Ministry for a decision on whether I should be permitted to
qualify for Royal Air Force Wings, another controversial issue.
Consequently I was astonished when almost immediately I
received a disarming invitation to join an advanced flying course
with the R.A.F. in order to qualify. Whether it was a case of
the right hand not knowing the left or a commendable touch of
sympathy I do not know. I was too conscious of the rare privilege
to care about its inspiration.

Rather anxiously – I had received a lot of Press publicity over
the Sound Barrier affair, including a picture of me in ballet tights
in a simpering pose that hardly suggested I was Wings material – I
reported to R.A.F. Training Command for a month's preparatory
refresher on advanced instrument flying and aerobatics before
joining up with the last two weeks of a Wings course being held
at No. 9 Flying Training School, Wellesbourne Mountford. My
anxiety was needless, for apart from one confirmed misogynist,

the staff and fellow students were, there is no other adjective for it, charming.

For two weeks, with the aid of enviably complexioned and gallant teenage air force cadets, I attempted to plug the gaps in my knowledge of military aviation in preparation for the formidable Wings examination. With these, I was warned, I would receive no mercy. Only one man, or woman, has ever worn R.A.F. Wings who has not qualified for them: Sir Winston Churchill. An exception that adds to their lustre.

On the day of the ground examinations, in the sepulchral silence of the examination room, I glanced at the other students, robustly healthy but biting nails and chewing pencils in agonized concentration. The invigilator looked at me sternly as I raised a hand.

'Yes?'

'Please, sir, I want to leave the room.'

There was a deafening guffaw as the invigilator perplexedly scratched his head, followed by an interested silence as he strove with the problem.

'All right,' he announced. 'But you are on your honour not to cheat.'

I accepted thankfully, returned after five minutes and completed the test papers on Navigation, Meteorology, Signals, Airmanship and Armaments. The following day I took the Wings flying test on an Oxford aircraft with the Chief Flying Instructor. What I hoped, with my experience, would be a formality turned out to be one hour and forty minutes of relentless appraisal. I landed bathed in sweat and exhaustion, quite sure that I had failed. The following day the results were pinned up on the notice board. The entire course, including myself, had passed.

After the ceremonial graduation parade, during which the Wings were formally pinned on, cocktails were served in the officers' mess.

'What are you going to do now, Jackie?' asked one with Wings as new as mine, in the hubbub of congratulations. He was a nice young man who had consistently refused to believe that I was a married woman of thirty-two, and had behaved accordingly during the course. It was a pertinent question and one for which I was unprepared in the momentary bliss of wearing Wings.

'I don't know,' I answered. 'Something will turn up.'

The following day in an end-of-term atmosphere that reminded me of Witney Flying College at the outbreak of war, I bade farewell enviously as the others left for Vulcans, Victors and Hunters, and drove home to a reproachful pile of washing-up and a martyred husband.

Nothing turned up. With a new flood of optimism born of the quaint belief that if I were capable enough to win R.A.F. Wings in addition to civil licences I was equally capable of a civil flying job, I retraced the arid path of refusals. Drove from bleak aerodromes in Scotland to opulent offices in Mayfair. Begged, cajoled, pleaded and, in desperation, contrived an appearance in the B.B.C. programme 'Down Your Way', hoping that Richard Dimbleby's avuncular unctuousness might provoke an interest in my plight. But it was hopeless. The answer was always a regretful shake of the head.

'Why do you make so much fuss, Jackie?' asked my mother-in-law. 'If you can't get a flying job, so what? There are other things in life.'

I tried to tell her it was true there were other things in life but, apart from my family, they came to nought. In those I was as

175

others, indistinguishable from the herd. I am, as is evident from this book, a commonplace person destined to hold a common place in life unless, by flying, I could achieve that distinction, that difference from others that surely is the most urgent reason for inhabiting this earth.

The final piece in the mosaic of misery fitted in diabolically soon afterwards. Owing to the drastic economy cuts of that time the V.R. flying training schools were closed down and only those pilots who had recently completed service in the regular Royal Air Force would be given an opportunity of flying service aircraft. The Wings that normally prelude a career in military aviation had, in my case, proved to be its epilogue.

It was typical. One moment I was moderately content. The sky was a garden in which I could pluck flowers and wander with the clouds. The next it was like a private enclosure hedged with signs baldly stating 'Trespassers will be Prosecuted'.

34

A FEW MONTHS LATER I LANDED AT PRESTWICK AERODROME after a charter flight from Weston-super-Mare and taxied along a tarmac bustling with the arrival and departure of international flights.

'Jackie,' shouted a voice as I climbed out of the cockpit. I looked across to the crew, disembarking from a Stratocruiser parked nearby, as one detached himself from the others and ran over to me. It was an old friend, a pilot in the A.T.A. during the early days of the war, now authoritative in the uniform of a B.O.A.C. Captain. A shadow of beard emphasized his tired but content eyes. He had just arrived from New York. We reminisced as we walked together to the Control Tower, lied to each other that we had not changed a bit and, as all pilots do who have not met for years, told each other who had been killed.

'Bit of a come-down, Jackie,' he observed sympathetically, looking back at my lilliputian Fairchild Argus parked in the shadow of his massive Stratocruiser. I followed his eyes and nodded wryly. 'What happened about that Sound Barrier business?' he asked. 'I read about it in the *Express*.'

I told him.

'You could still be the first British woman . . .' he suggested.

I shook my head. 'I need a job.'

'Have you tried ferrying? There's a lot of war surplus aircraft going overseas. I heard that Air Services have got a contract to ferry Spitfires out to Burma.'

'To Burma? In Spits!'

'Sounds improbable I know, but . . .'

I said good-bye hurriedly. I am always as reposed as a Chinese cracker when prospects loom, no matter how dim, and took off on the return flight to Weston-super-Mare. Turning on to a southerly course I sent my mind back twenty years, it was a shock when I realized it *was* twenty years, to the school atlas and the red blob in South-East Asia that denoted a far-flung outpost of Empire. It would be a different colour now. Teak, I remembered, and Tin and Temples. What else? Elephants and fabulous jewels and a faint memory of a picture of smiling flat-faced 'natives' in gay costume.

As the Bristol Channel glinted on the horizon like a symbol of foreign seas I wanted to go to Burma so badly I resorted to blatant bribery. 'Please, God, I won't eat meat or chocolates for three months if I get the job.'

Two days later I flew in a borrowed Proctor aircraft from Swansea to Air Services at Croydon. The secretary was kindly but not very encouraging. 'I want to see the Manager or Chief Pilot,' I insisted. Shrugging, she knocked on a door marked 'private' and edged it open.

'There is a pilot here, Mr Stock. Wants a job.'

'Christ! How many ferry-pilots are there in England? Must they all come here? Too busy; take his name.'

'It's a woman pilot, sir.'

'Oh. That's all I want.'

That voice. I knew it from somewhere. Emboldened I pushed the door open.

'Jackie! Jackie Sorour. Come in, come in.'

Though the link was tenuous, a casual meeting when I delivered a bomber to an R.A.F. squadron ten years before, I soon convinced him that we were very dear friends.

'Yes,' he affirmed, 'we have a contract with the Burmese Government to ferry Spitfires from Cyprus to Burma.'

He looked at my fingers and grinned. They were crossed.

'We need another pilot,' he admitted. 'You've flown Spitfires of course. What have you been doing lately?'

I told him.

'That seems to be all right,' he said. 'Insurance you know. Aviation is run by the insurance companies these days.'

I agreed. I would have agreed to anything he said. Make it six months without meat or chocolate.

He caressed the back of his neck thoughtfully. My face ached from its fixed smile. On the walls were neatly framed maps and charts. From the next office a typewriter tapped unconcernedly. 'I'm not sure that the Burmese will accept you. You'll have to fly right through the Middle East. For a woman it might be awkward . . . Purdah and all that, you know.'

'There isn't much Purdah on aerodromes,' I argued with a cringing mixture of obsequiousness and firmness. 'Even in the East.'

'Yes. But don't the Burmese take a poor view of . . . er . . . emancipation?'

'Do you?'

'Why me? No, I'm all for it.'

'Well?'

179

'O.K.,' he grinned. 'Leave your licence – it's valid.' I nodded, 'And a resume of your past experience with my secretary. I'll see what I can do. But', he warned, 'don't bank on it.'

A ghastly week passed before the telephone rang.

'Jackie?'

'Yes.'

'Bobbie Stock here. Can you leave for Cyprus in a week?'

'I can leave tomorrow if you want me to . . .'

'That won't be necessary,' he laughed. 'Can you come up to London tomorrow? Visas and things.'

'Of course.'

'Fine. Meet me at the Royal Aero Club, at three o'clock. Robinson and Pearce, the other two pilots, will be there with me. I want you to meet them. You *have* flown Jets?'

'Yes. Meteors and Vampires.'

'Good. There are four new Vampires to go out to Cyprus for on-delivery to India. You people can take them – I'm taking one – out as far as Cyprus and then carry on with the Spitfires. Good-bye.'

'How many flights to Burma?' I interjected quickly.

'I'm not sure yet. At least three. Maybe more. 'Bye. Don't forget your passport.'

'How long will I be away?'

'Oh . . . er . . . about six weeks.'

I TRIED MY BEST IN THE LOUNGE OF THE ROYAL AERO CLUB, against a background of trophies and signed portraits of illustrious names in aviation, to be as blasé as Stock and the others. As tea was served Robinson, who would be responsible for leading the ferry flights, scrutinized me over his cup with a faint hint of coldness in his eyes. Under his scrutiny I was as garrulous as a sparrow when I realized I had been too quiet and as taciturn as a tomb when I realized I had talked too much. I learned later that Robinson was relieved to discover that I was not the brash hermaphrodite he had anticipated but, on the contrary, a meekly obedient female.

I was too anxious to please to probe the evasive air of conspiracy that arose whenever anything other than immediate plans were discussed. Consequently I returned to Taunton that evening with only the haziest idea of the number of Spitfires to be delivered and how long I would be away. Two instructions only were definite: Report to London in three days packed and ready to leave. And bring my R.A.F.V.R. uniform.

Jill was home from boarding school for a few days and, with Reg, saw me off at the station. She was solemn, her face stiff from gainsaying tears as she clutched my hand. Reg wore the resigned look of one who sends others off to adventure and returns to an empty home. As they dwindled, waving furiously, on the platform and I settled in a corner seat I tried to be as conscience-free as a man leaving under similar circumstances. After all, it's only for a few weeks.

Stock, the two other pilots and I spent two days obtaining visas and fuel carnets, renewing inoculations and familiarizing ourselves with the Vampires at Hatfield. It was a vastly different Hatfield. The prosperous new buildings and hangars and the reverberating shriek of Jet aircraft eloquently told the story of aviation's progress since the piston-engined days of 1941. With a twinge of nostalgia I noticed that the wooden huts of A.T.A. had vanished under a new administrative building.

I looked at my Vampire, one of a neat row of four, in the same way one looks for oneself in a group photograph. The other three were unimportant. That one, number L.D.504 was mine. Mine. It looked wickedly sleek and low. The unfamiliar Indian Air Force markings gave it an exotic élan. Slipping away from the others standing on the tarmac I got into the cockpit and closed the hood. The instruments lay at rest but the pungent smell of jet-fuel and hydraulic oil were like the smell of the sea to a retired lonely mariner. This time tomorrow, I breathed, I'll be in Malta.

We were. And we stayed overnight, after a trouble-free flight from Europe's grey skies to the galaxy of blue and gold welcoming us to the fringes of the Middle East. Early the following morning we took off for El Adam where we had an early lunch and walked in the silent derelict North African desert. Its parched useless emptiness mocked the blood it had absorbed. In the afternoon, after changing into khaki, we continued in formation to Cyprus.

After clearing Customs and Immigrations formalities Pearce and I sipped tea in the restaurant. Robinson joined us later.

'Stock will be back in a moment,' he said as he sat down.

'I didn't see any Spitfires on the aerodrome,' I remarked, 'they are in the hangars, I suppose?'

'They are not here,' he said shortly.

I looked at him in astonishment.

'You'll have to know sometime,' he said. 'The Spitfires are in Israel.'

'Israel!'

'Shush!' he motioned with a pained expression.

'But why the secrecy?' I whispered.

'There's a war on over there,' he answered simply, 'and the Arabs are blockading Israel. That's why we are flying from Cyprus

182

and not direct from Israel. As long as the Arabs believe that the Spits have nothing to do with Israel we can fly over Arab territory and use R.A.F. bases in Iraq for refuelling. Incidentally that's why we are wearing R.A.F. uniforms.'

His eyes included us both as he summed up: 'You realize now why there's been so much secrecy. We have full clearance to fly over Lebanon, Syria and Iraq but if the Arabs find out these Spitfires originally came from Israel we'll be up the creek without a paddle. So keep your mouths shut!'

'What markings will the Spits have?' asked Pearce.

'Burmese Air Force.'

'The Arabs can't shoot down a Burmese plane just like that,' I protested. 'It's . . . it's piracy.'

'In the last few years, in this area,' Robinson explained with weary cynicism, 'umpteen aircraft have been shot down and questions asked afterwards.'

'When will the Spits get here,' asked Pearce.

'A couple of days. Israeli Air Force pilots are flying them over. They'll be wearing civvies, of course.'

After Stock joined us we drove to our hotel in Kyrenia to await the arrival of the first three Spitfires. During the drive Bobbie Stock enlarged on Robinson's brief outline.

The Israeli Government had sold thirty Spitfires including armaments and spares, to the Burmese Air Force. 'That's an odd thing to do when there's a war on,' I commented. He explained that, although there was a constant state of tension on the Israeli borders with resultant local scuffles, the war at the moment was more cold than hot and both sides were taking the opportunity of re-equipping with Jet fighters.

The Arab states surrounding Israel on three sides: Egypt,

Trans-Jordan, Lebanon, Syria and Iraq, though soundly beaten during the Arab-Israel war, refused to recognize the existence of Israel and, in an endeavour to give substance to this shadowy wishful thinking, had imposed a strangling economic blockade. To the West, of course, Israel had complete freedom of movement and trade via the Mediterranean, but she was completely cut off to the North, South and East.

The Israeli Government had suggested sending the Spitfires by ship but, as Egypt also blockaded the Suez Canal against Israeli shipping, the Spitfires would have to be shipped either through some complicated cloak and dagger subterfuge via Europe before going through the Canal or be on the high seas for weeks during the interminable voyage around the Cape. Either way would take too long. The Burmese required the aircraft urgently. 'That,' concluded Stock, 'is where we come in.'*

'What are you grinning at?' asked Stock later, as the car topped the mountains and revealed a superb sweep of azure coast before descending in a series of hairpin bends to the Dome Hotel nestling on the Mediterranean shore.

'Oh, nothing,' I lied. It seemed callous to confess after his sombre review of the situation in the Middle East that I was happier than I had been for years.

---

*Such is the sensitivity of the Arab States on the subject of Israel I have been asked by the company concerned to adopt assumed names both for itself and its pilots in order that their future relations will not be impaired. It is regretted therefore that the name of the company and of the pilots' mentioned in the original Spitfire ferry flights are fictitious.

35

ROBINSON'S ESTIMATE OF TWO DAYS BEFORE THE FIRST THREE Spitfires arrived from Israel proved to be optimistic. For ten days we sunbathed and swam in tiny pirate coves along the northern coast. At sunset, as the extravagant colours of the day relented and resigned to the soft-mood indigo of Mediterranean night, we sipped tinkling drinks on the hotel veranda flanked by bright villas and immediately backed by gaunt craggy mountains that rose steeply in monastic silence.

Pearce and I agreed at least twice daily as we compared our tans that this was the way to live, particularly when one's conscience was soothed by an expense account. Stock of course did not agree. He spent his days at the aerodrome sending blistering cables to Israel and attending to mail pursuing him from England. On the eleventh day, after Pearce and I had returned from an early drive to the Castle of St. Hilarian where Richard Coeur-de-Lion had done something or other, we were called to the telephone. It was Stock: 'The Spitfires have just arrived. Get down here as soon as you can. I want you to test-fly them today. You're leaving tomorrow.'

We changed from our tourist clothes and drove quickly to the airport. Stock, Robinson and the three Israeli pilots were waiting in Air Services' temporary office. I confess I stared at the

Israelis. I do not know whether I expected them to have horns growing out of their heads but I was faintly surprised that they were perfectly normal. Their leader, Hugo, had the physique of a rugby full-back and twinkling eyes that gradually closed to slits as his slow smile brought every muscle of his face into play. He spoke English with calm assurance, his imperturbable good humour undisturbed by the patronizing tone adopted by my colleagues and, probably, myself.

One of the pilots, fair and boyish, sensed our patronage and was taciturn as I walked out with him to my Spitfire to refresh my memory of the controls. He jumped on to the wing as I climbed into the cockpit. It had been a decade but the snug cockpit and the long nose, were instantly familiar. I closed my eyes and sucked the smell into my lungs before paying attention as the Israeli pilot leaned over my shoulder and pointed out the controls. I nodded and asked intelligent questions from the past; knowing the answers but trying to win a smile. I asked him about Palestine – 'Israel,' he corrected – but he preferred to explain the operation of the long-range auxiliary petrol tank: an extra tank slung snugly beneath the belly of the Spitfire giving it a mildly obscene pregnant look, and doubling the range from a normal 350 miles to approximately 700. It was a tricky business to change tanks and I followed carefully as he explained the procedure. We would need every gallon of fuel on some of the legs to Burma.

'The belly-tank doesn't feed too happily over 15,000 feet,' he warned. 'If it cuts, switch back to your main tank. The belly-tank will come on all right at a lower altitude.'

Stock came over: 'O.K., Jackie?' he asked. I nodded. 'Right. Take her up for half an hour and get used to her.'

The Israeli pilot watched closely as I started up. Hugo's face was screwed up into his irresistible smile as I taxied past.

I climbed to 20,000 feet and tried the belly-tank. It came on perfectly. With that over I dived in preparation for a loop when I suddenly recalled Hugo's warning: 'No violent manœuvres with the belly-tank.' Pity. I contented myself with lazy turns and a bird's-eye view of Cyprus.

'How was she?' asked Robinson after I landed.

'Fine,' I replied. 'A bit slow after the Jets.'

Pearce and Robinson then took up their Spitfires with similar results. That evening we moved to an hotel in Nicosia in preparation for a dawn start the next morning.

After dinner we had a final conference on flight tactics and 'our story' if we were forced down or interrogated. Robinson would lead, with Pearce on his left and myself on the right in open V formation. The route would be: Cyprus-Habbaniya-Bahrain-Sharja-Karachi-Jodhpur-Cawnpore-Calcutta-Rangoon. There followed a long complicated wrangle over what altitude we should fly. Pearce opted for 11,000 feet but Robinson preferred to take advantage of the higher favourable winds at 20,000 feet despite the discomfort of oxygen masks necessary at that height. I sat on the fence though secretly biased in Pearce's favour. Sitting for over three hours in a seat as cramped as the one-and-ninepennies at the cinema, in a temperature twenty degrees below zero and sucking at the same time on an oxygen mask, reminiscent of a war-time gas mask, was not an enviable proposition. But as Robinson was our most experienced Spitfire pilot and there was no authority on this matter, 20,000 feet it was.

'Our story' was that we were pilots under contract to the Burmese Government to ferry the aircraft from Cyprus to Burma.

True. When or how the aircraft came to Cyprus we had not the foggiest idea. *False*. If we were taxed with the suggestion that the Spitfires originally came from Israel we were to wear a look of astonishment and reply: 'Really?'

36

STOCK, A BURMESE ENGINEERING OFFICER AND THE ISRAELI pilots were at the aerodrome to see us off and helped us pack our luggage in the Spitfires' gun panels a few minutes before dawn. As the others sipped a farewell cup of coffee I slipped into the Ladies' Room and touched my forehead, chest and shoulders. Thirty minutes later I was glad that I had done so.

We took off and formed up into formation before turning east into the rising sun, and climbed steadily to 20,000 feet. The mountains cast long shadows on the sleepy plains that had the newly washed look of dawn. The dew had dried from my wings when my engine cut, roared and cut again. 'Belly-tank!'

'Catch up, Jackie,' ordered Robinson over the R/T.* I most earnestly wished that I could. I was too busy changing petrol tanks and hurriedly pushing and pulling knobs to reply.

'Jackie. What's going on? Catch up.'

'I can't. My engine's cut.'

'What's the matter?'

'Fuel pressure . . . belly-tank.'

'Switch back to main tank.'

'I have; she's still cutting.'

'Jesus,' murmured Pearce.

* Radio Telephone.

Too late. I had already solicited His aid. The fuel pressure warning light flickered ominously as Robinson and Pearce turned back and circled.

'Can you make it back to Nicosia?'

It was a pertinent question.

'I don't know,' I answered rather weakly, turning 180 degrees back to the aerodrome. 'I'll try.' I had lost about 3,000 feet when the engine made me jump by suddenly bursting into hearty unapologetic life. I checked the fuel-pressure warning light. It was out.

'She's O.K. now,' I shouted. 'Carry on.'

We had just turned back on to an easterly course when it cut again. The sweat was dripping into my eyes.

'Now what?' asked Robinson, an edge in his voice.

'It's cut again,' I cried.

'Make up your mind. Is she is or is she ain't?'

I giggled away the tension. 'I'll have to go back.'

'O.K. We'll follow you in,' replied Robinson encouragingly. I was down to 12,000 feet. The tourist's Mediterranean had lost its appeal.

'I can't swim,' I observed.

'Got your Mae-West on?'

'Yes.'

In fits and starts, moments of stark silence followed by bursts of healthy uproar, I straggled back to Nicosia and an emergency landing.

Hugo and his smile met me as I switched off and slumped in sweat in the cockpit. He had been listening in over the R/T in the Control Tower. Stock looked sour. The aerodrome looked delightful. It was good to be back.

After a cursory inspection of my Spitfire and a discussion of the symptoms that now, on firm ground, seemed unexciting, Robinson postponed our departure until dawn the following day for repairs and a short test flight. We tutted and vented our annoyance at this inauspicious start by muttering stock anti-Semitic clichés as we staggered back to Air Services office under a load of parachutes, dinghies, Mae-Wests, oxygen masks, helmets and goggles.

The following morning we got away to a successful start and climbed steeply towards the Syrian coast pin-pointed by the, as yet, innocuous sun. At 12,000 feet I tentatively switched over to the belly-tank and listened anxiously for any change of note in the engine. As I listened Robinson's voice startled me: 'Are you on belly-tank, Jackie?'

'Yes,' I replied.

'O.K.?'

'Yes.'

'You O.K., Pearce?'

'Fine.'

'We'll be crossing the coast in twenty minutes. Watch out for it.'

I peered ahead for the comforting glimpse of surf but the sun had reduced visibility to a few blurred miles. Oil pressure, oil temperature, radiator temperature. Monotonously my eyes swept those vital instruments. Once the coast was crossed they would receive only perfunctory glances.

'Coast ahead,' said Pearce. Three mouths pursed in relief. I checked the map. Pretty good. Right on track. Now for the Syrian desert, as bare of landmarks as the sea we had left behind. Four hundred miles of thirst. I looked over at Robinson a hundred yards ahead and to the left. Pearce formed the other side of the V. The sky, three aircraft and the desert. A fragmentary glint in the sky, a faint, elusive throb to the primitive Bedouin living below. It was difficult to believe Taunton and London, tubes and newspapers, money and death existed.

'O.K., Jackie?'

'Fine.'

'O.K., Pearce?'

'O.K.'

Nearly two hours later I was stiff and sore, wriggling from one cheek to another. Below, the land was scorched with centuries of heat. Up here it was bitterly cold. The oxygen mask chafed. 'How much longer?' I asked over the R/T.

'Twenty minutes,' answered Robinson, 'we can start letting down now.' He lowered his nose slightly and with Pearce and I following like obedient ducklings slowly descended. At 12,000 feet I whipped off the oxygen mask and relaxed as the warmth gradually enveloped us.

'Habbaniya Control. Uncle Baker 427. Do you read,' called Robinson. Faintly they answered. 'Uncle Baker 427. Habbaniya Control. Loud and clear. Go ahead.'

'Habbaniya Control. 427, Formation three Spitfires, 50 miles north-west. 12,000 feet. Estimate Habbaniya: Zero five. Transmitting for Q.D.M. One-two-three-four-five. Over.'

'427. Habbaniya Control. Q.D.M. 096.'

'Roger. 096,' confirmed Robinson.*

---

*I regret using technicalities but as the 'Q.D.M.' was the only navigational aid available on the Spitfire it warrants a brief mention. A ground station receives the voice signal sent out over the Radio Telephone, plots the direction of this signal on a special receiver and gives the course the aircraft should steer in order to reach the station. Having a short range and varied reliability, it is an aid rather than a primary means of navigation.

I checked my compass; we were steering 094. That put us about 5 miles off track. 'Nice work,' called Pearce over the R/T. I nodded agreement. It was admirable navigation. A few minutes later the muddy twisting Euphrates glinted dully on the horizon. Ten miles beyond lay Habbaniya, home of R.A.F. Middle-East Command but shortly, under revised treaty agreement, to be taken over by Iraq.

'Echelon starboard and tuck in tight,' ordered Robinson. Pearce swung over to my right as we closed up into tight formation and dived low over the runway before streaming in to land.

'Hello, Miss,' welcomed an R.A.F. sergeant. 'Any snags?'

'No. She's fine,' I replied as he helped me out of the cockpit.

'Long time since we saw Spits,' he commented. 'Mark IXs aren't they?' I nodded. Here and there an Arab head-dress warned against undisciplined tongues.

'Where are you from?'

'Cyprus.'

'Staying overnight?'

'I'm not sure. Depends on the flight leader,' I replied. Overhead the hot white sun looked down unmercifully, parching the soil into gaping cracks that looked like mouths begging for water. 'There's a dance tonight in the Sergeants' Mess,' he said hopefully.

Robinson walked over from his machine. 'I've got a few snags, Jackie. We'll stay overnight. Unpack your bags.'

The sergeant grinned happily.

'We are staying in the R.A.F. transit officers' mess,' added Robinson.

The sergeant's grin froze. 'Are you an officer?' he asked lugubriously. I assented sadly before stripping off my overalls.

We drove to the mess in the pick-up truck. 'Do the R.A.F. know the Spitfires originally came from Israel?' asked Pearce during the long drive to the far side of the aerodrome. I pricked my ears. It was a question I had not had the temerity to ask.

'I don't know,' replied Robinson easily.

I looked back at the Spitfires parked in a neat yet pugnacious line on the tarmac, their newly painted gold, white and green Burma Air Force markings sparkling exotically in the high noon sun. I hoped it was a good paint job. Hidden beneath were the Mogen Dovids of the Israeli Air Force.

37

THE FOLLOWING MORNING AFTER NORMAL CLEARANCE WE TOOK off with full tanks for the long 650-mile leg to Bahrain, a civil aerodrome on the Persian Gulf, and misfortune. Chattering happily over the R/T we climbed to 23,000 feet through the broken sleepy clouds not yet banished by the sun's magic wand. The tension that marked the first leg had gone. Robinson's leadership, at times irascible, had proven itself. The Spitfires responded obediently to our growing confidence. Below, four miles below, the rivers Tigris and Euphrates flanked us on either side like friendly sheep dogs pointing the way.

An hour and a half later we overflew Shaibah, the halfway mark and a possible alternate R.A.F. aerodrome if we had used more fuel than anticipated. Beyond lay the long haul over the Persian Gulf.

'How's your petrol, Jackie?' asked Robinson.

'O.K. I'm still on belly-tank. Main tank full.'

'Pearce?'

'Same. Still on belly. Main's full.'

'O.K.,' decided Robinson stoically, 'we'll press on to Bahrain.'

Pity. I was thirsty, stiff and cold.

A few minutes later the brilliant turquoise waters of the Gulf glinted relief to eyes surfeited with desert and scrub. I felt momentary surprise that it existed. The surprise that always accompanies my first view of a notable city, ocean or country. I do not genuinely believe that Rio de Janeiro, or Everest or the Yukon exist. They are ghosts until I discover them with my own eyes. Pearce's voice broke into my thoughts. 'Robinson,' he called. I glanced over; Pearce was porpoising slightly and trailing behind.

'Yes. What's up?' replied Robinson.

'Nothing much. My engine's a bit rough . . .'

'What's the matter with it?'

'Plugs I think. She's vibrating and . . .'

'Do you want to turn back to Shaibah?'

'Better.'

'Open up and try and clear her,' suggested Robinson.

Pearce tried it and sailed past.

'Any better?'

'No. She's still rough.'

'O.K. O.K. We'll turn back to Shaibah.'

With an alacrity that suggested we were all thinking of a cup of tea we turned our backs on the Persian Gulf and pointed our noses down for Shaibah, notorious throughout the R.A.F. as home of the plaintive ballad: 'I've got those Shaibah blues.'

Robinson landed first, vanishing in a miniature dust storm as he touched down and rolled along the natural desert runway. Pearce and I circled in formation for the dust to settle. 'You had better go in next,' I suggested.

I watched him as he broke off in a steep turn, the Spitfire's elliptical wings making a pretty silhouette against the egg-blue sky, and side-slipped towards the runway. The cloud of dust as he touched down was spectacular. I grinned. Must have been a lousy landing. The next moment the grin froze to horror as his tail reared almost vertically through the dust and hovered like the last appeal of a dying man before flopping back into the murk in another flurry of dust. With agonizing slowness the dust drifted away before the wreck emerged from its own funeral pall. A fire truck raced across the aerodrome, throwing up a bow-wave of dust like a destroyer at full speed. There was a confused babble of voices over the R/T before Robinson's voice broke in: 'Hold it, Jackie. Pearce has crashed.'

A few minutes later I landed on an alternative runway and taxied past Pearce's aircraft squatting grotesquely on its belly. Its sleek lines were blurred by jagged metal and wrinkled skin. The propeller was smashed. It was a write-off. Pearce waved ruefully as I taxied by.

'What happened?' I asked, as a very forlorn Pearce and an angry Robinson returned to the Control Tower in the fire-truck.

'I forgot my undercarriage,' he replied simply.

Poor old Pearce. I put my arm in his to cheer him up. 'It happens to everybody sooner or later,' I reminded him.

It is true. This humiliating kind of accident has plagued aviation since the introduction of retractable undercarriages, despite the devices installed to remind the pilot approaching to land that his wheels are still retracted. There is no excuse for it beyond human frailty, but no pilot would criticize another for the momentary aberration that has such disastrous consequences for, sooner or later, somewhere, sometime, the chances are that he will do it himself. If he has not done it already.

'I'll have to go and see the R.A.F. C.O.,' said Robinson. 'You two wait here. Keep your mouths shut,' he added.

'This is a bloody fine mess. I am a clot,' muttered Pearce

moodily as Robinson walked away. I clucked the useless don't worries of the helpless bystander and suggested tea.

Robinson returned an hour later, 'I've seen the C.O. We'll have to get out quickly before the Iraqis start poking around.' He turned to Pearce. 'I've cabled Air Services that you are returning immediately to London. There's an R.A.F. Anson aircraft leaving soon. They'll take you to Basra. From there you can make your own way back to England by air-lines. I'll give you travellers' cheques. Get cracking and unload your stuff from the Spit.'

'I'll help you . . .'

'No time for that, Jackie, we've got to refuel and get out. If the Iraqis start investigating and find out where these Spits came from the whole lot will be impounded.'

Within two hours of the crash Robinson and I were heading out over the Persian Gulf for Bahrain. I wished we could have spent a day or two with Pearce. The look of dumb misery as he waved from the Anson haunted me. 'Poor old Pearce,' I muttered involuntarily over the R/T.

'What was that?'

'I said, "Poor old Pearce."'

With a grunt he replied, 'Yep. Tough luck.'

Robinson and I completed the pioneering flight to Burma without further incident, rested for a day in Rangoon, too weary to explore beyond the cool fan-washed lounge of the Strand Hotel and gained only a fleeting impression of richly gilded pagodas rising from Rangoon's stifling squalor before returning by B.O.A.C. to Cyprus.

38

Two new pilots from England joined Robinson and me in Cyprus, amidst an alarming outbreak of rumours, for the next flight of four aircraft to Burma. In the hotel, in Nicosia's dreary night-clubs and on the aerodrome, total strangers offered the comment: 'Don't kid me old girl, I know your Spitfires come from Israel.'

Robinson, his face livid, joined us at breakfast the day before our departure and slapped a newspaper on the table. 'Look at that!'

We looked. Under the headline: *Israel Sells Spitfires to Burma*, not a detail was spared. At the end of the article were the significant letters 'U.P.'

'That means', observed Robinson angrily, 'it will be repeated in every damned newspaper under the sun!'

There was a moment's speculative silence.

'What do we do now?' I asked.

He shrugged. 'Nothing we can do but press on and hope for the best.'

'And what about us if the Arabs get nasty?' pertinently asked one of the new pilots.

Robinson grinned. 'We can always buy our freedom by flogging Jackie to the local sheik.'

'They don't like thin ones.'

'We can fatten her up with goats' milk.'

'Thanks!'

The goats' milk was unnecessary. We passed through Arabia without so much as a raised eyebrow. The Israelis, I decided, were exaggerating. The Arabs couldn't be less interested in the Spitfires.

We were the last flight to get through.

At Calcutta, Robinson, exhausted with a touch of mild but persistent fever, made an atrocious landing, damaged the undercarriage, promptly commandeered my Spitfire and continued to Rangoon with the other two aircraft, leaving me behind to supervise repairs. Swallowing my pique I did as I was told.

Ten days later I received a cable from Air Services instructing me to arrange for a Burmese air-force pilot to take over and to return immediately to Cyprus for the next flight.

After the long fifteen-hour flight westwards via B.O.A.C. I disembarked at Beirut for the B.E.A. plane to Cyprus. There was a two-hour delay. Tired and dishevelled I sat in the departure lounge idly admiring the abstract murals. Arab sheiks, impressive in white flowing robes and headdress ostensibly ignored me as is their unemancipated wont, but sneaked surreptitious glances at my legs. A sultry voice announced in Arabic and French the arrival and departure of planes for destinations at cold war with Israel. I glanced idly through the spacious windows. Parked in the far corner of the tarmac were three Spitfires in vaguely familiar markings. Absently I admired their graceful lines.

Spitfires!

I jumped up.

And sat down again.

It would be foolhardy to ask questions. Whatever the answer

it must wait until I reached Cyprus. They must have started the third ferry flight without me. Enigmatically the aircraft returned my glances. What had gone wrong? Where were the pilots?

The sultry voice announcing the departure of B.E.A. to Cyprus saved me from indiscretion.

In the trim B.E.A. Viscount the hostess got slightly snooty when I insisted on sitting on the side nearest the Spitfires. 'I want to see the Spitfires,' I explained.

'Yes, madam,' she replied in a voice reserved for the senile.

I looked at them carefully as they slid past the Viscount's large oval windows. Not a scratch. Not a bullet-hole. I was mystified. 'Do you know what happened to the pilots of those Spitfires?' I asked as the hostess fussily adjusted my safety belt. I did not add that I had been adjusting safety belts for nearly twenty years.

Maddeningly benign, she replied, 'What pilots, madam?'

Unkindly disgusted, I fell asleep.

'Nicosia, madam. Fasten your seat belt.'

I woke with a start and looked down as Nicosia aerodrome tilted into view. The mystery deepened. Meteors, Vampires, Dakotas. A Hermes. But no Spitfires.

Jones, an Air Services pilot met me in the Customs shed. 'Any news, Jackie?'

'Have *I* got any news!'

'You passed through Beirut . . .?'

'I saw three of our Spits there. That's all I know. What's up? What's happened?'

'Pity. I hoped you would have . . . Robinson decided not to wait for you and pressed on with the next flight. They ran into a packet of trouble. They were turned back at Baghdad.'

'Why on earth did they land at Baghdad? That's an Iraqi civil aerodrome.'

'We've been asked not to use the R.A.F. aerodrome at Habbaniya any more . . .'

'Why in heavens not?'

He shrugged. 'Orders from London. The Iraqis must have tumbled that the Spits are from Israel. Anyway, after landing at Baghdad, they were escorted back as far as the Syrian border by Iraqi fighters. Then they had engine trouble and had to go into Beirut. Emergency landing. They've been arrested and the Spits are impounded.'

'Couldn't they make it back here?'

'Apparently not. It was getting dark apart from the engine trouble.'

I looked at him gloomily. 'What do we do now?'

'Wait until we hear from London.'

'Is Hugo here?'

'Yes. He's waiting for us in the office. Let's go.'

'What does he think?'

'It's pretty obvious. The Arabs have clamped down.'

We picked up Hugo and drove to the hotel. 'I suppose Hugo, this means I'm out of a job,' I said as we drove through the airport gates.

'Yes, I guess so,' he replied curtly. I looked at him in surprise before the bitterness in his eyes brought home the monumental triviality of my remark. Momentarily I had forgotten he was an Israeli. 'I'm sorry, Hugo.'

Three days later a laconic cable arrived from Air Services:

'Remainder of contract cancelled. Return London immediately.'

202

Hugo saw us off. The smile had returned. 'Cheer up, Jackie,' he said enigmatically. 'We're not beaten yet.'

I looked at him hopefully. 'What . . .?'

He put an index finger vertically to his lips, winked and waved good-bye.

39

A MONTH HAD PASSED WHEN REG, HOME FOR LUNCH, unsuspectingly passed the telephone: 'It's for you. Trunk call.'

'Mrs Moggridge?'

'Yes.'

'Israeli Embassy here, Hayman Shameer speaking . . .'

'Yes.'

'This is in the strictest confidence. May I rely on your discretion?'

'Of course.'

'We are continuing the Spitfire operation.'

Bless Hugo.

'But how . . .?'

'I would prefer not to discuss it over the phone. Can you come up to London?'

Reg, his ear close to the phone, nodded.

'Yes.'

'Tomorrow at two o'clock at the Embassy?'

'Yes. What happened to the pilots at Beirut?'

There was a snort of disgust. 'They got out all right after they were searched, interrogated and fined.'*

*In answer to a subsequent protest by the British Government at this treatment of British pilots engaged on a lawful delivery flight of Burmese-owned aircraft from Cyprus

'And the aircraft?'

'Still there.'

I reported punctually at the Embassy, tucked away unobtrusively in a corner of Manchester Square. The blue and white flag of Israel billowing in welcome, added a touch of colour to the gloomy wintry scene. I looked at it curiously. Somehow I had not associated Jews with their own flag.

Inside, a dark attractive receptionist guided me to Shameer's office. He rose from his desk as I entered, apologized for the sniffles that contrasted oddly with his tan and introduced me to three pilots waiting in an adjoining office:

'Leo Kastner . . . He will lead the flights.' He was stocky, about thirty-five, tanned and puckishly easy. An American, I thought gloomily. He won't know anything about Spitfires. He was soon calling me 'Kid'.

'Sonny Banting . . .' The 'Howdoyoudo' was unmistakably English. He was of medium height, ruddy and looked about forty. He was fifty-seven. Had been flying since the 1914–18 war.

'Gordon Levett . . .' He too was English. Lean and hungry looking. Ex-R.A.F. He seemed to know Kastner and Shameer.

Kastner took charge immediately and shepherded us to an adjoining office littered with maps and charts.

'Here's the dope,' he said without preamble. 'As you know

---

to Burma the Lebanese Government stated that their action was justified in that the aircraft flew over Lebanese territory in a westerly direction instead of easterly as specified in the original clearances obtained by the Burmese authorities in London. In view of the fact that the aircraft were turned back from Iraq at gun-point this explanation is, to say the least, frivolous. The truth is, of course, that when the Lebanese (and Iraqi) authorities gave the original diplomatic clearance for these flights they were not aware that the Spitfires had been sold by *Israel* to the Burmese. Once this became known to them, as a result of newspaper reports, they immediately plugged this leak in the Arab blockade of Israel.

the Arabs (he pronounced it A-rabs) are determined to stop the Spitfires from getting through to Burma and have closed the old route via Cyprus. Air Services have, of course, cancelled their contract. The Israeli Government have decided to supervise the flights themselves using a different route and have appointed me as leader.' He smiled apologetically at me as though acknowledging that there was a remote case for my leading the flights.

'How many flights?' asked Sonny.

'I am not sure yet. Seven aircraft have already been delivered by Air Services. Right, Jackie?'

'Right,' I clipped in mimicry.

'That leaves twenty-three to be delivered. There's four of us; that's six flights with someone unlucky on the last trip.'

I looked carefully out of the window.

'Now,' he said seriously, 'for the route.' We crouched around him as he laid the maps on the floor and pointed to the route heavily scored with red pencil. 'To avoid Arab territory we'll be flying direct from Israel to Diyarbekir in Turkey for our first refuelling halt. From there due east over Turkey until we get to the Iran border then we can turn south for Kermanshah. From then on it will be plain sailing to Abadan-Sharja-Karachi-Jodhpur-Cawnpore-Calcutta and Rangoon. The trickiest leg is the first from Israel to Diyarbekir. We'll have to go well out over the Mediterranean to avoid Lebanon and Syria. If we get intercepted, they'll shoot and ask questions afterwards. We're all individually insured for ten thousand Sterling,' he added with a puckish grin.

I looked at the maps. The new route, 500 miles longer than the old, curved like a question mark around the Lebanon, Syria and Iraq.

'What do you think, Jackie?' asked Kastner, with the deference due to my recent experience.

'The Diyarbekir-Kermanshah leg looks a bit grim if the weather is bad.'

We pondered over the dark mauve shading, mountains, that flanked the route and surrounded Kermanshah.

'Yup,' agreed Kastner, 'but there's no alternative. We'll just have to make sure the weather is O.K. before we take off.'

Wise words, I thought, but Meteorology is not yet an exact science.

We discussed the route, visas and fuel carnets before Kastner closed the meeting. 'We'll have plenty of time to discuss details in Tel Aviv. I'm leaving almost immediately to test the Spits. You'll be leaving for Israel on the tenth of January, Gordon here will take you around to El Al's office to collect your plane tickets. Liaise with him and Shameer. O.K.?'

At El Al's office in Regent Street we sat waiting for our tickets. On the walls were stylized photographs of orange groves and antiquities. We were a little shy with each other.

'I'm glad we've got a contract. You have to be careful with these people,' I observed, for want of something better to say.

'What people?' asked Levett, eyebrows raised.

'Oh, you know. Jews.'

'I don't,' he replied. 'Tell me.'

Pedant, I classified him immediately, and changed the subject.

REG, RESIGNED, AND JILL SAW ME OFF AT TAUNTON. WE WERE blissfully unaware that it would be nine months before we met again.

In the El Al Constellation it was not long before we became

Sonny, Gordon and Jackie. Sonny, a raconteur, sipped coffee – 'I always go on the wagon when I'm flying' – and spun splendid tales of the good old days of flying. Gordon drank beer and was monosyllabic. I tried to make friends.

'Do you know Kastner?'

'Yes.'

I tried again. 'When?'

'During the war. The Arab-Israel war.'

'Flying?'

'Yes.'

Levett. Levett? Oh Lord, he's Jewish. I flushed at the memory of my gaffe in El Al's office.

'What's Israel like?' I asked meekly.

'Dreadful place,' he said ironically, 'full of Jews.'

'I'm sorry. I didn't really mean . . .'

'I know,' he said wearily. 'Some of your best friends are Jews.'

A little later the air-hostess served coffee and biscuits.

'Pretty girl,' I observed hopefully.

Levett grinned. 'Yes, she's Jewish. A Jewish girl in a Jewish plane flown by Jews to Jewland. You're in a tough spot.'

'*Touche.*'

We got along a little better after that. And slept.

LEO, WEARING AN OUTRAGEOUS MIAMI BEACH SHIRT, AND slacks, welcomed us at Lydda Airport. 'Hiya kids. Good trip?' I glanced at Sonny, old enough to be Leo's father, but his good-natured features smiled.

'I've got rooms for you at the Yarkon Hotel in Tel Aviv. It's near the beach,' he added. Overhead a Spitfire swooped low in welcome before climbing steeply away in the warm, brilliant sunshine. 'That's Hugo. He's helping with the testing.'

There was a crush in the airport reception lounge. A babble of German, French, Slav, Russian, tears and emotion.

'What's going on over there?' asked Sonny.

'New immigrants. It's like that every day,' answered Leo. 'The population of Israel has doubled in the last two years.'

'What does "Shalom" mean?' I asked.

'Peace be with you.'

Shalom. Shalom. I liked it and tried it out on the chauffeur, a German Jew. He was delighted and insisted that I sit next to him on the drive through eucalyptus and citrus groves to Tel Aviv. The six-figure number tattooed on his arm, he explained, was a concentration camp number.

During the drive he told me about Israel. Its conception was simple. A stroke of the pen by the British Government of 1917 who promised a 'National Home' in Palestine for the Jews scattered two thousand years before but still retaining their mystical yearning for their homeland. Gestation was uneasy as Arab and Jew fought bitterly over the interpretation of the words 'National Home'. For thirty years Britain administered the Mandate and was torn between the insoluble contradiction of establishing the Jewish 'Home' without prejudice to the rights of the Arabs already living in Palestine. This was a problem that only Solomon could solve. The British Government, a dubious rose, between militantly belligerent thorns, and certainly no Solomon, terminated her responsibilities by, in 1948, ending the Mandate and evacuating. An open invitation to the Jew and Arab to let force equate the irresistible and the irremovable. Birth, then, was bloody. The Jews, alone as Britain was alone in 1940 but with no English Channel or air force to prevent invasion, were attacked by Egypt, Trans-Jordan, Syria, Iraq and Lebanon. 'Don't ask me how,' continued the chauffeur, 'but we won.' The invasion failed and *Israel* was reborn after two thousand years. A unique atavism.

'Today,' concluded the chauffeur as the outskirts of Tel Aviv punctuated the sky-line, 'we are eight years old and still struggling for life against the Arab blockade.'

A few days after our arrival in Israel we drove out to the nationalized aircraft overhaul base – 'Bedek' – at Lydda Airport, to test the Spitfires. Sonny and Gordon had insisted that I wear my scarlet jeans and a white sweater that had shrunk a bit in the wash.

'Hiya, kid,' welcomed Leo, appraising me with a gleam in his eye. 'That's the stuff. It'll kill 'em.'

It did. Work stopped as we walked to the hangar to collect our flying gear.

'Hey, what are you doing?' shouted Leo as I scrambled into a pair of overalls.

'I can't walk around like this,' I protested.

'Nuts to that.' He grabbed the overalls and, with a cheer from the mechanics, threw them back to the storekeeper.

With a profusion of willing hands I climbed into a Spitfire, started up and taxied past the grinning mechanics and worried-looking executives.

After take-off I climbed in wide circles to 25,000 feet. Levelling off and looking down I felt a curious wave of anger and reverence. Beneath me was the land of the Bible where once walked the Son of God. Now the Son of Mars was rampant. At this height I could see in the brilliantly clear atmosphere the Egyptian border at Gaza and the Israeli communal farms where every man, woman and child sleeps with a rifle by his side after a day spent in the fields under the sniper's itching finger. To the east, sheltering in the Judean hills lay Golgotha, and Jerusalem; that sorrowful city of God split in two by a barbed-wire no-man's-land populated only by bullets and white-painted United Nations jeeps. Beyond the hills the salt waters of the Dead Sea reflected from a thousand feet below sea-level. To the north the Sea of Galilee pin-pointed yet another no-man's-land, the Syrian border.

I could see Israel; north, south, east and west. A cramped verdant sliver flanked on three sides by desert and with the Mediterranean completing the encirclement. Inside Israel's borders were the scars of industry, the rich promise of cultivated land. Beyond was the flat emptiness of desert and neglect. The Jews ask for very little, I thought. It was such a tiny piece of land for so much protestation.

Hugo met me after I landed.

'Be careful, Jackie,' he warned, after we had reminisced. 'Two of our Jets were sent up after you.'

'What on earth for?'

'You flew too close to the borders. "Radar" thought you were an Egyptian.'

We had lunch in the works canteen. It was a salutary experience for me. I wish every anti-semite could spend a day at 'Bedek'. There, on the aerodrome, was Israel. Every virtue, every failing, was there in cameo miniature. I entered the canteen with concealed patronage. I make no apology for that though there is no excuse for disliking the Jew. My parents should apologize; my school; my Church; and literature that has made the Jew the butt of man. I do make an apology that I had to have an emotional experience, a personal lesson, before I could attack the thick slime

211

of anti-semitism nestling in my subconscious mind. Not all can go to Israel, and leave humble and ashamed.

Sitting opposite Hugo and myself over lunch were Jews from Germany, England, Latin America and Yemen. At the next table were Russians and Slavs. Sprinkled amongst them were Nordic-looking youngsters, toughly built, blue-eyed and confident. 'Sabras,' explained Hugo. 'The Israeli nickname for the new generation of Jews born in Israel.' The Jew from England was an engineer. Ex-R.A.F. complete with moustache and a hearty manner. I looked around the sea of faces. Listened to the fascinating babble of seven, eight different languages. My eyes flitted from complexions Anglo-Saxon to African. From features classically Semitic to the refined decadence of the English aristocrat. From manner courteous to aggressive. But as every eye caught mine the twinkle and smile of welcome and friendship was unmistakable.

The dark-complexioned were from Morocco and Yemen explained Hugo. New immigrants pitchforked into the twentieth century from a way of life that had not changed since the greatest Jew of all had died. They spoke only Arabic. The language of their cousin-enemy. 'One of them had a nasty accident this morning,' said Hugo. 'They won't *sit* on toilet seats; they think it's unhygienic. They insist on standing on them despite orders to the contrary. One of them slipped, broke the porcelain and gashed himself to the bone.'

I shuddered. Hugo nodded. 'Just another of our problems.'

After lunch I rose to return my dirty plates to the counter when a passing mechanic, his hands calloused with work, took them from me with an exquisitely expressed: 'Allow me.' I sat down, bewildered.

I left the canteen, as I left Israel a few months later, knowing that to dislike the Jew is not only cruel. It is stupid. For what *is* a Jew?

On the beach a few days later Gordon and I lazed as Sonny swam. The next day we were taking off for our first flight to Burma.

'It's a funny thing,' I said. 'I'm beginning to forget that you and all these people are Jewish. I've never had such a warm welcome. They're all the same, the "Bedek" crowd. The staff at the Hotel Yarkon. Do you think they are *trying* to impress me?'

'Maybe. Unconsciously. I don't know,' he answered. 'Most of them earned the right to sympathy by what they went through in the concentration camps. But they want to forget that, want to be judged by what they have done here in Israel. They are glad that you are here, that you can see what they've done. That you can return to England realizing that a Jew isn't an usurer or a wide boy in the East End but a chap who can build this,' he waved his arm, 'out of the desert. Sorry,' he concluded, 'I've got a bit of a fetish about Israel.'

'By the way,' he added, as Sonny joined us and we got up to leave, 'not that it's important, but I'm not Jewish.'

PART FOUR

DESERT INTERLUDE

Now think of all the good it does,
To cross so many lands;
Remember that the world is yours,
You hold it in your hands.

1955

NOTE

In the remainder of this book I have selected and described only one – the fourth – of the six ferry flights that I completed from Israel to Burma (in addition to the two flights from Cyprus undertaken with Air Services). I should point out that Banting and Levett have given me permission to use their proper names whereas Kastner, being a Jew, had no option but to request the use of a pseudonym.

40

DRAGGED FROM OUR BEDS AT 3 A.M. WE DROVE MONOSYLLABIC-
ally to the aerodrome. Our emotions dominant; our intellect still
asleep and unable to resist the atmosphere of tension and irritation
that presaged all the flights. Gordon, at his most acid before dawn,
met Leo's incorrigible cheerfulness with verbal violence. We
usually had at least one blistering row before we arrived at the
aerodrome and were silenced by the dramatic impact of the four
Spitfires, floodlit by the fluorescent light bursting from the open
hangar doors, waiting silently on the tarmac.

In those moments of pre-flight bustle: 'Got your emergency
kit?' 'Where are the spare plugs?' 'Who the hell's got my Mae-
West?' 'Did you check that oil leak?' and the final: 'All set?'
spoken by envious-eyed mechanics; we were supreme. I nodded
and laughed with those who would be left behind. Tried to
understand them. But felt only a profound sorrow that they
could not share my exaltation. In a few minutes I would be
alone; would triumph over pettiness; become one with the sky.
I would become the Spitfire, joyous, fully dimensional, adrift
from a world of logical values. The world at my feet; and death
in my hands.

With night still lingering in the west, and flame visible from
our exhausts, we took off from Lydda and climbed across the

coast of Israel for the turning point, 30 miles out to sea, that would keep us clear of Lebanon and Syria.

With Leo in the lead we straggled in lazy formation, each with his own thoughts; together, but separated by unbridgeable space should mishap occur. I looked down as we passed the sleeping coast. No natural border separated Israel from her bellicose neighbours. The land flowed in brotherhood giving, as a book does, freely to those in need.

As the coast disappeared and we were alone with the sea and sky I felt the first symptoms of unease that attack all pilots when flying single-engined aircraft over long sea crossings. I checked and re-checked the instruments, refusing to be comforted by their assurance of all's well.

The engine lost its smooth, untroubled beat. The Spitfire became a host of individual parts. Cables that could fray, bearings that could parch and seize, filters that could clog, a million nuts and bolts that could work loose and bring catastrophe. Perhaps even the theory of flight would collapse, leaving me hurtling into the sea, 12,000 feet below.

Simultaneously with the appearance of the Turkish coast my engine cleared and throbbed sweetly. The Spitfire, in a remarkable metamorphosis, became a sleek entity speeding through the air with the grace and omniscience of a bird.

An hour later Diyarbekir aerodrome lay spread out on the plain as though awaiting our arrival. In a confused babble of Turkish and English tongues over the R/T we landed and scurried quickly off the runway as Turkish Air Force F-84 Jet fighters zoomed and buzzed waspishly in their urgent impatience to land. The scene, ten minutes from the Russian border and painted with lavish American aid within the aerodrome boundaries, contrasted ruthlessly with the poverty of peasants working primitively in the fields beyond.

We were met with that grave formal courtesy and efficiency characteristic of the Turkish Air Force, and Leo was advised, owing to a warm front moving in from the south-west, to stay overnight. With his delightful tact he discussed the matter with us before deciding to concur.

The following morning, after a firm promise of clear skies and favourable winds, we took off on the long leg for Kermanshah and spiralled steeply to 20,000 feet before heading due east over the gaunt mountain range where, traditionally, Noah's Ark rests. As with the sea, so the peaks brought unease. Rising to 14,000 feet and spreading to Kermanshah and beyond, they waited. Waited.

In a spurious attempt to ignore what lay beneath, we chatted inanely over the R/T. Leo who was prone to burst into song at the slightest provocation, sang an aria. I sang another, enjoying the sound of my own voice in the earphones. Sonny muttered something that by its metre I took to be verse. Gordon, as usual, maintained a pointed silence.

Within an hour we were in trouble. The moving warm front of yesterday had not dispersed. High above us the ominous streaks of cirrus cloud had joined into a lowering blanket that slanted down to the peaks straddling the horizon. The fickle sun had deserted us to shine elsewhere.

'Um,' said Leo significantly over the R/T.

Silently I agreed with him as the first rain mixed with the film of oil on my windscreen. Tuck in. We'll have to go through it,' ordered Leo. Metaphorically we hitched up our sleeves and obeyed as the clouds curled around us in a blinding embrace. I put my useless maps away and clung to Leo's ghostly silhouette. The mountains had vanished.

'Where's Sonny?' called Leo anxiously.

'It's all right,' answered Sonny, casually. 'I'm in the box.'

I envied his nonchalance as the rain burst into furious uproar as though determined to purge us from the sky. We carried on, eyes fixed to Leo. One thought unspoken. What was the weather at Kermanshah? We had no radio equipment to guide us down if the clouds reached in a solid blanket to the ground.

'Time's up,' said Leo, twenty minutes later, a contrived coolness in his voice. 'We should be over Kermanshah.'

'Kermanshah. Spitfire Uncle Baker 430 calling Kermanshah,' he called, a moment later.

'Kermanshah. Spitfire Uncle Baker 430 calling Kermanshah,' he repeated. We waited for an answer from those hidden below, without whose guiding help we could not descend. Leo repeated the call as we circled in blind turbulent loneliness, in an orbit reduced to artificial horizons and airspeed indicators and the unechoed voice of Leo appealing for help. The sweat was dripping into my oxygen mask.

'Jackie; you try,' ordered Leo.

'Spitfire formation calling Kermanshah. Do you read?'
Silence.

'Spitfire formation calling Kermanshah. One-two-three-four-five-four-three-two-one. Spitfire formation calling Kermanshah. Come in please,' I called, putting a siren-like appeal in my voice.

Silence. Damnable silence that brought the first twinge of panic.

'It's useless,' called Leo. 'They must be on a different frequency.

What do we do now? We can't turn back, we haven't enough gas.'

'Turn south towards the plains. We can let down there,' suggested Sonny.

'But that's Iraq,' protested Leo.

'Who the hell cares!' exploded Gordon.

We turned south and flew deeply into forbidden territory away from the mountains before descending through the clouds. Gradually the gloom lightened to an opaque light as the wayward sun returned and shone weakly. At 2,000 feet we broke out of the cloud and found ourselves over desert. I threw the hood open and wiped my hands on my thighs.

'Anyone know where we are?' asked Leo optimistically after four distinct sighs of relief had echoed over the R/T.

'Ha!'

'Ha!'

'Ha!'

'You're a great help,' answered Leo acidly. 'Try and find out. And watch out for Iraqi fighters.'

We edged out into open formation and got out our maps. Our conflicting and irascible observations confirmed that we were completely lost.

'O.K.' said Leo decisively. 'We'll fly due east until we hit the railway . . . or run out of gas.'

I looked at my maps. The Iranian State Railway ran due north and south. It was a good tactical move (the railway would pinpoint our position) *if* we were west of it.

We flew steadily eastwards beneath the lingering clouds. Twice mirages provoked a cry of 'There it is' followed by bitter disappointment. Impersonally the desert slipped by. The tired parched rivers that were its only relief were impossible to identify. There were too many with the similar features of those born from the same womb. I glanced at my watch; our season ticket for flight was fast expiring.

'How much petrol have you?' asked Leo.

'Eighteen gallons,' said Sonny.

'Twenty,' I said.

'Fourteen,' said Gordon.

'I have less than ten,' commented Leo dryly.

Ten minutes, before gravity asserted calamity.

'WE'VE HAD IT,' ANNONUCED LEO COOLLY. 'WE'LL HAVE TO crash-land. After I've stopped, land as close to me as you can. Stick together. Land with your hood open and your straps tight. Keep those wheels *UP*. No heroics, Jackie! Keep those wheels *UP*. You'll go over on your back if you land with them down.'

'Roger,' I answered.

'Roger,' echoed Sonny and Gordon. 'I hope it's Iran,' added Leo.

We were absurdly cool as we circled and watched Leo descend in a wide arc towards his shadow on the desolate plain. It was like a typical British film scenario with everyone keeping a stiff upper lip. I wanted to laugh. And cry.

We all saw it at once. The R/T burst into a shrieking babble.

'Leo . . . Leo. Runway. On your left.'

'. . . runway . . . Leo . . . Don't land.'

'LEO . . . on the left!'

'O.K. O.K. I've seen it.' He turned sharply. I saw his undercarriage coming down. Oh God, let him make it, I prayed as he turned steeply towards the runway dancing like a mirage in the heat. The spurt of dust as his wheels touched down on this miraculous refuge answered my prayer.

'Thank God,' I shouted shamelessly over the R/T.

'With reservations,' said Gordon dryly. 'He was responsible for the weather as well, you know.'

'Oh shut up,' I shouted as he turned and landed with Sonny and I following him in.

We climbed out of our cockpits and gaggled together. The runway cut starkly and incongruously through the silent desert. Nothing else was witness to our fantastic escape. Nothing but this gaunt concrete, this exquisite tableau. Gordon knelt and kissed it. 'You beautiful thing,' he grinned, 'I love you.'

'How much petrol did you have left, Leo?' I asked.

'None. The gauge showed empty.'

'I had twelve gallons left.'

'Eight,' said Sonny.

'Five,' added Gordon.

We were silent for a moment.

'We are not out of the woods yet,' reminded Sonny. 'We may be in Iraq.'

I looked at the Spitfires, unmarked and silent as walls, parked in an impressive line along the runway; their perfection no credit to us.

A tarmac road bordered the runway and ran south through the desert towards a village perched on the horizon. To the north it straggled towards our recent foes, the weather and the mountains. We sat patiently by the roadside awaiting the messenger of incarceration or freedom. After twenty minutes of silence a lorry passed by, ignoring our signals.

'Did you notice the number plate . . .?' asked Leo.

'Yes. I think it was Arabic . . .'

'That's Iraq.'

'No. It was Persian.'

'That's Iran.'

A small truck approached from the village and sped furiously towards us.

'This is it,' I ejaculated. 'Handshakes or rifles.' It stopped opposite us. The driver, sans rifle, stepped out on to the sand with a smile and, with unconscious theatrical melodrama, said: 'Welcome to Iran.'

Simultaneously we burst into hysterical laughter.

'Sorry,' I giggled. 'We thought we were in Iraq.'

'Where are we?' asked Leo.

'Andemeshk,' he answered. 'I am the manager of a petrol storage plant down there,' he continued, pointing to the village. We checked the map; Andemeshk was 150 miles south-east of Kermanshah!

'Have you any 100 octane petrol?'

'Yes,' he answered. 'We've had it for years. Three hundred gallons. Can't get rid of it . . .'

'How lucky can we be,' murmured Sonny.

With the aid of a primitive chamois-leather filter we finished refuelling from four-gallon cans as the sun flirted with the horizon and sent blood-red beams across the desert. It was too late to take off for Abadan.

Our good fortune continued. The manager invited us to stay for the night in his guest house. It was air-conditioned, had a first-class Indian cook and running hot water. Aware of what might have been, we revelled in luxury.

There were only two bedrooms. Accepting the necessity of

avoiding Sonny's reverberating snores, we forced him protesting, into one whilst Leo, Gordon and I shared the other.

The following morning we drove out to the runway and prepared for our take-off to Abadan, 150 miles to the south. We were worried about starting. There was no auxiliary method in Andemeshk should our batteries fail.

Gordon and Sonny started easily, took off immediately and circled the runway. I waited for Leo and watched him fuming in the cockpit as his propeller turned slower and slower and finally stopped with infuriating resignation.

'Gordon and Sonny, go on to Abadan. Jackie and I will meet you there,' instructed Leo, over my R/T.

'Roger,' acknowledged Gordon, as they turned towards the south. I watched them until they disappeared. At that time I did not know why. I climbed wearily out of my cockpit, the sweat oozing uncomfortably across my lipstick. I envied the men their independence of unnatural enhancement. A shave and they were ready for the day. I hid behind my sunglasses and walked across to Leo.

'Flat?' I asked.

'Yup,' he answered briefly before adding two words that brought a blush to my sodden cheeks.

We tinkered uselessly with Leo's battery until a solitary diesel-engined petrol lorry left the village and headed north towards the mountains. Leo pounced on it, contrived a complicated series of wiring from the lorry's battery to the Spitfire's starter and grinned triumphantly as his aircraft burst into song.

With a dive of thanks and farewell we left the manager to his oasis in the desert and followed Sonny and Gordon to Abadan.

41

LEO WOKE US UP IN THE MIDDLE OF THE NIGHT, IN THE TRANSIT mess at Abadan, groaning with pain and vomiting.

'What's the matter, Leo?' I asked.

'Beats the hell out of me, Lieutenant,' he moaned from the bathroom.

The noise awoke Gordon. 'What's going on?' he asked sleepily.

'Leo's sick,' I said as Sonny poked his head enquiringly round the door.

With a final despairing belch Leo returned from the bathroom, clad in startling pyjamas. He was pale and dishevelled, the twinkle missing from his eyes.

I tucked him in, gave him some pills and switched off the light. Two minutes later he was back in the bathroom, hawking piteously.

We spent an unhappy night with the lights going on and off like traffic signals. Next morning an Iranian Oil Company doctor pronounced nothing more serious than cramp. By this time, however, it was too late to take off, so Leo rested in bed, Sonny washed his smalls, if such a giant can be considered to have smalls, and Gordon and I took a taxi to the bazaar to buy odds and ends. This was one of those days when he decided to be friendly and charming and we chatted gaily as we escaped the sun and wandered through the cool dark passageways sheltering under canvas roofs. We found a stall that sold Japanese imitation Ronson lighters embellished with voluptuous nudes. Only one appealed to us and we were on the point of bickering once again when I suggested we toss for it. I won, but such is human perversity, I felt little pleasure in my small victory.

The next day Leo felt better, though still weak. To relieve him of the burden of navigation, we persuaded him to let Gordon lead on the next leg to Bandar Abbas. Bandar Abbas had been chosen as an alternate aerodrome as we had received a hint from the British Government, just before taking off from Israel, that we were no longer welcome at Sharja. The local sheik objected to Jewish or ex-Jewish planes passing through his territory.

Before taking off we checked the facilities chart for information on the aerodrome at Bandar Abbas. No one knew very much about it except that it had no radio facilities, had not been used for years and was difficult to find. Doubtfully we checked with the Iranian Oil Company who assured us that petrol had been specially shipped there for us.

We took off soon after dawn with Gordon leading, myself his number two and Leo and Sonny numbers three and four. The weather was perfect and, as we climbed through the heat haze to the coolness above, I felt again the emotion of flight and wondered why such a subject had failed to produce a writer worthy of its elusive quality. The sky, that holds the inspiring grandeur of sunset over the Himalayas, sunrise over the reflecting glaciers of Greenland, that was the stage for tragedy and valour during the war, still awaits its interpreter.

On Gordon's right and adjusting the throttle to hold this position, I glanced at the others. The sun glinted sharply on the perfect elliptical symmetry of their wings, and provoked a sad reflection on the day when this historic and graceful aircraft disappears from the skies. Gordon looked over to me and waved his map. On his left Sonny straggled behind, determined as usual, to keep a fatherly eye on me.

We climbed to 11,500 feet before levelling off. Below us the Persian coastline grew faint and disappeared, leaving us suspended in a symphony of blue. Only the air-speed indicator registering 195 m.p.h. confirmed motion and achievement. I loosened my straps, wriggled to a more comfortable position on the dinghy seat and wished I had left off my overalls. My parachute straps persisted in slipping off my shoulders and the perspiration struck coldly against my back. Around me the slim cockpit fitted as closely as the latest fashion line. I sympathized with Sonny; he was twice my size.

We flew comfortably above the haze that cut a sharp line on the horizon. Above this line the sky stretched to infinity; below, visibility dropped to a dusty blur that concealed the sea and separated us from reality. I reflected on the slight differences of technique of Gordon's leadership, slight unimportant differences that pointed out the differing methods of American and British military flying. He flew confidently and his confidence induced me to put away my maps. A foolish act, for should Gordon suffer mishap I, as number two, would take over the leadership.

After two hours we began letting down into the haze and tucked closely together in echelon starboard formation before sweeping over Bandar Abbas at two hundred feet to signal our arrival to the local petrol agent. The small port flashed by in a second before we followed Gordon faithfully as he twisted and turned in unison with the dusty track that straggled across wadis and desert and led to the aerodrome. I got out my maps and tried pin-pointing our position but there was nothing significant enough on the ground to relate to the maps. There was an anxious ten or fifteen minutes before Gordon's voice came over the R/T.

'There it is. Spread out. It's below us now.' I looked down into a barren wilderness and saw nothing but sand dunes, patches of scrub, and an unherded cluster of black goats.

'Where?' I asked peevishly. 'I can't see it.'

'Hello, hello.' There was a babble of voices and a high-pitched scream over the radio as two of us tried to transmit simultaneously; followed by a mild altercation between Gordon and Leo who felt we were too far north. We broke formation and circled independently like buzzards, until a chorus of 'O.K., I can see it,' broke from us all. The field was natural sand and shale distinguished only by whitewashed stones that marked its boundaries. At its northern end a wind-sock hung limply as though asleep. There were no buildings. No sign of activity. To the north, stark, treeless mountains rose sheerly to 6,000 feet. To the south the Persian Gulf shone dully.

We circled at 2,000 feet whilst Gordon flew low over the field and selected the best landing path. 'It looks O.K. I'll land towards the south,' he commented as he lowered his undercarriage and turned in for the final approach. I positioned myself to go in next, my throat parched with thirst, and eyes tired from the unrelenting sun.

'Christ, he's crashed!' Leo shouted over the R/T. My heart pounded. I looked down and saw Gordon's Spitfire on its nose, the tail pointing grotesquely to the sky. There was no sign of movement. There was silence over the R/T. I was stunned. What had happened down there with such unnerving suddenness?

He needed help.

'Shall I go in next?' I begged, over the R/T to Leo.

'O.K.,' he answered, not knowing, as none of us knew, the cause of the accident.

Ignoring the niceties of flying, I jerked the throttle closed, turned steeply and, with my imagination conjuring Gordon's face smashed in a horror of blood against his instrument panel, landed short. Just as I touched down I heard a shout over the R/T that gradually penetrated the wall of heartache and anxiety. It was Gordon's.

'Don't use your brakes, don't taxi! The other two don't land!'

Disarmed and trembling with relief I obeyed and slithered to a halt without using my brakes. At the last moment I swung violently through 45 degrees and came to rest leaning heavily to one side. My left undercarriage leg had sunk deeply into the treacherous bog. I looked over to Gordon's aircraft. Both wheels had disappeared into the mud. The propeller was smashed. He ran over to me, waving violently. I looked at him, at his face livid with anger, and bowed my head in the cockpit, concealing from his agnosticism my thanks, the sign of the Cross. He was unhurt.

He jumped up on my wing, unceremoniously snatched my helmet and spoke over the R/T to Leo and Sonny who were circling warily above. 'I'm all right. Stand by.' He turned to me aggressively. 'What the hell did you land here for? Couldn't you see there was something wrong?'

I hated him and answered hotly, 'We thought you were hurt. I didn't know the field was like this.'

The thick mud on his shoes was mute testimony to the condition of the field. He looked at me stubbornly. I was uncomfortably aware of my shiny nose, the rings under my eyes, my hair flattened by the helmet, lips ungraced by lipstick. He, as usual, looked absurdly immaculate.

'I think the others should go on to Sharja, don't you?' His request for agreement was disguised apology.

'Yes,' I answered, travelling half way to reconciliation.

He squeezed my helmet on to his head and spoke to Leo:

'Hello, Leo. Hello, Leo. You can't land here. It's a bloody quagmire. My prop's smashed . . . No, I don't think the engine is damaged. But I'll need a complete prop unit . . . Go on to Sharja . . . To hell with the sheik, this is an emergency. Course about 198 . . . No, only the prop, and tools of course . . . No, she's all right. A Roman Catholic built this field . . . Yes, I'll send her on to Sharja as soon as the field dries out . . . Don't know. A week at least, providing it doesn't rain again . . . Push off, you haven't too much fuel . . . Good-bye . . .'

With this he switched off. Leo and Sonny zoomed low over the field, their superchargers screaming with the Spitfire's characteristic high-pitched whistle, and vanished over the southern horizon, leaving the world to Gordon and me.

'Get unpacked,' he ordered. 'Take everything. We are here for a week at least,' and he walked over to his own aircraft.

I stripped off my overalls and felt cool rivulets of sweat oozing between my shoulder blades. We were on the northern shores of the Persian Gulf; sixty degrees warmer than Diyarbekir. I looked around me and felt the silence, the isolation, the heat that enveloped us like an exotic flower that closes its petals around its prey. We were completely alone.

A half an hour passed before, with startling suddenness, we were joined by two raggedly dressed sinister-looking peasants who must have appeared from the bowels of the earth. As usual I was the object of intense scrutiny and Gordon, no doubt to his extreme annoyance, was being consistently ignored. I tried looking demure but their eyes were fastened on the more feminine perquisities of my body. Gordon left me for a moment and fiddled around in his cockpit. He returned carrying a bulky object wrapped in a towel. 'Cartridge pistol,' he explained. 'Go and get yours, just in case. Load it but don't let them see it,' he ordered conversationally and with an irrelevant smile on his face.

I returned carrying the pistol in my overnight bag. There was a great deal of argument going on. I smiled at Gordon fuming in frustration. 'Eenglish. Eenglish,' I shouted helpfully, accomplishing nothing but frankly appraising stares and knowing grins. Gordon was equally unsuccessful and, turning to me in exasperation, shouted: 'Where on earth is the petrol agent?'

'Must be in Bandar Abbas,' I answered.

'And how do we get there? It must be 12 miles from here,' he replied.

At this moment of deadlock a lorry appeared in a shower of spray and skidded to a spectacular halt a few inches from my Spitfire. This gratuitous appearance was not to be scorned so as the driver climbed out we climbed in and with an arrogant attempt at *fait accompli*, gesticulated and shouted: 'Bandar Abbas, Bandar Abbas.' We were only mildly surprised when we drove off in the right direction towards the south.

We drove interminably over a road mined by nature and neglect. The driver, a maniacal grin on his face, searched diligently for the larger pot-holes and drove into them at furious speed. We climbed precipitously, dived concomitantly and charged with violent impact through swollen streams that cut the road. He was trying to impress his pilot passengers. He did. Gordon with some embarrassment carefully put his arm around my shoulder and protected me from the worst of the jolts. The moment the road appeared tolerably flat, his arm, with scrupulously correct behaviour, lifted from my shoulder and rested on the back of the seat. He looked, perhaps a shade too carefully, straight ahead, glancing at me only when an excessive jolt sent us both bouncing perilously near the roof. Conversation was impossible.

Eventually we arrived at a drab, miserable collection of mud huts sparsely interwoven with more permanent-looking buildings. This was Bandar Abbas or what remained of it. Torrential rains had transformed it into swirling muddy islands, capped by roofless remains of primitive houses. The roads were unnavigable and littered with the debris of collapsed walls and rotting vegetation. Such a pitiful scene in Europe would have provoked relief and emergency aid measures. (In fact the local inhabitants had thought our aircraft had brought such assistance but laughed wryly at their *naïveté* when later they confessed these hopes to us.)

We stopped before a relatively imposing two-storeyed building, home of the local representative of the Iranian Oil Company, and squelched into the mud as native women passed by, one hand holding their skirts, the other balancing the perennial earthenware jug on their heads. Their eyes peeped curiously through the dramatic black masks that concealed their features. We dithered helplessly until a tall, European-dressed figure forced his way through the chattering crowd and held out his hand to Gordon.

'Good afternoon. I was expecting you two weeks ago.'

'Sorry,' muttered Gordon as, leaving our shoes on the portals, we followed our host into his house. 'We were delayed.'

We sank gratefully into Lloyd Loom chairs and sipped the sweet, milkless tea that appeared with thought-reading alacrity.

'What can I do for you?' asked our host, Dustmalchi.

'About thirty-seven million different things,' answered Gordon, unhelpfully.

'Everything,' I translated as our host looked puzzled. 'First of all we need a crane . . .'

'A what?'

'Crane, you know the thing that er . . .' I appealed to Gordon. With eloquent hands he conveyed our meaning.

'But why do you need a crane to put petrol into aeroplanes?'

We both laughed.

'Sorry,' I explained. 'Of course you don't know. Captain Levett crashed on landing.'

A look of horror passed over Dustmalchi's handsome features.

'It's all right,' interpolated Gordon quickly, 'nothing serious, but my aircraft is stuck on its nose in the mud and we need a crane to lower it.'

'But there isn't a crane for 200 kilometres,' answered Dustmalchi, 'and the roads are blocked.'

'The things I do for Israel,' muttered Gordon with mock weariness.

'Look, let's get first things first,' I interjected. 'We will need accommodation for a week or so. Can you arrange it? We will worry about the other things afterwards.'

Dustmalchi eyed us doubtfully. After the drive we looked like ruffians.

'Yes,' he answered gallantly. 'You may stay here with me. There is nowhere else to stay in Bandar Abbas. Come, I'll show you your room.'

The singular was ominous though its significance did not register immediately as we followed him along a stone veranda that overlooked the surrounding desolation. At the end of the corridor he opened a wire-mesh door, revealing a cool bedroom furnished with two shameless beds.

I felt myself blushing and turned hurriedly to the window to examine intently the dusty bodies of dead flies trapped between the wire mesh and glass panes. Dustmalchi left innocently to attend to our luggage.

'He thinks we are married,' said Gordon, and continued neutrally: 'There is no alternative accommodation.'

I nodded in reply, too tired to select a thought from the kaleidoscope of my mind.

'Get unpacked and washed. I'll go and see the police. Let me have your passport and health certificates.'

I gave them to him and he left. Wearily I pulled off my socks and stretched out on the bed. Gradually the objects in the room focused. Two bedside tables, a wardrobe. On the wall a garish pin-up revealed the Eastern taste for buxom women. Two lizards waited motionless on the ceiling for their prey. Outside I heard the ugly croak of Dustmalchi's pet parrot. Pervading all was the gentle, yet inexorable pressure of the heat.

I dozed in perspiration and dust for what seemed only a moment but awoke suddenly to see Gordon looking down at me.

'Hello, lazybones,' he said gently. 'Everything's under control. The army are guarding the Spitfires. The police have our passports. Dustmalchi has arranged for your Spit to be refuelled tomorrow, and the local works engineer is going to help out with mine.'

He unpacked.

42

EARLY THE FOLLOWING DAY WE WERE AWAKENED SUDDENLY BY the roar of a Spitfire circling overhead. Startled, we jumped out of our beds in a flurry of mild panic. Looking out of the window, we saw Leo circling very low, waggling his wings violently and blipping his engine.

'Good God,' said Gordon, 'he's not going to land! Quickly, get the Very pistol and a red cartridge,' and he rushed out to the balcony, frantically waving a towel. More inhibited than Gordon, who stood revealed to Bandar Abbas in his pyjamas, I snatched a precious second to don a dressing-gown.

'Hurry, hurry,' he shouted from the balcony. I found the pistol, loaded it with a red signal cartridge and passed it through the window to Gordon. With a deafening report the cartridge soared steeply into the air leaving a trail of brick-red smoke and sparks.

'He's seen it,' I said as Leo dived towards us, his propeller cutting and scattering the arc of smoke into cavorting eddies. 'He must want us to go out to the airport and talk to him over the R/T.'

Dustmalchi arrived on the balcony at this moment.

'Have you got a jeep or something to take us to the airport?' I asked.

'Quickly,' interpolated Gordon as Dustmalchi nodded and disappeared, 'he hasn't got much petrol.'

Gordon and I dressed hurriedly and stood by the roadside waving to Leo with towels and trying to indicate that we were awaiting transport. The ant-like file of masked women water carriers had stopped and gazed entranced, wondering what on earth we were going to do next.

Anxious minutes passed until Bandar Abbas's only doctor and his wife arrived in a jeep. We drove at a snail's pace until Gordon, in a nail-biting frenzy of impatience urged him to go faster. An hour later we arrived at the aerodrome. Gordon jumped out before we had stopped, ran to my Spitfire, switched on the radio and squeezing on my helmet, spoke to Leo, now circling overhead.

'Hello, hello, Leo. Do you read . . .?'

Gordon lifted up one side of the helmet and motioned me to listen. I heard Leo's voice: 'How's Jackie?'

'She's fine,' answered Gordon. 'Watch your language. She's listening in.'

'Hiya kid . . . Sonny and I are staying at Sharja until your new prop is laid on. I've cabled London but no reply yet. Are you absolutely sure there's no other damage?'

'Nothing,' assured Gordon. 'I was only doing about two knots when she went over. The mud took most of the shock.'

'Fine. When do you think Jackie can take off?'

'A week at least. We had more rain last night and there's no drainage.'

'Any communications?' asked Leo.

'Nothing. The floods have washed away the lines. We are cut off completely.'

'Where are you staying?'

'With Iranian Oil. We are married.'

'Who's married?' queried Leo, startled.

'Jackie and I.'

'Churched?'

'No, but there's only one room and our host has assumed . . .'

'You dog. You have all the luck!' commented Leo with exaggerated envy.

'Huh, you know Jackie,' commented Gordon sourly.

'We only just made it at Sharja,' said Leo.

'What happened?'

'Bogged. Only 700 yards available for landing. Just dried earlier. An hour sooner and we would have had it,' replied Leo. 'The sheik's on holiday,' he added.

'Snafu.'

'Negative. Fubar,' laughed Leo. 'Look, here's what to do,' he continued. 'Sonny or I will fly over from Sharja every morning after tomorrow at ten o'clock your time, and give you what news there is. There may be a Rapide aircraft laid on to fly in a prop from Abadan, any day after Wednesday. Stand by all day at the field from Wednesday onwards and give him a red if it's still unsafe to land. Can you do that?'

'O.K.,' answered Gordon. 'I'll lay out a "T" at the beginning of the best landing run.'

'Good idea . . . Got enough money and cigarettes?'

'Yes.'

'I'm off.'

'Good-bye,' I shouted into the microphone. 'Give my love to Sonny.'

'What about me?' answered Leo.

'You, too,' I laughed.

Gordon glanced at me quizzically as I switched off the radio.

As Leo disappeared into the haze Gordon and I walked over to his Spitfire still perched drunkenly on its nose with the pathos of a bird with a broken wing.

'Perhaps we can rig up sheer-legs,' he commented.

'Yes,' I answered dutifully. What are sheer-legs, I wondered silently.

The doctor and his wife joined us.

'Would you like me to show your wife the cockpit?' I offered.

'Please,' he answered.

I sat in the cockpit and pointed out the instruments and controls.

'Where does your husband sit?' asked the doctor, translating his wife's question.

'In the other aircraft,' I said.

'But how does he drive both aeroplanes?'

'He doesn't. We fly one each.'

This was too much for her and she subsided into bewildered silence.

We returned to Bandar Abbas.

THE FOLLOWING MORNING GORDON BORROWED THE DOCTOR'S jeep and we drove alone to the landing field. The solitary guard eyed us suspiciously but intimidated by Gordon's supercilious nonchalance, he let us pass and followed warily as we walked across the field to the Spitfires.

'There's the engineer,' nodded Gordon. 'I wish they wouldn't drive on the landing path. Damn it. Look at them.'

With a flourish a small truck, followed by a larger lorry, slid to a halt, their wheels scoring the mud. Chattering happily Indian labourers climbed out of the lorry and, the sun glinting on their thin, hardened bodies, stared curiously at the aeroplanes.

A tall, wiry man detached himself and held out his hand to me. 'Hello,' he said, his thin hand firm, his swarthy classic features showing centuries of wind, sand and stars. He turned to Gordon. 'I couldn't get any poles for a sheer-leg but I have a better idea.'

'What?'I asked.

'Sand,' he answered.

'Sand?' queried Gordon.

'Sand,' he answered with a smile.

'All right,' grinned Gordon, 'I'll buy it. How?'

'Quite simple. My boys will build a pile of sand under the tail, leaving a gap of a yard or so. Two boys will then climb on to the tail so that their weight will force the tail down on to the sand, whilst the remainder will slowly shovel away the mound of sand, so lowering the aeroplane.'

'Now why didn't I think of that? How long will it take?' said Gordon.

'Half a day,' answered the engineer.

Within the stipulated half a day the Spitfire was lowered without incident except that Gordon tore his trousers whilst climbing perilously on to the tail to add his spindly weight to the two labourers. We checked the oil, glycol and hydraulic fluid levels. To our relief they were normal despite the unusual angle of the aircraft for the last two days. We drove cheerfully back to Bandar Abbas, applauding without reserve as the engineer, who had decided to return with us, sang a mixture of Italian lullabies and incomprehensible Turkish love songs.

241

Our gaiety was short-lived for Dustmalchi was waiting for us when we returned, his habitually solemn expression even more lugubrious than usual. 'I'm dreadfully sorry,' he apologized. 'The auditors are arriving from Abadan by boat and I need your room.'

'Where else can we stay?' I asked, thinking sadly of the bathroom.

'At Point Four. I have arranged accommodation.'

'What's Point Four?' asked Gordon, morosely.

'A guest-house run by the American Point Four programme,' he answered. 'It's not bad,' he added encouragingly.

'When do we move?'

'Not until tomorrow. You can use my truck . . . See you at dinner,' and he returned to his office.

'Damn, damn, damn,' muttered Gordon.

An hour or two later, after a delicious hot bath, we lay on our beds listening to the sounds of twilight. The raucous honking of mules retreated to the monotonous distant yapping of pariah dogs. The lizard's appealing mating call served as an antidote to the petulant whine of the mosquitoes. I turned on my side and glanced at Gordon as he lit a cigarette. He smokes too much, I thought. The match silhouetted his sharp features against the window and the purple-hued mountains beyond. We lay silently as the day died with his cigarette. It should have been a moment of peace, but there was tension in the room.

Dustmalchi knocked with embarrassing discreetness on the door. 'Dinner,' he called. A little regretfully I switched on the light and mopped the moisture from my nose.

Dinner was excellent, though indescribable. Mrs Dustmalchi, emancipated and with the plump prettiness of a milkmaid, con-

242

tinued to eye us shrewdly. She was uncommonly fair and contrasted strikingly with her olive-skinned husband and two children.

After dinner, Gordon and I borrowed Wellington boots and walked to the tiny harbour. Sitting on the creaking jetty that thrust feebly on spindly legs into the Persian Gulf we spoke of ourselves.

Overhead, the niggardly moon threw weak shadows. Beneath, the sea nibbled patiently against the rusted supports. Timidly, as we talked of the years and circumstance that had contrived to bring us both to this backwater, a sweet compatibility was born. His voice relaxed from the patronizing irascible tone he normally adopted towards me. My mind was purged of dislike and hovered tensely, like a wild deer ready to flee at the slightest false move, over the quicksands of regard.

We walked home in comradeship. As usual I went to bed first whilst he waited in the lounge. Later, I heard his 'good-nights' to our hosts and his footsteps approaching the bedroom. He switched on the light as I covered myself in a flurry of bedclothes. The pause before his second shoe dropped heavily and carelessly to the floor was filled with the flapping of moths in their universal imbecility against the light. He switched off the light and creaked into his bed.

'Good-night.'

'Good-night,' I answered, trying to impose finality in the wish.

We lay in our beds aware of each other's breathing. I thought longingly of Reg and Jill. It was still early evening in their world. Of Reg's patient courting and his determination that I would marry him. Of the bliss of our early married life. Of the fight to protect that bliss from the relentless drip, drip, drop of patriarchal taste and plebeian income that seems so much a part of life today in England.

43

THE NEXT DAY, AFTER AN EXTENDED FAREWELL TO THE BATHROOM we moved sadly to 'Point Four'. Our new host, an Iranian youth whose favourite word was rascal, clucked proudly as he showed us his establishment. Walls crumbling and windows broken it protruded from the surrounding desert like the last defiant tooth in an expanse of empty gums. Decay had reduced this former British Consulate to a haunted Bleak House sinking in the sands of memory.

Cobwebs clung lovingly to peeling walls adorned only with the shadowed memory of picture frames. Cupboards echoed hollowly. Sand rasped protestingly and foretold eventual victory by the encroaching desert as we walked on the bare stone floor. Gordon was silent as we walked from room to room. I smiled wanly at our host as he told tales of its former glory. On the bathroom door was a neatly typed notice informing us of the cost of board and lodging. At the bottom of the page flourished the signature of an American official.

A bath! I rushed to it and turned both taps. Rusty water gurgled and spat as though resentful of release. I felt my feet getting wet and glanced at the other end of the bath. At its lowest extremity a jagged hole leered at us with the malignancy of Cyclop's solitary eye. The toilet, a hole in the ground, crowned this dismal inspection and nearly brought me to tears as our host dismissed these limitations as another amoral example of those rascals in Teheran.

The bedroom was gloomy and musty; the Valhalla of deceased ants, moths, mosquitoes and a baby lizard, and the happy hunting ground of persistent flies. Through the uncurtained French windows we could see sand dunes footing the distant mountains, with Bedouin style lean-to tents offering stepping-stones to Bandar Abbas, shimmering distantly on the horizon.

Too depressed to unpack we drove immediately to the landing field with our host. His jeep, with its unyielding springs and un-upholstered seats, added further to my woes. Sitting on numbness I day-dreamed nostalgically of beauty parlours and glossy women's magazines. Images of elegant models langorously reclining against sleek cars brought a snap of disloyalty, like a trusted dog turning on its master, towards my chosen profession. Gordon to my disgust looked infuriatingly cool and immaculate.

Punctually at ten o'clock Sonny arrived from Sharja, roared low over us and pulled up sharply into a steep climbing turn that silhouetted his Spitfire's graceful lines against the cloudless sky, before settling down to a sedate circling of the aerodrome.

There was little news. Leo had communicated with Abadan by wireless to confirm the arrangements for bringing a propeller by charter aircraft but without success. It might come and we were to remain standing by. Evidently Sharja, London, Rangoon, Abadan, Teheran and Tel Aviv were all working furiously, and independently. 'No doubt,' commented Gordon sourly, 'six propellers will arrive simultaneously.'

If we could possibly locate a W/T set we were to try and contact Leo at Sharja by wireless telegraphy at 1400 hours G.M.T.

Gordon passed the helmet to me and climbed out of the cockpit. I replaced him and spoke to Sonny as he continued circling overhead like a motherly hen guarding its chicks. 'How is it?' he brooded tenderly. 'Could be worse,' I answered, envying him his transport to fitted bathrooms, good food and air conditioning.

'What about Gordon?' he continued, the inference obvious.

'All right so far,' I replied.

Gordon waved me to switch off.

''Bye, Sonny. Battery is getting low.'

'Cheerio. See you tomorrow,' and his voice faded.

Gordon watched me guardedly as I climbed out of the cockpit, as though aware of Sonny's implied reproof. His face cleared as I smiled at him and we both watched Sonny vanish in the haze, leaving the silence to return and enfold us as though he were no more.

We returned to 'Point Four' to find a few grains of sand swept into corners and the appetizing aroma of cooking halting the desert's stealthy approach. Our bags were unpacked and a broken mirror leaned crazily on the bathroom mantelshelf.

That evening we spent an abortive and farcical hour at Army headquarters trying to contact Sharja by wireless. All pilots learn Morse code, but years of neglect had reduced Gordon and me to a dubious five words or so a minute. We coped adequately with 'a's and 'b's etcetera, but 'k's, 'w's and xyz reduced us to giggling hysteria. Eventually we wrote our message down in Morse and operated the key on what we hoped was the correct frequency. We achieved precisely nothing but pained anguish on the face of the Iranian radio operator who spoke only Persian and, no doubt, confusion throughout the ether.

Walking home along the lonely shores of the Gulf, Gordon groped for my hand. I let him take it for refusal would have been more significant. In my mind's eye I looked at us both. Two solitary figures leaving footprints in the sand. I saw them stop, look at each other and kiss as the soft ripples curled around their feet.

We did stop and looked out over the Gulf that shimmered like silver lamé. We waited. The past seemed divorced, the present a gossamer thing protected by isolation, the future not thought of though intangibly present.

I don't know how long we waited for the other to make the first move; wanting to kiss not each other but the companion who shared the beauty of the night, before he broke the mood by lighting a cigarette.

THE FOLLOWING DAY, WEDNESDAY, WE PACKED SANDWICHES, borrowed a thermos flask which we filled with lemonade and drove out to the field for the possible arrival of the Rapide aircraft from Abadan. The jeep returned to Bandar Abbas, leaving Gordon and me alone apart from the solitary sentry who retired tactfully to the other end of the field.

We inspected our two Spitfires, by now covered with a thin film of sand that emphasized their insignificance in the patient desert. The silence was intense and, allied with the shimmering heat that produced convincing mirages, joined us together in a natural intimacy that made us speak in whispers, unwilling to shatter the solemn atmosphere that made nonsense of the passage of time.

'Look,' I whispered and pointed towards the mountains that danced in the heat. We both watched the peasant, astride his donkey, come from nowhere and vanish behind a sand dune. He was asleep, his head nodding, his legs dangling a few inches from the ground. The donkey, seemingly oblivious of the burden that should have pressed him to the ground, moved intently and neatly on his delicate hooves and flicked viciously at the flies with his tail.

'I wonder where he came from . . .'

'And where he's going to,' added Gordon.

We were silent and both, I think, a little envious. Gordon raised his eyebrows and nodded slowly, his face thoughtful.

'What's the matter?' I asked.

'Oh nothing . . . I sometimes wonder . . .'

'What?' I encouraged.

'Who's right. They or us. The donkey or the Spitfire.'

I looked at the aircraft, incongruous in their desert coat, far from their halcyon days of 1940 as the sole defenders of a way of life that, in this moment of truth, had become as insignificant and petty as the squabbling of pampered children. There was no other sign of human endeavour except the windsock, motionless and hanging vertically to the ground, to mar this solitary antiquity. This scene, this horizon, had not changed since the earth was born. And now, it had not changed but was changing us.

'Let's walk.'

We walked over the dunes and wadis. Over alternating mud and burning sand. Walked until the aircraft and the windsock were out of sight.

'I think this is you,' I observed suddenly.

'Say again,' he grinned cynically, breaking the spell. It was cruel and the anger that always seemed near when I was with him, rose again to the surface. 'Sometimes I think you are stupid!'

We returned without speaking to the Spitfires, sat on our parachutes and picked idly at the arid sandwiches.

'Talk,' I ordered.

'About what?'

'Anything. You must have something to say about something.'

'Well, here we are ladies and gentlemen, lazing under the tropical skies, watching the vast panorama of nature . . .'

'Oh, shut up!' Suddenly he turned to me. We stared at each other, hovering. Simultaneously we dropped our eyes and I swallowed the piece of dry bread that had lodged in my throat.

'What about the "T"?' I reminded.

We walked to the northern end of the field and selected a position for the "T".

'I'm glad it isn't a "W",' he observed.

'I don't see what difference . . .' I said, striving to maintain the change of subject.

'I'll draw a picture,' he said. 'The "W" goes down, up, down and up again. The "T" . . .'

'All right, pedant.'

We plucked some of the whitewashed stones that bordered the landing area and began laying out the outline of the "T". Obstinately I selected large stones and staggered under their weight, whilst he then ostentatiously gathered tiny fragments. This farce went on for two minutes before I surrendered and collapsed in a crumbled heap on to the sand. Gordon leered malignantly, murmuring something about the emancipation of women, and carried on working.

After two hours the 'T' was finished and we lay down beside it, admiring our handiwork.

'It isn't straight,' I pointed out.

'It is,' he argued. I got up, walked fifty yards along the landing strip, knelt on the sand and sighted my eyes down the shank of the 'T.' It *was* two or three degrees out of parallel with the runway. 'It isn't,' I shouted. He joined me, lay flat on the ground and squinted at the 'T.' 'You win,' he smiled, turning to me, 'but it stays that way.'

I agreed with a nod and we returned to the Spitfires.

We lay on our parachutes, dozing and sipping the blood-warm lemonade. The sentry joined us and stared curiously. I offered him a drink. He appraised it dubiously, sipped it, spat with a grimace and smiled apologetically. He looked at my legs and thighs stretched tightly in the khaki slacks, moved his eyes to Gordon, back to my thighs, shrugged and trudged off to the farthest end of the field.

'Wonder what he dreams about,' commented Gordon idly before we dozed.

Gordon's voice woke me. 'We've had it for today. The Rapide isn't coming.'

'Nor Leo,' I added, glancing at the sun and my watch. It was three-thirty.

'I've enjoyed today,' remarked Gordon, without preamble.

I nodded in assent. 'I've enjoyed it too.'

Promptly at four o'clock a cloud of dust signified the arrival of the jeep.

That evening, after an austere supper, we sat on the veranda overlooking Bandar Abbas. The unshaded fight swung gently in the evening breeze, like an incense burner, and threw shadows across our faces. The distant murmur, of the Persian Gulf emphasized the calm of the sky as I sang snatches from light opera; the lyrics adding poignancy to the extraordinary peace that I felt.

251

44

THE FOLLOWING MORNING GORDON DROVE OUT ALONE TO THE airfield whilst I attended to our smalls. He returned, to my surprise, shortly after noon, streaked with oil and mud. 'The bloody jeep broke down,' he said.

'Must you swear?'

'Sorry. You can take the bloody thing next time and I'll do the washing,' he answered vehemently.

I laughed, despite myself.

Leo had flown over from Sharja. A propeller was being flown from Israel to Abadan by a *Sabena* aircraft chartered to bring Jewish immigrants from Bombay to Israel. From Abadan the arrangements were still vague. The cost of chartering the Rapide aircraft was prohibitive and, consequently, this idea had been dropped.

'That means,' commented Gordon, 'we won't have to go out to the field every day.'

Leo was still receiving a stream of contradictory cables, one of which ordered that I should leave Gordon behind and join the others at Sharja as soon as possible.

'That's stupid,' I protested.

'Why?'

'Why don't Leo and Sonny go on to Burma and you and I

continue as soon as your prop arrives? Supposing you go down, nobody will know where you are. If the two of us fly together, at least we will be able to pin-point the position if one of us should crash.'

'True enough,' replied Gordon, 'but enough time has been wasted already. The Burmese want at least three Spits as quickly as possible.'

'Why three? Why not two, or four?' I interjected heatedly. 'One Spitfire isn't going to make all that difference.'

'Well, Leo's the boss and that's the way he wants it. Anyway I can fly to Burma in short hops. I'll land at Jiwani to refuel . . .'

'What about Calcutta-Rangoon?'

'I can land at Akyab.'

I felt a little happier about it. By landing at these intermediate aerodromes he could cut down on the long sea crossings and fly closer to the coasts. 'All right,' I admitted reluctantly, doubting that he would in fact detour. 'When do you think I can leave?'

'I suggested to Leo about three days' time, provided we have no more rain. I checked the field this morning. It's still dangerous. If you don't arrive at Sharja by Monday Leo will fly over to see what's happening. He won't come again otherwise.'

'Fine. What about the batteries?'

'Blast! I forgot them. The radio was weak this morning. I meant to bring them in. I'll have to drive back to the field. Pop over to Dustmalchi and see whether he can arrange to have them charged somewhere.'

'Yes, sir!' I replied formally.

He grinned and left.

On Saturday we drove out to the field, accompanied by

the engineer and a few labourers, to prepare the strip for my departure.

After examining the field we chose a take-off path a few yards to the left of centre of the north-south strip. The labourers scrutinized every inch and filled in the treacherous soft patches with dry shingle. We walked and worked with them, their dignity bringing lustre to the comradeship. The engineer swore vehemently at one who accidentally knocked his spade against the wheel of my aircraft. Gordon walked quickly over to the labourer, patted him on the back and offered him a cigarette. He walked back to me, saw my eyes and blushed furiously.

'Why?' I asked, knowing the answer but wanting his admission of sensitivity.

'He looked hurt,' he replied, avoiding my eyes.

'You have hurt me many times.'

'You can take care of yourself,' he answered neutrally, walking away.

'It is strange that you two are married,' observed the engineer.

I reddened. 'Why do you say that?'

He looked at me shrewdly. 'You both behave as though you are still courting.'

I turned uncertainly to the aircraft, as the engineer left to drive his truck for over an hour monotonously up and down the field, the wheels crushing the surface into some semblance of firmness. Gordon and I checked my Spitfire before we washed the mud from the undercarriage and radiators, checked the level of the oil, petrol and glycol, polished the windscreen and fitted the newly charged battery.

'Do you want to run the engine?' asked Gordon.

'What about the battery?'

'You're right. We should save it until you are ready to go. I'll pull the prop through.' He struggled, like Laocoön with the snake, turning the propeller until the sweat dripped from his aquiline nose. 'Seems O.K.,' he gasped. 'She's ready to go.'

We tied the Spitfires down for the night and walked slowly along the strip on a final inspection. It was a serious moment. 'I still don't like it,' commented Gordon, with a frown, stamping his heel into the surface. 'If you go over on your back you haven't a chance. There is nothing here to get you out.'

'I'm not leaving until tomorrow. It will be better then.'

The engineer drove up in his truck. 'What do you think?' I called as he jumped down from the seat.

'I know nothing of flying,' he replied with a shrug. 'These are the first aeroplanes I have seen here in three years. The last one was a Russian. They also were bogged . . . for three weeks. What do they weigh?' he added, nodding to the Spitfires.

'About seven thousand pounds with the present fuel load,' I answered.

'Hum, just over three tons.' He pursed his lips. 'It's a pity we haven't got a roller. Can you not wait a few more days?'

'I'd rather she left as soon as possible,' said Gordon.

'Do they gain speed quickly?' asked the engineer.

'Yes,' I answered.

'She should be airborne in a 150 yards,' added Gordon.

'Is she a good pilot?' enquired the engineer, appraising me dubiously.

'Lousy,' grinned Gordon.

'Ah. I have met the English before. That means she is good. I think,' he continued, 'that tomorrow will be difficult. Perhaps the next day . . .'

'Well try taxi-ing tomorrow,' answered Gordon firmly. 'If she can taxi, then she can take off. Two o'clock. That will give the sun more time to dry it out. Will you be here?'

'Of course,' answered the engineer.

'And about fifteen labourers, a fast truck, axes, ropes, buckets and shovels. Just in case.'

'Right.'

'Will you call the men? I'd like to explain tomorrow's programme and what I want them to do.'

'We should give them something,' I suggested.

'Would you mind if we did?' enquired Gordon.

'It isn't necessary,' answered the engineer.

'But we want to,' I insisted.

'As you wish,' shrugged the engineer. He called them over.

'The lady pilot is taking off tomorrow,' commenced Gordon, nodding to the engineer to translate. 'The ground is not very satisfactory but it will be many days before the surface is completely dry and she must leave immediately.'

The engineer continued translating volubly. The labourers whispered amongst themselves, shaking their heads.

'There is', continued Gordon, 'a very slight possibility that the aeroplane may suddenly stick in the mud and go over on its back. If it does, it may catch fire, with the lady pilot trapped inside.'

After the engineer translated this, with suitable gestures, the men shook their heads violently. We had become good friends.

'Therefore if an accident does happen, we haven't much time. Before she starts her take-off we will all get into the truck with axes, ropes, poles and buckets of sand. When the lady pilot starts her take-off we will follow her in the truck. If she crashes we must get this side panel open,' he pointed to the emergency release panel, 'with axes if necessary and pull her out. If there is a fire we will use the sand buckets. If we can't get her out that way then we must lift one wing and try to release her from underneath . . . We will need about fifteen men to lift the wing,' he added. He waited until the engineer completed his translation. 'Just one more thing. If there is a fire, it is possible that the petrol tanks may explode.' There was a mutter, almost of rebellion, as they looked accusingly at Gordon. 'It is the lady pilot's wish that she leave as soon as possible,' he explained hurriedly.

'Will you detail two men for the axes and three for the buckets. The remainder are to stand clear until I give other instructions. Explain to them they must not get in each other's way.'

The engineer assented.

'Everything clear?'

'Perfectly. They offer their prayers.'

'I prefer their sinews,' replied Gordon sardonically.

'I think I should be the one to decide that,' I interjected. 'Tell them I return their prayers.'

Gordon raised an eyebrow and stared coldly at me. For fully fifteen seconds we glared at each other. Finally he sighed, rummaged in his pockets and gave the men our tokens of gratitude. They accepted the money graciously, without servility.

'Sorry by the way, to make that speech of mine so melodramatic. I wanted them to understand that tomorrow will be no joke,' explained Gordon.

'I understand,' I answered, furious with myself that he could soothe my ruffled feelings so easily. His mastery of insult, followed by the soft manner, left me swinging like a pendulum between active dislike and regard.

We collected the shovels and other equipment and got into the truck. The labourers climbed in the back and braced themselves for the rough ride back to Bandar Abbas. I looked back at my Spitfire straddling the desert, its potential returned. Tomorrow I would fly again . . . perhaps.

That evening I said good-bye to our friends. Gordon bought some beer and we sat on the veranda with Dustmalchi and his wife; the engineer; the army colonel who returned my passport; the doctor, and his wife who still stared at me with a puzzled frown. It was a sad gathering, for most of them were exiled in Bandar Abbas and politely envied my impending departure. After they left, Gordon and I continued sitting on the veranda, I with my thoughts, he with the last bottles of beer. I waited for the aggressiveness that always followed whenever he drank beer in my presence.

'I'm going to miss you,' he said.

'It won't be for long. Your prop should arrive within a week. You will probably meet up with us in Rangoon,' I answered, pleased with his admission.

'Maybe. You might start on the next trip before I return to Tel Aviv.' He poured another glass. 'I wouldn't like that,' he added.

'Neither would I,' I observed, the words echoing significantly in the soft midnight air. I savoured them again like a wine merchant tasting an unexpectedly pleasing vintage.

He got up and leaned against the balustrade that overlooked Bandar Abbas. Turning, he beckoned me to join him. For the last time I gazed at the feeble lights and listened to the painful honking of a nearby mule. I knew that this was a moment that would be recalled many times in my life. Overhead the moon, its valleys clearly visible, tugged treacherously at me as though I were the tides to be pushed and pulled at its command. Defiantly I returned to my chair. He turned, his ally the moon mocking me from his shoulder. It seemed as though he commanded nature; the sea glittering with silver; the sky with stars; the dark mountains isolating Bandar Abbas from the rest of the world; even the zephyr breeze had calmed, awaiting the outcome of this moment.

'I think you should go to bed,' he announced baldly, flicking his cigarette over the balustrade.

Without a word I left.

As I lay in bed I could hear him pacing overhead. His footsteps echoed hollowly, like a drum. Suddenly the footsteps ceased their monotonous indecision and clumped downstairs. There was a determination in them that frightened me. Quickly I turned on my side and feigned sleep.

'Are you asleep?' he whispered.

I did not answer. Neither did I answer the sigh that followed. His lips brushed my temple like a shadow before he creaked into his camp-bed. I lay silently, secretly touching my temple.

'Good-night,' I said quietly, wanting him to know I knew he had kissed me. But it was too late. He was asleep.

45

At noon the following day we ate a Spartan lunch of cheese, olives and goat's milk, packed my luggage and drove to the airfield. Behind us, invisible in the cloud of dust, trailed our friends in a convoy of jeeps and lorries. Ahead, the horizon shimmered in the heat, making the palm trees look like women dancing with their skirts held high. Gordon sat beside me, his face inscrutable. Unable to emulate his example, I hid my emotions behind my sunglasses. My stomach was tight with the vicarious thrill that presages all my flights.

As my Spitfire appeared, parked on the edge of the airfield, as though born of the desert, I felt grateful for its uncompromising appeal; its ability to soar with me into the waiting sky, to cut the umbilical cord of care and transport me to a world of ego, simplicity and space.

Gordon squeezed my bags into the gun panels as I gave the aeroplane a cursory inspection. Everything was ready; the bond already welded that separated the Spitfire and me from those who were to be left behind. I strapped on my parachute and helmet and climbed into the cockpit. By now we were surrounded by peasants. Gordon motioned them back until they stood in a long thin line like spectators at a football match. I waved good-bye to them as Gordon jumped up on the wing to help me with my straps.

'All set?' asked Gordon.

'Yes,' I answered.

'O.K. Start her up and taxi down to the other end of the field. You'll have to switch off there and let her cool down.'

'O.K.,' I replied. I adjusted the controls; petrol on, parking brake on, mixture set to idle cut-off, throttle slightly open. 'All clear?' I shouted.

'All clear,' answered Gordon.

'Contact!' Impatiently she burst into life. The instruments rose sluggishly into action. Anxiously I watched the oil pressure gauge; she had been sitting idle for a long time. Slowly it rose, 50,60,70 . . . 75. Just right. I signalled Gordon to pull the stones away from the wheels, and gingerly opened the throttle. Would she move? Like a jockey I urged her on. Slowly she inched forward; I gave her more throttle as she lurched uncertainly through the clinging top-soil. Gordon and the spectators had vanished in the sand driven from my slipstream.

I taxied slowly to the end of the field, turned, lined up carefully with the take-off path and switched off. The silence was deafening. The field had disappeared in a cloud of sand. I sat, waiting patiently, until Gordon and the others appeared dimly through the cloud.

Gordon jumped up on the wing, his face and hair covered with dust; his eye-lashes exaggerated as though with beige mascara. 'How was it?' he asked anxiously.

'Not bad,' I answered encouragingly. 'I needed about 1300 revs to keep her moving.'

'As much as that?' he frowned.

'Yes.'

'Do you want to try it? It's up to you.'

261

'Yes.'

'How are the temperatures?'

'A bit high. Radiator's about a hundred and five. I'll wait a few minutes.'

'Do you want to jump out?'

'It isn't worth it. I'll sit here.' I eased off my helmet and loosened the straps. We waited with the embarrassed suspension of waiting for a train to leave. The engineer's truck was parked nearby.

'Don't forget, keep your brakes on as long as you can as you open the throttle. As soon as you feel the tail coming up slam on full throttle, through the gate, and watch out for the swing. She'll swing like hell at plus eighteen boost. Use full right rudder bias on your trim. Keep the stick back when you open the throttle. If you go over, cut your switches and petrol. We'll be right with you.' His face was creased with worry; he couldn't keep still.

'Stop fussing. I'll be all right.'

'Keep your carburettor air filter open, that will give you another inch of boost'

'What about the sand?'

'To hell with the sand.' We waited another five minutes. 'She's cool enough now.'

He helped me with the straps, trussing me up like a chicken.

'Hey, that's too tight,' I protested.

'It won't be if you go over on your back.'

I put my helmet on.

'All set?'

'All set,' I replied.

He grasped my hand, squeezed it and fussed with my harness.

Deliberately I left my oxygen mask off. The spectators and labourers watched silently. The doctor's wife wore a look of worried comprehension.

'You had better kiss me good-bye,' I suggested as lightly as I could. 'We are supposed to be married.'

He leaned down into the cockpit and kissed me. It was an awkward kiss. The helmet strap disciplined my lips, the struggle for balance his. But there was a delicacy and honour in the kiss that was a fitting tribute to our relationship. And a fitting end. I felt proud that we had resisted turning an elusive yet profound intimacy into something of which at this moment, now that it must end, we would have felt ashamed. It had been a parenthesis in both our lives. We acknowledged its significance, and its demise, as our eyes lingered in farewell.

'Call me on the R/T after you take off,' he said shyly. 'I'll be listening out on my Spit. Tell Leo to fly over if there is any change of plan. Otherwise the three of you carry on. I'll see you when I see you. And watch the swing!' He jumped down and stood on the running board of the engineer's truck parked parallel with me.

She started easily as though anxious to be off. Mechanically I went through the vital actions necessary before take-off and, with a final wave, slowly opened the throttle. Minus 3, minus 2, zero, plus 1. She shook and trembled with frustrated power, as I still held on the brakes. More throttle. More until she shook with rage. At plus 2 I felt the tail lighten . . . This is it! I released the brakes. With a jerk the Spitfire charged into exultant action. I slammed the throttle fully open to emergency power and kicked full right rudder as she began to swing. Come on. Come on! Out of the corner of my eye I saw the truck racing with me. 40 . . .

50 . . . 60. Still she clung to the topsoil, the long nose swaying and bobbing violently. I fought against the temptation to ease the control column forward. The truck had gone. Suddenly the lurching ceased . . . I was airborne, free. We soared violently into the sky.

Shaking, I throttled back until the panic roar of the engine subsided to normal climb power and switched on the radio.

'Hello, Gordon. Jackie here,' I called.

'Are you all right?' he replied instantly, his voice metallically different, over the radio.

'Fine,' I answered.

'I can't see you. You blew up a dust storm.'

I looked down. The aerodrome was covered with a long trail of dust that billowed high into the air. To the south I could see Bandar Abbas sandwiched between the Gulf and the desert.

'How was the take-off?'

'Not bad. I swung . . . couldn't see a thing with the tail down.'

'You are in the air. That's all that matters. It's clear now. Come down and do a beat-up,' he said.

'Roger,' I replied and dived steeply at his white shirt.

'Take it easy. You've got a belly-tank on you know.'

'O.K.'

'Push off. You haven't got too much petrol.'

'O.K. I'm on course for Sharja now.'

'Good-bye.'

'Good-bye,' I answered. 'Take care of yourself.' There was a metallic click. He had switched off.

I climbed to 7,000 feet before crossing the coast and heading out over the Gulf. I checked the instruments carefully as Bandar Abbas slipped past under my wing and kept myself unnecessarily busy with map-reading. I swallowed and kept swallowing the lump that had lodged in my throat. I loosened the strap of my helmet. It made it easier.

Fifteen minutes later I called on the R/T: 'Sharja Tower; Uncle Baker 437. Do you read?'

They came back immediately. 'Uncle Baker four three seven, Sharja Tower. Read you Loud and Clear. Hello, Jackie. Come on in; we're waiting for you.'

'Four three seven. Thank you. Are Captains Kastner and Banting there?' I replied.

'Sure thing, kid,' answered Leo's voice. 'What's your E.T.A.?'

'About twenty minutes,' I replied.

'Hurry up. We've got a party laid on for you tonight.'

I thought of Gordon returning to Bandar Abbas; to an empty, silent room, as I followed the Trucial Oman coastline until the white sands of Sharja appeared. Parked by the Control Tower and standing out sharply against the bleached sands were the other two Spitfires. I landed, taxied next to them and saw the familiar figures of Leo and Sonny running out to me. Hurriedly I put on my sunglasses and climbed out of the cockpit.

'Hey, you look wonderful, kid,' shouted Leo, grabbing me by the shoulders.

Sonny smilingly agreed. 'Bandar Abbas has agreed with you.'

I forced a smile and left it at that.

46

I HAD ALWAYS LIKED THE REMOTE APPEAL OF SHARJA PERCHED on the shores of the Trucial Oman peninsula and dominated by mountains to the east, but I was in no mood now to enjoy its extravagant colour and exotic beauty as I joined the others in the tiny air-conditioned transient mess. I wore a ubiquitous nylon dress, after a salt-water bath, and knew that I looked my best. Not a particularly exciting phenomenon in Europe but adequate for woman-starved Sharja. Gallantries and compliments fell on me like spring showers. The 'Doc', scruffy and unorthodox; the C.O. newly arrived and shy; a locust-control officer sadly reminiscing over his predecessor murdered in nearby Dubai for a few paltry rupees; a bank clerk; a mildly supercilious army officer and a few incredibly youthful air force officers made up the party. I commented disparagingly on the Doc's moustache. Two minutes later he returned, bloody but unbowed, with half of it shaved off. He raised his eyebrows enquiringly. 'Yes,' I nodded. 'Decidedly better.' He vanished and returned clean shaven.

'What's happening about Gordon?' I asked Leo during a lull in the dancing. He shrugged his shoulders and pulled out a batch of cables from his tunic. I read them quickly, anxiously.

'Surely it should have been sorted out by now?' I said peevishly.

He shrugged. 'As far as I can make out from the cables they are flying a propeller to Kerman and then by road to Bandar Abbas.'

'By road!'

'Yes.'

'That's 200 miles,' I replied, appalled by the thought of driving over those impossible roads with a propeller.

He nodded. 'They expect to arrive in Bandar Abbas within a week.'

'How are we going to let Gordon know?'

'Well, how can we?' riposted Leo.

'We could fly over on our way to Karachi and drop a note.'

Leo shook his head. 'No. We haven't enough fuel.'

'We could refuel at Jiwani,' I pointed out encouragingly.

He smiled mockingly. 'What are you so anxious about, kid?'

'Leo,' I protested, blushing with innocent guilt, 'he's marooned there alone. No one to talk to. No idea of what is happening. It won't be so bad if he knows when he's going to get out.'

He shook his head firmly. 'Sorry, Jackie. I don't want to land at Jiwani, they haven't got a battery cart. If we can't start up on our own batteries, we're stuck.'

'Couldn't just one . . .' I argued weakly.

'No. We stick together.'

'Are we leaving in the morning?'

'Yes. Dawn. Call at four o'clock. It's time we went to bed.'

There was a flattering chorus of protests as we left the party. I said good-night to Leo and Sonny, waited for them to retire and sneaked out of the gates of the fort to the Spitfires parked outside. It was a perfect night. The red hurricane lights marking out the parking area gleamed weakly in the liquid moonlight that caressed the aircraft and threw their elongated shadows on the sand. I touched the wing of my plane like a lover. It felt cool and clean; the leading edge as sharp as a knife, ready to thrust its way through to the glittering infinity above. Intoxicated with the night's beauty I turned north to Bandar Abbas, then west to Taunton and wavered like a compass needle between them both before returning reluctantly to my stuffy bedroom.

47

THE FOLLOWING MORNING WE CLIMBED AWAY STEEPLY TO THE east with the sun plunging blindly into our cockpits. After an hour I felt uncomfortable. After two I knew that I shouldn't have had that second cup of tea at breakfast. After three I was desperate and opened up the throttle to maximum cruise and jumped into the lead.

'Hey, Jackie!' shouted Leo over the R/T. 'What are you doing?'

'I er . . . I've got to get to Karachi quickly . . .'

'What's the matter?' asked Leo anxiously. 'Something wrong?'

'Yes.'

'What?'

I kept eloquently silent. 'O.K.,' replied Leo, chuckling. 'Go ahead, we'll follow.'

Intently I urged my Spitfire on as the Pakistan coastline crawled sluggishly by. At last Karachi aerodrome loomed up in the haze. I called the Control Tower over the R/T.

'Karachi Tower. Uncle Baker 437. Three Spitfires approaching from the west. Request landing clearance.'

'There are two aircraft ahead of you. Stand by,' they answered.

'I can't stand by,' I answered urgently. 'I want to spend a penny.'

There was a stunned silence over the R/T before an aircraft replied: 'After you, madam.'

'You are clear to land number one,' ordered Karachi Tower dryly.

I landed, taxied to the tarmac and had to sit, fuming, for three interminable minutes whilst the health authorities let off a D.D.T. bomb inside the cockpit. Officers standing on the Control Tower waved encouragingly as I ran past.

After a brief lunch we took off again for Jodhpur, a relatively short flight of two hours across the barren featureless Thar desert that forms a natural barrier between Pakistan and India. It was an uneventful flight and we landed, parched but content, as the sun threw its longest shadows.

After a prolonged battle of two hours with the Customs authorities who, still unable to understand that Spitfires were fighter aircraft incapable of carrying either freight or passengers, instituted a new form or a new procedure every time we landed there, we checked in at Circuit House, a small quiet hotel nestling in its own grounds on the outskirts of Jodhpur. After a disappointingly European dinner Leo, Sonny and I sat on the veranda overlooking the drive and listened to the unwavering croak of the frogs, the appealing tch-tch-tch of the chameleons and the bloodcurdling howl of the pariah dogs. We were all overtired and spoke desultorily. Leo cross-examined me fitfully about Bandar Abbas, before suggesting that we make it an early night.

At dawn we drove in a jeep to the aerodrome. It was cold and we huddled up in our flying overalls as we passed laden ox-carts plodding steadily along the road, their drivers wrapped in coarse calico sacks and nodding in sleep. Slowly, as dawn lifted the pallor of night and splashed a thin daub of crimson in the eastern sky, brilliant peacocks strutted from the undergrowth, ruffled their feathers in a cascade of brilliance and preened conceitedly. In violent contrast ugly misshapen vultures hopped clumsily in search of carrion breakfast.

We were late taking off. Unaccountably my booster pump had fused and I could not start. Leo fumed irritably over the R/T. 'I can't help it,' I protested. 'It's not my fault if the fuse blows.' I was sorely tempted to add to this but by now I had become reconciled to the others' tendency to blame me for any hitch in our schedule. We climbed out, found a spare fuse, fitted and checked it and took off in a flurry of perspiring bad temper an hour later.

We cruised at a higher throttle setting to make up for lost time and the indefatigable Merlin engines soon spanned the 400 miles to Cawnpore.

Narrowly avoiding an invitation for a lethargic curry lunch at the officers' mess we refuelled and took off again in the heat of noon for Calcutta, 600 miles to the east.

The Meteorological officer had warned us of monsoon storms and severe turbulence along the route though, when we levelled out at 11,000 feet, the skies were crystal clear and pacific. Perhaps, I thought cynically, a little too clear and pacific.

My cynicism was well justified, for within an hour I felt the first touch of turbulence that shook our formation in gentle warning like a nanny chastising a too adventurous child. Ahead, blocking our path, towered majestic cumulonimbus clouds in unmistakable challenge. Like gigantic cauliflowers they boiled and blustered into fantastic silhouettes. I tightened my straps and watched Leo warily as he veered left and right in search of an opening. I edged closer to him as though his nearness could help.

271

He gave me a quick look, grinned encouragingly and pointed to his oxygen mask. I nodded, grinned feebly back and turned on my oxygen. We climbed as the storm blackened the sky and loomed closer. Climbed and struggled for height until, at 27,000 feet the Spitfires floundered and responded sluggishly in the rarefied air. But it was futile. The squall leered at us from Olympian heights; we were like salmon battling against Niagara Falls.

'It's no good,' shouted Leo over the R/T. 'We'll have to go underneath.'

We spiralled steeply, discarding thriftlessly the hard-won altitude, until we were a few feet from the ground, twisting and turning through the valleys that tossed us like shuttlecocks in an uproar of turbulence and hail. Dimly I could see Sonny, on the other side of Leo, rising and falling sickeningly in a violent series of gusts that threatened to tear loose his long-range belly-tank. The ground flashed by in a series of kaleidoscopic sketches; forests, rivers and the upturned faces of startled villagers. Suddenly, as though a door had closed, we were through and I felt sheepish, like a man who finds himself shouting in a sudden hush, as I still struggled unnecessarily violently with the controls in the magically smooth air.

'O.K., Jackie?' asked Leo as we climbed back to cruising level, blinking in the brilliant sun.

'Yes.'

'Sonny?'

'O.K.'

'Now where the hell are we!' added Leo.

Being lost seemed a comparatively minor event after the turmoil of the storm and our chatter over the R/T possessed the mild inanity of a drunken trio as we tried to identify the swollen rivers and flooded fields two miles beneath. After we had come to three violently conflicting conclusions Leo surrendered and called for a Q.D.M. from Calcutta. The course that Calcutta gave us to steer for the aerodrome proved all three of us to be conclusively wrong – not, under the circumstances, very surprising.

Calcutta soon appeared on the horizon, looking fresh and clean like a small boy from the heavy showers. The Hooghli river, stained with soil, curled heavily through the city and pin-pointed Barrackpore aerodrome.

We were met by Indian Air Force officers who quickly supervised the manhandling of our Spitfires into the hangar before the next storm broke over the aerodrome, drumming the corrugated tin roof of the hangars with a deafening deluge. Two cows munched placidly on the concrete apron, oblivious of the torrent that bounced off their backs in tiny angry waterspouts and dripped from the tails still mechanically flicking though no flies could survive that waterfall.

'Only three this time?' questioned the engineering officer. 'Who's missing?'

'Levett,' I answered. 'We left him behind in Bandar Abbas. Have you heard anything?' I added.

'Not a word.'

I unpacked miserably.

48

WE STAYED OVERNIGHT IN THE OFFICERS' MESS AND WERE received with that humble courtesy characteristic of the people of India. The accommodation was primitive, the beds mattressed with lump straw that smelled of damp stables and betokened the fakir's bed of nails. I stripped and revelled in the cold shower, eyed curiously by a jet-black crow perched impudently on the window ledge. I tried to make friends but he flew away with a haughty flurry of wings. It was close and humid as I flopped wearily on the bed with a towel wrapped around me and dozed fitfully with the roar of the Merlin engine still echoing in my ears like sea-shells. Images of Bandar Abbas and Taunton rose before my eyes as I listened sleepily to the wur-wur-wur of the fan creaking uselessly on the ceiling.

I awoke suddenly to find my bags unpacked, their intimate contents laid neatly on a small table by the window. Standing by my bed was the 'bearer' eyeing me gravely and holding a steaming cup of tea:

'Tea, Memsahib. Your dress will be ready in a moment.'

I snatched hurriedly for the towel but it was unnecessary. I was covered modestly with a coarse white calico sheet. He disappeared as silently as he had come whilst I stared bemusedly at the sheet.

I dressed for dinner and joined the others in the dining-room. Tall bearded Sikhs imposing in coloured turbans, and wiry young officers rose graciously as though it were the most natural thing in the world for a woman to assume equality in their eyes. I smiled at them trying to show that I was aware of the honour they accorded me as we sat down to dine.

I listened happily to the boisterous conversation that took me back to the comradely days of war-time in the A.T.A. Fighter pilots sneered unmercifully at the transport pilots who replied with unkind references to 'Brylcreem Boys'. Eagerly they talked shop: 'He's a damn good pilot . . . it wasn't his fault . . . It's a lousy aeroplane over 25,000 feet . . . They collided right over the aerodrome with forty paratroops on board. Only two got out. Their wives and families were watching from the aerodrome. Crashed right in front of them . . . Peter has got his second stripe at last.' Obsessed with flying, they looked quickly at me to see whether I was listening and smiled happily when I nodded encouragingly. I felt part of them; my memories theirs. My fears known to them. In each one I knew the tablet of fear that dwelled, deeply concealed in their hearts, of their mistress waiting in the air to whom they must return. A mistress of beauty and moods, sullen in cold grey shrouds or radiant and innocent in a superb ensemble of infinite blue and gold. Demanding, voracious, fickle; luring with a Judas kiss and snubbing with imperial disdain and death those whom she had subjected.

After dinner we drove into Calcutta through streets choked with desperate poverty where naked children playing in filth underlined the grim statistics of death from cholera and smallpox written in our aircraft log-books. India has inherited a formidable burden with her independence. I did some shopping; vulgar brassware from Benares, silks from Kashmir and unlikely trinkets from Birmingham before we went to the Princess cabaret on Chowringhee. We stayed far too late in an exotic atmosphere of lamé saris, determined tourists, and imported English chorus girls that would have brought an appreciative gleam to Gordon's eyes. We drove back in the early hours of the morning, the streets miraculously empty except for the silent forms, covered in wretched rags, sleeping on the pavements.

It seemed that my head had barely touched the pillow when the bearer arrived with another cup of tea: 'Five o'clock, Memsahib. Time to get up.' I sipped the tea drowsily, aimlessly swotting at the mosquitoes that buzzed petulantly, determined to get their quota of blood before daybreak. Leo knocked heartily on the flimsy partitioning that separated our bedrooms.

'All right,' I cried peevishly. 'I'm up.' I hated him. I hated everybody at this grisly hour. We ate a melancholy breakfast in the silent empty mess and climbed clumsily into the truck.

The Spitfires were ready, immaculately washed and polished, for the last leg of our journey, Calcutta to Rangoon across the Bay of Bengal. By the time we had completed the Customs and Immigration formalities the sun had caught us up and reduced me to a limp rag. I put on my parachute, climbed into the narrow cockpit, wriggled into the seat, fastened the safety straps, stuffed my unkempt hair into my helmet, fitted the oxygen and radio mask tightly over my mouth, plugged in the radio socket and sat steaming, staring balefully at Leo who, as was his wont, shook hands and said a prolonged good-bye to everyone in sight.

We took off individually from the long narrow runway and formed up over the aerodrome before climbing towards the Bay. The heat was intolerable and shimmered from the engine cowling.

276

I eased open the cockpit hood, poked a few fingers into the slip-stream and diverted a little of it on to my face. 'Phew,' I croaked over the R/T.

'What?' said Leo.

'Phew,' I repeated.

'I don't understand. Say again.'

'Phew. Peter-How-Easy-William,' I replied, determined to make the point though realizing the length of this conversation had now become out of all proportion to the original observation.

'Phew what?' shouted Leo querulously.

'It's hot.'

'Christ. Is that all!' he replied irritably. I subsided into injured silence, mulling over the probability that if either Sonny or Gordon had offered a similar observation Leo would have replied chattily: 'Yes, isn't it.'

We cruised steadily at 11,500 feet between two broken layers of cloud that sandwiched us neatly and concealed the forbidding green waters of the bay. I eyed the clouds suspiciously. Even the most innocuous clouds give a message that pilots are foolhardy to disregard.

'The Met report was rather optimistic,' observed Sonny suddenly.

'Yes,' answered Leo, 'but I think we should press on. We can alternate to Akyab if necessary.'

With the approach of the Arakan coast and the rich jungled mountains of Burma, the occasional showers forecast by the meteorological officer united into a purple-hued swathe directly in our path. This time last year, I thought wistfully, I was sitting in Maynard's drinking a genteel cup of coffee.

'We can't go above it,' crackled Leo's voice over the R/T.

'We'll go underneath and follow the coastline south until it clears.'

'Roger,' I replied and waited for Sonny's affirmative.

'Sonny. Did you hear?' called Leo. No reply. Only a crackle echoed in our headphones.

'That's great,' said Leo succinctly. 'Sonny's radio has packed up.'

Throttling back, we dived through the broken layer of cloud beneath us towards the sea now tossing white-capped waves that seemed to reach up in a wave of welcome that belied the eternity lurking beneath. Our horizon had shrunk to an embracing grey blanket that cocooned us with menace. Like a swarm of angry wasps the monsoon storm stung us with driving horizontal rain as we skimmed over the waves, isolated and lonely like submarines trapped in enemy waters. Even the stupidly confident roar of the engine was lost in the uproar of spray and gusts that thrashed like a whiplash and brought groans of protest from the Spitfires. 'Occasional showers' I recalled sourly as the rain seeped through the cockpit hood and dripped steadily on to my lap. I peered towards Leo; he was staring intently ahead, leaning forward, his face almost pressed against the windscreen. Sonny, a faint camouflaged shadow, oscillated violently and showed a brief flash of colour, like a woman's slip, as his sky-blue underbelly turned nakedly towards us. Anxiously I watched the narrow gap between the low broken scud and the sea. I looked at my hands clenched tightly on the control column, the nails white with pressure. 'Relax Moggridge. Relax.' I watched the blood returning as I loosened my grip.

My success was temporary for within a moment I was tense and rigid again. Suddenly to our left a faint shadow loomed and

278

vanished like Hamlet's ghost. 'Leo,' I shouted over the R/T. 'The coast,' and turned towards him to head him off. He veered to the right; on the other side Sonny sheered off like a startled fawn as Leo turned towards him.

'Leo,' I repeated, 'the coast's on our left.'

No reply. I waggled my wings hurriedly and pointed to my helmet. Leo shook his head. My transmitter was not working. The shadow appeared again in the driving rain and Leo caught it, nodding his head violently. It was Ramree Island.

'We'll alternate to Akyab,' shouted Leo turning slowly towards the north. Suddenly a voice crackled deafeningly in my ears. I turned the volume down:

'Akyab Control . . . Jet Uncle Baker-XYZ . . . Transmitting for a Q.D.M. I'm coming in . . .'

'Jet UB-XYZ . . . Akyab Control . . . Impossible land here. Heavy storms . . . Visibility and ceiling zero.'

'Roger,' answered the Jet easily, probably 30,000 feet above us in clear blue sky. 'I'll alternate to Bassein.'

The sands were fast running out on the last lap of our flight. I scanned the maps again, searching for an alternative aerodrome. We had to get down, quickly. On the tip of Ramree Island a tiny blue circle promised a haven. I ignored the ominous word *abandoned* printed tersely underneath, gesticulated to Leo and turned south again. Throttling back I lowered my undercarriage and flashed a glimpse at the others. Leo was nodding indefatigably in agreement as his undercarriage unfolded like the legs of a bird. Sonny was sticking like glue at the end of a lash that swung violently as we twisted and turned through the steaming valleys and flashed across new-born rivers. Floods had made the terrain unrecognizable. The rich green on my maps had become muddy swirling lakes on the ground. I felt a tension almost sexual in my legs as the first pangs of panic gripped me. Miraculously like an oasis of sanity in a lunatic bedlam, a black sliver of runway cutting its way through the tight jungle appeared fleetingly to the left. I cut the throttle and fish-tailed violently towards the runway as Sonny and Leo banked vertically around the perimeter of the aerodrome, their wing-tips flirting with the tree-tops. In less than a minute we had landed, our wheels shooting up a cloud of spray, like the bow-wave of a destroyer at full speed, as they touched down on this sanctuary. I looked again at my nails; they were healthily pink.

We sat in our cockpits, waving foolishly to each other as the full frustrated fury of the monsoon bombarded us in ineffectual malignant anger. We had got down just in time. Like a child safely at a distance I jeered at the theatrical melodrama of rain and wind that bent the trees into hunch-backed caricatures and blotted out all but the gaggle of Spitfires and the threshold of the surrounding jungle.

Silence and peace descended as violently as they had departed and only the drip of water, the glistening runway and the low clouds racing over the tree-tops remained of the tempest that had been defeated by a perilously close margin.

Feeling exhausted and battered I climbed out of the aeroplane and with firm solid ground beneath my feet felt for the first time in my life the urge to smoke a cigarette.

The aerodrome was deserted and abandoned. Built by the Japanese as a base for their bombers and fighters to harass Allied shipping in the Bay of Bengal it was now a memory slipping back into the jungle from which it had been rudely hacked. I looked apprehensively into the whispering trees and mangrove swamps that bordered the runway. The silence was uncanny. Uneasily I walked over to Sonny, robust and solid, standing by his aircraft. I was quite prepared to forego the privileges of emancipation. Suddenly a horrifying thought brought a shout to my lips:

'Leo. We may be in rebel territory!'

'Where are we?' he answered quickly.

'Kyaukpyu, Ramree Island . . .' I answered.

'Jesus . . . I don't know . . . It may be. Get back. Quickly. . . . Let's get out of here!'

We ran for our aircraft but it was too late. A score of figures had appeared silently and, rifles held negligently in their hands, were watching us from the edge of the jungle. As we watched tensely, more figures appeared until we were completely surrounded. In the oppressive silence I heard a jeep approaching; it was still hidden by the dense undergrowth.

'Leo . . .'

'Shut up. Let me do the talking,' ordered Leo sharply.

The jeep swung into sight, covered in mud and careering recklessly through the deep puddles. Driving it was a tiny elderly woman, dressed spotlessly in white. 'Good morning,' she smiled.

'Is this Government territory?' rapped out Leo.

'It is now,' she answered. 'It wasn't a few weeks ago,' she added dryly. Sitting next to her was another woman, young and pretty. Leo grinned sheepishly. They were the missionary and nurse in sole charge of a tiny church and hospital in the nearby village of Kyaukpyu.

'These are Burmese Air Force aircraft ma'am. Is there a military unit here?' asked Leo politely, his eyes straying to the nurse.

'Yes. But they are out on patrol. Won't be back until this evening.'

281

'Is there anywhere here we can stay the night? I'd like to get our radio repaired before we push on to Rangoon.'

'I will be happy to accommodate you in my house,' offered the missionary. 'And who is this young lady?' she added, nodding to me.

'She's a pilot,' answered Leo in the sepulchral tone he invariably adopted when introducing me and which made me feel like adding, 'It's nothing really.' She smiled at me, looked at my filthy overalls and said: 'You look as though you could do with a bath.'

It was a short drive to the magical little village, standing on stilts, that nestled picturesquely in a setting of rich golden pagodas. The entire population had turned out to receive us. The women gay in vivid coloured longyis and tight-fitting white bodices, the men in check longyis, shirts and incongruous brown trilbys that gave them an extraordinarily spiv-like appearance. They were all laughing and waving pungent-smelling cheroots as the children, goggle-eyed, clustered around the visitors from the skies.

We spent the evening in mellow mood, lazing on the veranda with our hosts, the only Europeans on the island. In this remote corner they had found a vocation that brought a remarkable serenity to their eyes and a slow grace to their movements as though time had stopped for them. I felt myself slipping contentedly into the mystical soothing clutches of their world as I listened to tales of myth and war, legend and peace from Burma's history.

Here was the desert island to which the mind's eye turns when nerves scream with the tempo of modern life and the heart asks with every beat: 'Why, why, why?' Like the drowning man's, my life flitted through my thoughts in a series of newsreel flashes the peak of which seemed to be worrying about oil pressure at 15,000 feet or a new dress for the annual regimental ball at Bath. I seemed to have spent my life chasing my own tail.

Reluctantly, as the murmur of noise hushed in the village and the twinkling lights were slowly extinguished, I said good-night. In bed, under the silken folds of the mosquito net, God – Buddhist or Catholic – seemed very close.

Early the following morning we awoke to the chatter of monkeys and the melodious tinkling of bells from the village temples. I glanced, mechanically writing a meteorological report, at the sky. It was a beautiful morning. The trees were motionless, smoke rose vertically from the village and wisps of cirrus cloud signed a truce in the sky. Later, Leo, Sonny and I headed a large convoy bound for the aerodrome, where Buddhist monks, striking in saffron-yellow robes, who had left their meditations to bless our departure, listened gravely as their mortal theological enemy, the missionary, translated Leo's warning on the danger of getting too close to the Spitfires' propellers.

As we tinkered with the radios, repairing quickly the loose connection in mine, but baffled by Sonny's, an Argonaut airliner cruised overhead on its way to Calcutta.

'Perhaps we can get the weather at Rangoon,' I suggested to Leo.

'Go ahead,' agreed Leo. 'Keep your helmet off,' he added with a grin, indicating the children gathered around the aircraft.

I winked understanding, turned on my radio to maximum volume and spoke into the microphone: 'Hello aircraft passing over Ramree Island. This is Uncle Baker 437 calling from Kyaukpyu Aerodrome. Do you read?'

Immediately they answered: 'Uncle Baker 437. This is Fox Peter How reading you loud and clear. Go ahead.'

The children's eyes popped out of their heads as the voice from the skies echoed from the head-set. A few ran screaming down the runway. There was a buzz of awe and astonishment as I replied:

'Morning Peter How. Can you give me Rangoon's weather?'

'Delighted,' answered the unmistakably English voice. 'Are you the Spitfires?'

'Yes.'

'Weather's fine. Broken cloud at 4,000. Visibility unlimited.'

'Thank you Peter How. Good morning.'

'Not at all. They are waiting for you in Rangoon. Good luck.'

I switched off amidst a circle of dumbfounded faces that turned from me to the vanishing speck in the sky and back again. The monks, interpreters of life to the villagers, wore superbly non-committal expressions as their wards appealed for explanation.

We took off violently from the short strip and circled the village in salute before climbing to altitude. Rapidly, as we headed for Rangoon, the village became a speck that lingered on the landscape and then vanished, becoming a memory. Yesterday, visibility had been a few yards. Today, 50 miles of rugged splendour unfolded like a map beneath us. Stark mountains, cousins of Everest, thrust without preamble into the air. Rivers darkly stained with soil, curved like arteries through the impacted jungle. To the west, the limpid waters of the Bay glistened like glass. It was a magnificent canvas, but not a happy one when flying a single-engined aeroplane. I blew my lips in

284

relief when the flat plains of the Irrawaddy delta lent a more hospitable vista.

Like horses headed for the stables the Spitfires eagerly spanned the last few miles. Soon, the gigantic Shwe Dagon pagoda, a fabulous Buddhist shrine plated with gold, rose massively three hundred feet from the squalor of Rangoon and glinted like a rising sun on the horizon. In its jewel-encrusted peak rested Buddha's tooth and a lock of hair, ornaments of faith that drew pilgrims from the scattered corners of the world and sign-posted *finis* to our flight.

We flashed across the aerodrome in tight V formation, peeled off and beat-up the hangars, before side-slipping in to land. I switched off with a curious mixture of elation and sadness and slumped in the cockpit as the instruments dropped slowly to zero.

'Hi,' shouted a Burmese supply officer laconically, as though we had just completed a meek little flight from an airfield nearby.

'Hi,' I answered, determined to be equally unceremonious. Little earth-bound mortal. How could he know that parched deserts, proud mountains and the conquest of fear sat with me in the cockpit, binding me closer to this inanimate thing of metal than to him, denizen of a smaller world.

'Any news of Gordon Levett?' I asked as I handed him the delivery documents.

He frowned.

'The other Spitfire,' I prompted.

'Oh. Yes. He left Bandar Abbas yesterday.'

'Is the pilot all right?'

'U-huh. We expect him in a few days. Where are the spare radio crystals?' he added nonchalantly.

I pulled off my helmet, pushed my hair back and pointed to the wing panels. He shrugged and disappeared under the wing.

So, on a note of absurd anti-climax, ended the fourth ferry flight.

EPILOGUE

HOW TO END THIS BOOK WHEN THERE IS NO ENDING? I AM TOO young to sum up, too old to end with a hint of a new beginning. There seem very few ends that need gathering. Gordon Levett arrived safely at Rangoon and joined us at Tel Aviv in time for the remaining two ferry flights.

At the end of the Spitfire contract I hitch-hiked back to London on an Israeli Air Force freighter. As we crossed the Alps at night I sat at the controls. The rest of the crew were dozing when the clouds broke like a curtain to reveal the splendid sweep of the Bernese Alps. The moon, luminous as a pearl in the oyster of night, caressed the snow-clad peaks with shafts of quicksilver that lent depth by giving shadows to the valleys between. Peak upon peak reached for the sky like silvered pagodas. Swiftly the broken clouds sped past the moon switching its spotlight from one superb peak to another. New peaks rose to be admired, posed for an instant, then slipped into shadow. The slopes in the reflected light from the glaciers looked like the tinselled skirts of ballerinas. The frozen lakes like a hundred moons. And, I thought, as the peaks spotlighted the horizon for a brief moment before being snuffed out by distance, people ask me why I do not give up flying.

287

Here then, a copy of a recent advertisement, is the end:

'Woman pilot, 35, Commercial Licence
and Instrument Rating, 3500 hours.
Recent experience Far-East ferrying.
Seeks flying post Home or Overseas.
Box 467.'

AFTERWORD

In 1979, Nick Grace, design engineer and qualified pilot, acquired Spitfire ML407 from a museum. Over the next five years he painstakingly restored the aircraft back to flying condition, and in 1985 Nick finally had his Spitfire airborne again. When Nick died tragically in a car accident in 1988, his wife Carolyn, a relatively inexperienced pilot, took on learning to fly the Spitfire in order to keep a Grace in the cockpit.

The historian tracing the history of their Spitfire told Nick and Carolyn that it was first flown by ATA Pilot Jackie Moggridge on 29 April 1944.

As a pilot myself, I have found all the ladies who flew in the ATA to be a huge inspiration. What they achieved in a male-orientated environment, during a time when women weren't expected to drive a car, let alone pilot an aircraft, is incredible. When the historian Hugh Smallwood told me that the famous woman pilot, Jackie Moggridge, had been the first to fly our Spitfire I was deeply moved.

I first met Jackie when we were making *The Perfect Lady*, a documentary about our Spitfire. She came to Land's End Airfield where we were filming and I was so in awe of her I could hardly speak, but she immediately put me at ease.

Looking through Jackie's logbook entry from the 29 April 1944, it's possible to re-visit the aircraft's first flight. ML407 was one of two Spitfires Jackie delivered that day – and it was supposed to be her day off! On the 27th and 28th she had delivered a Beaufighter (Bomber), Hawker Typhoon (Fighter), another Spitfire as well as flying the transport aircraft Oxford and Anson. Quite a schedule! Jackie delivered ML407 to 485 New Zealand Squadron where it became the 'mount' of Flying Officer Johnnie Houlton DFC who was accredited, whilst flying ML407, with the first enemy aircraft shot down over the Normandy beachhead on the 6 June, D-Day.

I decided to recreate this first flight: Jackie and I would re-deliver the Spitfire to its original pilot fifty years after its first flight. I had gathered together twenty members of the original 485 Squadron ground crew to be with Johnnie to receive their Spitfire again. On 29 April 1994 there Jackie was, standing beside 'her' aircraft that embodied so much history, looking wonderful in her ATA uniform which still fitted her perfectly.

Jackie was, by her own admission, not a good passenger! She had told me she didn't want to pilot the Spitfire herself. As we took off from North Weald for our 'delivery' I decided something must be done. Once we were airborne, I told Jackie that I had dropped my map so she would have to take control of the aircraft. As a Spitfire has no floor, Jackie knew this was a potentially serious situation and immediately said, 'I have control'. Of course I hadn't really dropped anything, but I knew this was the best way to make her fly her Spitfire again. As we approached Duxford, another Spitfire pilot suggested we fly together for a flypast down the runway. Jackie flew ML407 beautifully low down the runway in formation with the other Spitfire.

After this flight, Jackie and I formed a bond I treasure to this day. In what is still a male-dominated profession, she would be sure always to look her best, having her lovely hair flow free when she removed her flying helmet to accentuate her femininity. She would ensure her make-up was perfect and carried a pair of high-heeled shoes to put on when she alighted from her aircraft. I remember her telling me at the Duxford Air Show to change into my slimmer-fit flying suit in order to show my figure off better. In an environment where everything is practical and serves a purpose, Jackie injected some much-needed glamour.

But Jackie was also an expert pilot, capable of flying a wide variety of aircraft types. She would have ferried these war machines unarmed, usually in dangerous circumstances. By the end of the war Jackie had delivered more aircraft than any other member of the ATA, male or female, an incredible achievement. All this she did whilst managing the complications of family life – what a lady!

It was with great sadness but immense honour that I scattered Jackie's ashes from her Spitfire on 1 August 2004: an appropriate ending to an inspirational life.

Carolyn Grace, May 2014

APPENDIX A

Below are expanded lists of the people featured in some of the photographs included in the image section. Many thanks to Richard Pode and his team at the Maidenhead Heritage Centre for all their hard work identifying faces.

'The women of No. 15 Ferry Pool relax in the sunshine…', (p.4 of image section):
LEFT TO RIGHT Kay Van Doozer (USA), Cecile Power, Anna Leska (Poland), Unknown, Unknown, Margot Duhalde (Chile).

'The full team of No. 15 Ferry Pool…', (p.4 of image section):
FRONT ROW (LEFT TO RIGHT): Pam Marsh, Phyllis Farquharson, Kay Van Doozer, Maureen Dunlop, Grace Stevenson, Emily Chapin, Rosemary Bannister, Pat Parker, Philippa Bennett, Rachel Nickalls, Margot Gore, Alison King, Rosemary Rees, Barbara Murray, Margaret Murray, Doreen Williams, Jean Bird, Anna Leska, Veronica Innes, Mary Wilkins , Betty Grant. MIDDLE ROW (LEFT TO RIGHT) Dora Lang, Jackie Moggridge, Tanya Whittall, Diana Barnato. BACK ROW (LEFT TO RIGHT) Bobby Leveaux, Mardi Gething, Margot Duhalde, Anne Walker. TOP Vera Strodl.

'**The ATA's forty year reunion**...', (p.12 of image section):
BACK ROW Lettice Curtis, Veronica Volkersz, Pete Wither, B. Hale, Mary (Guthie) Cunningham, Doreen (Williams) Ulstey. Joy (Gough) Lofthouse, Zoe Jener, Rosemary (Bannister) Seccombe, Marigold (Dean Drammond) Saville. THIRD ROW FROM FRONT Helen (Kerly) Storm Clark, Alison King, Freddie (Leaf)Sharland, Monique Agazarian, Maggie Fost (hidden). SECOND ROW FROM FRONT Anne (Walker) Duncan, Pam Tulk Hart, Maureen (Dunlop) de Popp. Betty (MacDougall) Evans, Molly Rose, Phillippa (Bennett) Booth, Bernie Willis, Mary (Wilkins) Ellis, Cecile (Power) Moger. FRONT ROW Diana Barnato Walker, Margot Gore, Margaret Murray, Jackie Moggridge.

Photo on back cover of No. 15 Ferry Pool:
LEFT TO RIGHT: Betty Hayman Diana Barnato, Maureen Dunlop, Mary Wilkins, Freydis Leaf, Unknown, (Driver) Pamela, Doreen Williams, Grace Stevenson, Emily Chapin, Kay Van Doozer, Margaret Murray, Veronica Volkersz, Margot Gore, Unknown, Rosemary Rees, Philippa Bennett, (in cockpit) Chile and Anne Walker, three ladies sitting on wing unknown, above them Tania Whittall, Mardi Gething, Jackie Moggridge, Vera Strodl.

All of the images used in this edition have been kindly provided by Jackie Moggridge's family from their personal collection.

I miss the beauty of that world above the earth,
Where winds have curled the tops of clouds,
And tossed them into frilly forms;
The sunlight sweeping o'er them
Warms my very soul.

And I behold a vision there of silver wings,
Swift, cutting through the cumulous mass,
And listen to my heart it sings,
Until with pain I see, alas!

It is not I that feels that thrill,
Though yet the memory lingers still;
It is a younger one today
Who's flying now, o'er my skyway.